FROM PAGAN TO CHRISTIAN

BOOKS BY LIN YUTANG

Kaiming English Books (3 vols.)
Kaiming English Grammar
The Little Critic (2 vols.)
Confucius Saw Nancy (drama) and Essays About Nothing
A Nun of Taishan
A History of the Press and Public Opinion in China
My Country and My People
The Importance of Living
Wisdom of Confucius
Moment in Peking
With Love and Irony
A Leaf in the Storm
Wisdom of China and India
Between Tears and Laughter
The Vigil of a Nation
The Gay Genius
Chinatown Family
Wisdom of Laotse
On the Wisdom of America
Widow, Nun and Courtesan
Famous Chinese Short Stories
Vermilion Gate
Looking Beyond
Lady Wu
The Secret Name
The Chinese Way of Life

Lin Yutang

FROM
PAGAN
TO CHRISTIAN

CLEVELAND AND NEW YORK

THE WORLD PUBLISHING COMPANY

PUBLISHED BY The World Publishing Company
2231 West 110th Street, Cleveland 2, Ohio

PUBLISHED SIMULTANEOUSLY IN CANADA BY
Nelson, Foster & Scott Ltd.

Library of Congress Catalog Card Number: 59-11534

THIRD PRINTING

Grateful acknowledgment is made to the following for quotations used in this book:

From *The Wisdom of Confucius,* edited and translated with notes by Lin Yutang, copyright 1938 by Random House, Inc. Reprinted by permission.

From *The Wisdom of China and India,* edited and translated with notes by Lin Yutang, copyright 1948 by Random House, Inc. Reprinted by permission.

From *The Wisdom of Laotse,* edited and translated with notes by Lin Yutang, copyright 1948 by Random House, Inc. Reprinted by permission.

From *Gay Genius* by Lin Yutang, by permission of The John Day Company, Inc., Publisher.

From *Looking Beyond* by Lin Yutang, copyright 1955 by Lin Yutang. Reprinted by permission of Prentice-Hall, Inc.

From *On a Chinese Screen* by W. Somerset Maugham, copyright 1922 by W. Somerset Maugham. Reprinted by permission of Doubleday & Company, Inc., and Heinemann, Ltd.

From *A Buddhist Bible,* edited by Dwight Goddard. Copyright, 1938, by E. P. Dutton & Co., Inc. Reprinted by permission of the publishers.

To My Wife

Contents

CONTENTS

FROM PAGAN TO CHRISTIAN

Preface

THIS is a record of one man's experience in his quest for religion. It is a record of his adventures in belief, his doubts and perplexities, his encounters with different philosophies and religions of the world, and his explorations of the best that has been said and thought and taught by the sages of the past. It is, of course, an exciting voyage, and I hope to make it clear and simple. I am sure that in this quest for the noblest truths, every person must travel by his individual road, and these roads are all different. It did not matter that Christopher Columbus never landed on the continent of North America; the essence of Christopher Columbus was that he did make the quest, and had all the excitement and the suspense and the happiness of a voyage of discovery. It did not matter that Magellan took a different and a much longer and more circuitous route around the Cape of Good Hope to reach India. Roads must be individual and different. I have no doubt that today a much simpler way to go to India is by jet plane. You get there faster. I doubt, however, that there is very much advantage in taking a jet plane to salvation, in getting to know God quicker and more safely. I am sure there are many Christians who never made this quest; they found the Christian

God when they were in the cradle, and, like the wife of Abraham, they took this God with them wherever they went; and finally, when they reached the grave, the same God was with them still. Religion sometimes becomes too comfortable, and has even been associated with smugness. Religion of this kind is like a piece of furniture or a possession that you can tuck away and take along in your journey wherever you go; and among the atrocities of modern American English I must mention the phrases that one can "get religion" or "sell religion." I believe that many churches prefer to sell religion in a "package." It's compact, and so much more convenient to carry around. That is a comfortable and easy way to come by religion.

I doubt, however, the value of religion of this sort. I have come by religion the hard way, and I think this is the only way, and do not think there is any other way to give it the necessary validity. For religion is, first and last, an individual facing up to the astounding heavens, a matter between him and God. It is a matter of individual growth *from within*, and cannot be "given" by anybody. For religion is a flower which is best grown in a field, and the pot-grown or hothouse variety is apt to be pale-colored, as well as fragile and friable.

This is therefore necessarily a story of personal experience, for all worth-while accounts of this kind must necessarily be based on personal inquiry, on moments of doubt and moments of insight and intimation. Though this book is not an autobiography, there are places where I find it necessary to touch on certain personal circumstances and backgrounds in order to make the story of the evolution comprehensible. It is by no means a smooth voyage of discovery, but one full of spiritual shocks and encounters. There is always something of the story of Jacob's wrestling with God in his dream; for the search for truth is seldom a pleasure cruise. There were storms and shipwrecks and puzzling deviations of the magnetic compass which frightened the sailors on Christopher Columbus' boat. There were doubts, hesitancies, and threats of mutiny, and the desire to turn back. I had to sail past the Scylla of a damning hell-fire and the Charybdis of Pharisaism, Scribism, and Caiaphatism of organized belief. I finally got through. But it has been worth while.

I do not write for those who never join the search, who have "no time for religion," for this book will not interest them. Nor do I write for the smug Christians who are perfectly satisfied with what they've got, who have, as it were, a guaranteed salvation, people who never had any doubts. I have no sympathy for those who believe that they have a reserved seat in heaven. I speak only to those who ask the question, "Where are we going on this voyage?" There are passengers on every ocean liner who find it necessary, for their peace of mind, to look at the log of the steamer on which they are traveling and find out the exact longitude and latitude of their boat. It is to these people that I speak.

The modern world and the development of contemporary history have always seemed to me like the odyssey of men who do not know where they are going, and the first sign of salvation is the willingness and the desire to ask, "Where are we going now?" I can conceive of a ghost ship, a pilotless submarine driven by the power from nuclear reactors and run entirely by automation. And I can imagine that sometimes on this ghost ship there is a great argument among the passengers as to who is running the ship and where she is going, for apparently there is no pilot. Some will essay the opinion that the submarine runs itself, while other, more speculative minds will start to argue that perhaps the submarine even built itself, by a fortuitous conjunction of mechanical parts, without any designing engineer. And amidst the heat of argument, I can detect a sense of frustration and of puzzlement and discontent, and there will be those who say, "We did not ask to come aboard; we merely found ourselves here." That, I believe, is a picture of the modern world. There will be no evidence of any pilot who is running the ship, and much evidence that the ship is running by itself without a pilot. The great speculative minds will essay the opinion that probably the nuclear-powered submarine built itself. Such speculation will give the sponsors of the theory much intellectual satisfaction and pride; for in their flights of speculation they have seen the awful beauty and grandeur of such a conception of the fortuitous conjunction of events, the lucky coincidences of screws fitting holes and congruence of the diameters of the main shaft and the hole of the main driving wheel, and so on, of which they believe the lesser minds have no conception. But the majority of the sailors and the passengers on board will be occupied with the more practical question of where they come from and where they will ultimately land.

I write to please no one, and may displease some, for what I say will be strictly from an individual viewpoint. Tolerance is a rare virtue among followers of religions. There is so much about the religions of the world, and Christianity in particular, which has been hardened and encased and embalmed and which admits of no discussion. For, curiously, in this matter of religion, every individual likes to think that he has the monopoly of truth. In his speech asking the Great Convention to pass the Constitution of the United States, Benjamin Franklin wrote: "It is therefore that, the older I grow, the more apt I am to doubt my own judgment of others. Most men, indeed, as well as most sects in religion, think themselves in possession of all truth, and that wherever others differ from them, it is so far error. Steele, a Protestant, in a dedication, tells the Pope that the only difference between our two churches in their opinions of the certainty of their doctrine, is, the Romish church is infallible and the Church of England is *never in the wrong*. But, though many private persons think almost as highly of their own infallibility as that of their sect, few express it so naturally as a certain French lady, who, in a little dispute with her sister, said, 'But I meet with nobody but myself that is *always* in the right.' *'Je ne trouve que moi qui aie toujours raison.'* "

Perhaps there are too many people who want to give us a "packaged" salvation, too many people who want to overprotect us from heresy. The anxiety for our personal salvation is entirely laudable. On the other hand, in such a "packaged" salvation, people are apt to put too heavy a load on our beliefs.

That is what is called dogmas and the dogmatism of spirit; and it is not so much the dogmas individually and specifically as the spirit of dogmatism which I object to. The overprotection and the burden of belief may crush many a young mind.

In this connection, I remember a story my father told me of himself. We lived in Changchow, on the South China coast. There was a preacher who lived some five or six miles from Changchow, and who came back to the city regularly twice a month. My father was twelve or thirteen at the time. And my grandmother, being a Christian, offered the services of her son to carry the luggage for the Christian preacher without charge. My father was at the time the only son living with his widowed mother, and they were very much devoted to each other. He used to sell sweetmeats and, on rainy days, fried beans. The residents of Changchow loved to eat fried beans on a rainy day, for the beans were crisp and tasted somewhat like American popcorn. He was a good carrier, and obeyed my grandmother's injunction to carry the luggage. The preacher's wife traveled with him, and my father told me that this woman would put everything into the baskets which were suspended from both ends of the pole on his shoulder. There were not only clothing and bedding and laundry, which made the load heavy enough for a boy of thirteen, but the woman would also put in some pots and pans, and finally even a clay stove which must have weighed three or four pounds. And she would say to my father: "You are a good boy, a strong boy. This is nothing. I am sure you can carry it." There was no strict necessity for carrying the clay portable stove back and forth between Changchow and his station. I can still remember seeing the scars on my father's shoulders, which of course were not entirely due to these trips alone. But I have always thought of those baskets of luggage and pots and pans and the unnecessary portable clay stove. They remind me of the burden of beliefs which the priesthoods of different religions like to place on the shoulders of young minds, saying to them: "You are a good boy, a strong boy, you can take it. If you will only believe, you will find that it is true." Sometimes the shoulders of these young minds develop blisters.

CHAPTER 1

Childhood and Youth

I WAS BORN toward the end of the nineteenth century. It was 1895, the year of the Treaty of Shimonoseki between China and Japan, which ceded Formosa and recognized the independence of Korea, after the disastrous war with Japan in the previous year. The crushing defeat suffered at the hands of Japan was due to the fact that the Manchu empress dowager had diverted the money set aside for building a modern Chinese navy to the construction of the now famous Summer Palace outside Peking. The old Summer Palace had been ruined and sacked by the allied European soldiers in 1860, and this ignorant but stubborn woman with her antiforeign feeling was to help precipitate the Boxer Uprising a few years later. I remember hearing my father tell about the flight of the empress dowager and the emperor during the Boxer crisis, when I was five. Consulting the almanac, I found that the year of the Treaty of Shimonoseki was also the year in which the German physicist Roentgen discovered the X ray.

One of my earliest recollections as a child was that of sliding down the roof of the church. The church was a one-room affair, and directly adjoining it was the vicarage, two-storied, so that by standing on the balcony of the vicarage one was able to look down through a small window at the back of the church into the church itself. There was a very narrow space between the top of the church roof and the beams of the vicarage above, and a child could climb up the roof on one side, squeeze through the space, and slide down on the other side. I remember standing on the balcony as a small boy and wondering about the omnipresence of God. It bothered me, and I wondered whether God was a few inches directly over my head if He was omnipresent. I also remember arguing with myself about the idea of thanking God for our daily bread, and I came to the conclusion that this meant the general bounty of life for which we should be grateful in the same sense that the residents of the empire should be grateful to the emperor for the peace and order which made the people's livelihood possible.

Childhood is an age of wonder, and standing on the balcony of the vicarage I found much to wonder about. For in front of me were the ten peaks of the Southern Hill and behind was the stony crevice of another high mountain. Our village was so far inland and so completely surrounded by tall mountains at all points of the compass that locally it was called a "lake." It was some sixty miles from the nearest port, Amoy, but in those days a voyage by river junk took about three days. The junk voyage was another of the great spiritual experiences that have been permanently imprinted on my mind. For we were of the South, and the valley of the West River from my village to Changchow was inexpressibly beautiful, unlike the denuded bare loess hills of the North. But we were so far inland that at a point some six miles from my village of Poa-a, the river had become unnavigable by the usual junks, and we had to change into a much smaller craft, a kind of skiff, which was literally lifted over the rapids by the boatwomen, their trousers rolled way up their legs, who jumped into the river and carried it on their shoulders.

There is something about living in the country so close to

the high mountains, for to be close to them is to be near God's greatness. I used to stand fascinated and wondering, looking at the changing gray-purplish hues of the mountainsides and at the fanciful, wayward meanderings of the white clouds on the mountaintops. It gives one a contempt for the lowly hills and for all that is artificial and small and made by men. Those high mountains have become a part of me and my religion, for they give me a richness and inner strength and sense of independence which no man can take away from me. It gives reality to the Biblical line, "How beautiful upon the mountains are the feet of him . . ." and I am inclined to believe that no man who has not known the pleasure of letting his toes touch the wet grass can truly know God.

We were a family of six brothers and two sisters, and we boys used to take turns drawing water from the family well. There was fun in learning the art of swinging the bucket when it reached the bottom of the well so that it would overturn and catch the water. Mechanical gadgets were unknown, for it was the age of the kerosene lamp; we had two such lamps at home and also a few pewter lamps that burned peanut oil. Soap did not come into our lives until I was about the age of ten. My mother used a kind of "bean cake" made from the residue of soya beans; it gave a very meager lather. When soap was introduced, it came in the form of long bars and squares, and the farmers used to dry it in the sun so that it would harden and, at the time of washing, not be used up too quickly.

My father was a pioneer progressive of those days. He was a dreamer, keen, imaginative, humorous, and eternally restless. He communicated to us children a passionate zest for all that was new and modern, the knowledge of the Western world, which was called "the new learning." My mother, on the other hand, was a simple, guileless soul, surrounded by her adoring brood of children, and we brothers and sisters used to conspire in what I may call the benevolent bullying of our mother. We used to make up stories and tell her fantastic tall tales. She would listen, a little incredulous, until we burst out laughing, and then her face would crease up and she would say, "You have fooled your silly old mother." She had labored a great deal in bringing up the children, but by the time I was ten my sisters had taken over the household chores of cooking and washing. We had daily family prayers in the evening before going to bed, and it was in a home of Christian piety and love and harmony, with a well-ordered routine of work that we grew up. We brothers were never supposed to quarrel, and we never did.

My father was unconventional. As boys we did not wear queues like the other children, but had a kind of page bob, and my sister used to knit us tam-o'-shanters which she had seen French sailors wear on the streets of Kulangsu, opposite Amoy. My father was a very active man. On a summer night when there was a clear moon, he would sometimes on the spur of the moment go out to the bank and preach near the head of the bridge where he knew the peasants would gather and sit in the summer breeze, enjoying the moon. My mother told me that once he almost died of pneumonia, for during a harvest moon he went out and preached and perspired and came home without a good rubdown. He was always building churches, for he had built one when he was stationed at Tongan. When I was ten or eleven, I saw him building the new church at Poa-a. The church was made of sun-baked mud bricks, covered with tiles cemented on the surface. There was great excitement when the weight of the roof gradually began to push the walls apart. Hearing of the situation, the Reverend A. L. Warnshuis,* then stationed at Sio-khe, six miles away, ordered some steel beams from the United States. These beams were joined in the center by a pin which could be screwed to allow for the exact length required. They were attached to the wooden support of the roof, and when the screw was tightened the beams pulled the woodwork together

---

* Later Secretary of the International Missionary Council, London and New York, 1921–1943.

and visibly lifted the top of the church a few inches. It was a great, memorable moment.

That he was a Christian pastor did not mean that my father was not a Confucianist. By no means. And I remember helping to trace the calligraphy of the great neo-Confucianist Chu Shi, which was to go up in the form of literary couplets for the walls of the new church. My father had made a trip to Changchow to obtain these samples of calligraphy, the characters being about one foot square, for Chu Shi had been a magistrate of Changchow. Chu Shi lived in the twelfth century and was supposed to have brought "civilization" to our province by introducing the binding of women's feet. His work was not too successful, so far as I could see, for the bound feet of the womenfolk were neither small nor shapely.

My first contact with the West was when a missionary couple came to stay at the vicarage during a visit, leaving a can of sardines and a shirt stud with a shining gilt globule in the center. We used to keep this shining stud in the drawers, and I used to wonder greatly at it, not knowing what it was for. The smell of butter also hung round the room after they left, and my sister had to open the windows to let the air blow it away. My first contact with the English language in print was a copy of some American women's magazine, probably the *Ladies' Home Journal*, which somehow had drifted to our home. My mother used to keep it in her sewing basket, using the pages of the slick magazine for holding embroidery threads. I believe no copy of the American magazine was made use of for such a number of years. During the building of the church, Dr. Warnshuis had also sent us a set of Western carpenter's tools, including a rotating drill, and I marveled greatly at them and thought they were extremely well made.

In Reverend Warnshuis my father had met his match, and they became great friends, for Reverend Warnshuis had discovered in my father a voracious appetite for all that was Western and new. He introduced us to a Christian weekly called the *Christian Intelligence*, printed on very shiny paper, with greasy, oily ink. He sent us all kinds of pamphlets and books, both Christian literature and books about the Western world and Western science which the Christian missions in Shanghai had put out. In this way Western learning came to our family. My father, I believe, read all that was available about the Western world. I remember his saying one day, with a cynical laugh: "I read all about the airplanes, but I've never seen any one of them. I do not know whether to believe or not." This was about the time of the Wright brothers. I do not know how he came to know about it, but he used to speak to us children with a bright light in his eyes about the universities of Berlin and of Oxford as "the best in the world," hoping half in jest and half in earnest that some of us might be able to study there one day. We were a family of incorrigible dreamers.

When I was the age of ten, I left with two of my brothers to go to Amoy for schooling; the local school, my father had decided, was just not good enough. As the voyage took several days and cost a few dollars, we did not come home for the winter vacation, and it meant separation from my mother for a whole year. But a boy is a boy, and I soon learned to forget about home and became immersed in the various activities of the school, which included kicking bare-footed a wooden ball which was cut from a dumbbell. This was the regular sport of the schoolchildren. But nothing quite equaled the thrill of returning to my mother. A mile or so from home, after having entered the mountain-circumscribed valley called Poa-a, we three brothers would get impatient with the slowness of the boat and start to walk. And we would plan how to announce our arrival to Mother, whether to scream outright at the gate, "We have come back!" or to practice "benevolent bullying" of Mother by calling, in the voice of an old beggar, and asking for some water, or to sneak silently into the house, find where she was, and then suddenly burst in upon her. I think sometimes the universe is not big enough to hold the heart of a child. This is what some Westerners, long-time residents in China, call the phlegmatic temper of the Chinese.

During the holidays, our home turned into a school. I have said that my father's being a Christian pastor did not mean that he was not a Confucianist. After we boys had swept the floor and the girls had washed the breakfast dishes, a bell would ring and we would clamber to our seats around the dining table to listen to Father expounding the Confucian classics and the Confucian *Book of Poetry*, which contained some exquisite love songs. (I remember a shy young schoolteacher whose face turned all red when he had to explain the love songs which Confucius himself had edited and selected for our edification.) We would go on studying, and then toward eleven o'clock, my second sister would watch the sun's shadow on the wall and rise slowly and reluctantly with an expression of rebellious submission on her face and say, "I must go and cook the lunch." Sometimes in the afternoons we would be studying together, and then again she would have to stop her studies and rise and say, not too willingly, "Now I have to go and take in the washing."

I must write about my second sister not only because she was very much a part of my childhood but also to show what a college education meant in our family. I remember that my second sister loved me (all Freudians, get out!) because I was a brilliant but rather erratic and mischievous boy. While my brothers were still conning their lessions dutifully, I would dash out to the garden and play. I remember her telling me when I was older that as a child I was very naughty, and that in one of my tantrums, after a quarrel with her, I threw myself into a muddy hole in the back garden, and wallowed there like a hog, to revenge myself upon her, and on getting up said, "Now, there, you have to wash it!" I must have looked terribly dirty and adorable at that moment!

My sister had read Sir Walter Scott and Dickens and Conan Doyle and Rider Haggard's *King Solomon's Mines* and the

Arabian Nights, all translated into Chinese by a fellow provincial of mine, Lin Shu. Lin Shu did not, in fact, know a word of English, but depended entirely upon one Mr. Wei to put it into Foochow dialect for him. Then this man, this great writer, put the whole story into the beautiful classic language. Lin Shu was enormously popular, and he went on to translate Maupassant and Dumas' *La Dame aux Camélias,* which took Chinese society by storm largely because the heroine was a beauty suffering from tuberculosis, very much like Taiyu in the Chinese romance *Red Chamber Dream.* The Chinese ideal of beauty seemed to be a lady who was either a tubercular patient or extremely emaciated and all but about to die. Even in classical times, the most famous Chinese beauty was a lady suffering either from angina pectoris or from a kind of neuralgia, and her most famous pose was when her eyebrows were knitted in a moment of excruciating pain. Now, after reading about Sherlock Holmes and about a certain French detective whose name I have forgotten, my sister and I would inveigle and amuse my mother by concocting a long detective story of our own from day to day as we went along, a story full of hair-raising escapes and adventures. My sister was talented and had an expression of intelligent delicacy like Deborah Kerr, so much so that when I first saw the latter on the screen a few years ago, my heart skipped a beat and I clutched the arm of my daughter and exclaimed, "There, that is how my second sister looked!" and my wife, who knew her, confirmed it.

Having graduated from high school in Amoy, my sister wanted to go to a girls' college in Foochow. I heard her pleas after the family prayers. But it was all futile. She did not want to be married right off; she wanted to go to college. And it is for that reason that I am telling the story. My father would not think of it. My sister pleaded and coaxed and made promises, but my father said, "No." To me it was dreadful. I do not blame my father. He really did not mind having a talented and well-educated daughter, for I remember that after reading a certain article by a girl writer in a Shanghai magazine, he commented, "I wish I had such a girl for my daughter-in-law!" But, dreamer that he was, he saw no way to do it. College education for a girl was a luxury which our family simply could not afford. Furthermore, this was the time when even the sons of rich families in Amoy did not go to Foochow or Shanghai to study. My father, largely through his reading in the *Christian Intelligence*, I believe, had heard of St. John's College, Shanghai, as the best college for studying English in China. I heard my father himself telling a friend that when he signed the deed for the sale of our only house in Changchow to enable my second brother to go to St. John's, a tear escaped and dropped on the paper. That was the limit of a pastor's power. A son, yes, but a daughter, no, not in those days. It was not a question of tuition, for she would have been able to get a scholarship in the Christian college, I am sure. It was just a question of the traveling and pocket expenses, which might come to fifty or sixty Chinese dollars a year. And so my sister drifted and drifted, teaching in Amoy and waiting to get married. Girls of those days had to marry in a hurry once past the age of twenty. My sister had a long-standing suitor, but every time my mother approached her at night and broached the topic of the suitor, my sister blew out her candle. But she could not go to college and she was already twenty-one.

When it was suggested that I go to St. John's because my second brother would soon be graduating and would be able to support me, the question was not decided until the very last day, on account of the awful gamble of Father's asking for a loan of a hundred dollars from a devoted friend and former pupil. According to the custom of ancient China, a teacher was a master for life, a member of the Confucian trinity of "emperor, father, and teacher." This former pupil of my father had now become rich, and I remember that whenever my father was passing through Changchow, he stopped at his old pupil's home. For there was more than an ordinary relationship between master and pupil in this case; this rich man was once a bright but poor boy, and when he studied under my father, Father gave him a hat as a present, a gift which this man remembered for life, for when it was worn out he swore he would never wear another hat in his life, and he didn't. Such were loyalties in ancient China—the fierce loyalties taught in Chinese romances and on the stage, whether of generals and officials or of common household servants or just between man and wife. My father knew that he could get the loan if he would only open his mouth. To this day, I do not know whether it was repaid or not.

And so it happened that my second sister and I went with our family on the same junk down the West River, she to her wedding at a hamlet called Mountain Town, and I presumably on my way to my first year of college at Shanghai. The question of the hundred-dollar loan hung like a sword of Damocles over my head, but I was jubilant. I was sixteen. After the wedding was over, my sister took forty cents from the pocket of her bridal dress and gave it to me. She said at parting, with tears in her eyes, "Ho-lok, you have a chance to go to college. Your sister, being a girl, can't. Do not abuse your opportunity. Make up your mind to be a good man, a useful man, and a famous man." That was all a part of the idealistic mold of the family.

She died of bubonic plague two years later, but those words are still ringing in my ears. I tell these things because they have so much to do with the influences that shape a man's moral being. What is trying to be a Christian but trying to be a good man, a useful man, as my sister told me? All the knowledge of the laws and the prophets and all the learning of the scribes are as nothing in the sight of God, to a humble, simple man struggling to find the best in himself, to stumble, perhaps, and pick himself up again. This is the teaching of Christ in all its uncomplicated simplicity. I still think of myself as that boy wallowing in the mud to revenge myself upon my sister, and I believe God must have loved me even for that. The extraordinary thing about Jesus, the unique thing about Him, is that the publicans and harlots felt closer to Him than all the doctors of philosophy and the learned scribes of His day, who would not allow a man to raise a fallen calf on the Sabbath.

❋

St. John's College had at that time already achieved considerable national distinction as one which produced several Chinese ambassadors, W. W. Yen (from my home town of Amoy), Alfred Sze, and Wellington Koo. It was without a doubt the best college for learning English, and that was what St. John's existed for in the minds of the students. Though it was Episcopalian, its sacred mission for the majority of the students was to produce successful compradores as aides to the Shanghai tycoons. Actually, the quality of English of the average student was no more than that expected of a compradore. The president was Dr. F. L. Hawks Pott, a truly great man whose conception of his own task, I think, was much like that of a master of Rugby or Eton. His paternal influence over the students was unmistakable. Every morning, after the morning service, he would go over the whole campus with a black bag in his hand, accompanied by the shroff. I am sure that was his morning constitutional before he sat down in his office at nine. He was such a methodical man that he was reputed to have read a novel in a year by giving himself an hour a week for that peculiar relaxation. As for the library, it held no more than five or six thousand volumes, a third consisting of theological books. It really does not matter at all to what college a man goes; the important thing is a good library. The quality of learning, like the kingdom of God, is within you, and it must come from the inside of your mind. The mind is a monkey: all you need to do is to let the monkey into a forest; you do not have to tell him where the nuts are to be found. You don't even have to guide him toward the good nuts. I roamed in that meager forest, and read Darwin, Haeckel, and Lamarck and the novelist Winston Churchill's

The Inside of the Cup. For the rest, I learned to play tennis and football and even to pitch baseball with some schoolmates from Hawaii, though I never could learn to throw a curve. I made the rowing team and the track team for the five-mile run. It is fair to say that one of the things I got from St. John's was a fairly developed chest—which I could not have got if I had gone to some government school.

My adolescent mind was now on the rampage, looking about for what it could find and devouring whatever was edible, like a squirrel in the park. Whatever it ate was absorbed, and nourished. The thinking mind, once launched, voyaged upon an endless and sometimes tempestuous sea. One looked up at the stars and wondered, while the ship was buffeted and battered and tossed about and pitched on the waves. I remember returning for the summer in my sophomore year. My father made me preach a sermon (which I had often done even in my teens; for my father, as I have said, was an unconventional man, and I suppose I was garrulous and he wanted to show me off). I chose the topic "The Bible To Be Read as Literature." There is really no sense in talking to the peasant Christians about the Bible as literature, but it was at the time very much in the forefront of my consciousness, and out it came. I think I said that Jehovah was strictly a tribal god who helped Joshua to smite the Amalekites and Gideonites, and that there was an evolution in the idea of God from a tribal idol to a monotheistic God of all peoples and all nations, no one in particular being "chosen." You should have seen my father's face that Sunday at dinner! The harm, he could see, was already being done. Was I going to travel the road of atheism? He very much feared so, for he had known a man in Amoy who was good in English and who was also an atheist. It was an ominous cloud: being "good in English, and an atheist."

I enjoyed the college and ignored the classes. Usually, I was fishing in the Soochow Creek during the examination week when others were cramming. The thought of failure at examinations never entered my head. In school and at college I always graduated second, because there was always some fool who took his classwork seriously, and who came out first.

Here it is important to mention the classes in Chinese, because they were to react in a most peculiar manner on my Christian beliefs later. I remember, for example, reading Houston Stewart Chamberlain's *The Foundations of the Nineteenth Century* under the desk in a Chinese class in civil law. Why there was such a class in civil law I never could understand. The Chinese teacher was an old *Shiutsai* (B.A. in the imperial examinations) who wore large glasses and weighed a maximum of about eighty pounds. Now, a *Shiutsai* had never learned to conduct a class or to lecture. The textbook on civil law was a matter of a hundred-odd pages in big print, which one could finish in one sitting but which was supposed to last us a whole semester. But so it stood on the curriculum, and so we had to drag it out. Each week the "professor" of civil law would read to us some ten or fifteen lines which took at most fifteen minutes, and for the rest of the hour he was absolutely speechless and immobile, huddled in his seat, and he was supposed to look at us through his heavy glasses while we also looked at him in silence. Unfortunately, it was a performance that I could not go through with; an absolute vacuity of mind was really difficult to maintain. I was not going into a Buddhist *chan* meditation. This was typical of the classes in Chinese at St. John's, and the worst thing was that one could obtain a diploma at St. John's after flunking year after year in Chinese. The study of things Chinese was, in fact, largely ignored at the school. This state of affairs changed only after 1930.

I had just begun to get interested in Chinese history when my entry to St. John's abruptly terminated it. A mind could not serve two masters, and I was in love with English. I dropped the writing brush for the fountain pen, and even when I was studying in Leipzig, my father still wrote letters saying how ashamed he was of my calligraphy. Chinese calligraphy is an art which takes half a lifetime to bring to perfection. This had closely to do with the real process of unlearning that must be a part of a man's education after college. Most minds continue to grow and mature by tossing about what one has learned from school and college. In my case, this process of unlearning consisted in going back to Chinese studies with a curse, and throwing out my Christian beliefs along with it.

Meanwhile I was, by my own choice, studying for the ministry, and I enrolled in the Theological School at St. John's. Here I was buffeted by the first storm. Exegesis was for minds other than mine; I was after the great thoughts and ideas. Very soon, I was the Zapata of Voltaire, though I did not make direct acquaintance with Voltaire until I had left St. John's: I found contradictory answers to my queries, and sometimes no answer. I was buffeted, and I retreated; again I was buffeted and again I retreated. All the theological hocus-pocus was an insult to my intelligence. I could not be honest and go through with it. I had lost all interest, and made poor grades, which was a rare thing in my studies. The bishop thought that I was not fit for the ministry, and he was right. I dropped out of the Theological School.

CHAPTER 2

The Grand Detour Begins

AFTER graduation, I went to Peking to teach at Tsinghua. To live in Peking then was to come into contact with authentic Chinese society, to see, as it were, ancient China made manifest. The clear blue sky of Peking, the glorious temples and palaces and the gay, cheerful, contented working people gave one a feeling of the sufficiency and adequacy of a way of life. Ages had changed and centuries had passed, and Peking was still there. There the Lying Buddha slept in the Western Hills, the Jade Fountain Hill gave forth crystal-clear springs, and the Drum Tower intoned the watches of the night. What did man want of God? What more could man ask on earth, having the gift of life? Peking was China, authentic China, with its yellow-roofed palaces and terra-cotta temple walls and its Mongolian camels and nearness to the Great Wall and the Ming tombs. It was paganism with pagan cheerfulness and content.

Now what did being a Christian in China mean? I had been brought up in the protective shell of Christianity. St. John's was a continuation of that shell. We moved in a world of our own, intellectually and, I am sorry to say, esthetically cut off

33

from the—if you like—heathen community—that satisfying, glorious community, full of wickedness and corruption and poverty, but also of good cheer and content, even of gaiety. To be brought up as a Christian was synonymous with being progressive, Western-minded, and in sympathy with the New Learning. It meant, on the whole, acceptance of the West, with particular admiration for the Western microscope and Western surgery. It meant taking a clear, firm stand for education of women and against concubinage and foot binding. (Christian women were the first to unbind their feet; and my mother, who had been brought up as a "heathen" girl, had unbound hers and wore socks.) It meant an attitude favoring popular mass education, and some notion of democracy and "speaking English" for the better educated. It meant also, in Amoy at least, Romanization and ruination of the knowledge of Chinese characters and sometimes ruination of all knowledge of authentic Chinese folklore and folk literature and the theater. Romanization was a wonderful thing: we in Amoy had a perfect Romanization system with seven tones, which made a mockery of all Sinologists' arguments against it. My mother could read the whole Bible in Romanization, besides having taught herself to read the hymn book in Chinese characters, and she wrote letters to me in a perfectly clear Romanized script. It isn't that Romanization is not feasible, but psychologically we don't want it.

But there were also disadvantages to a Christian education which soon became apparent. I had cut myself off not only from Chinese philosophy but also from Chinese folklore. Not to know Chinese philosophy as such was excusable in a Chinese, but not to know the common ghosts and spirits and folk tales of China was obviously ridiculous. What had happened was that my Christian upbringing was too perfect. There was an element of Calvinism in it. I was not permitted to listen to the age-old beautiful stories sung by the blind minstrels of Changchow to the accompaniment of a guitar. These blind singers, sometimes men but more often women, would go through the streets at night, with a clapper in hand and a lantern, and tell the magic stories and historic romances of China of old. My mother, who had been brought up in a heathen family, told me some of these stories, but I never heard the tales from the minstrel singers themselves. When we boys passed a theatrical show in the square of Kulangsu, we were supposed to look straight past the stage and not to loiter. Now, the stage is the universal medium for educating the Chinese people, both literate and illiterate, in their history. Any Chinese laundryman was better acquainted with the heroes and heroines of the *Three Kingdoms* than I was. I had known even in my childhood that Joshua's trumpets had blown down the walls of Jericho. When I discovered that the tears of Chi Liang's widow, on finding her husband dead as conscript labor to build the Great Wall, had melted away a good section of the Great Wall, my rage was terrible. I had been cheated of my national heritage. That was what a good Puritan Christian education could do to a Chinese boy. I determined to plunge into the great stream of our national consciousness.

The grand detour of my spiritual voyage began. As long as we lived and moved and had our being in the Christian world, we were sufficient, too, as sufficient as the pagans of Peking. But being a Christian Chinese moving into what I call an authentic Chinese world, with one's eyes and mind open, one was stung with a sense of shame, blushing up to the tips of one's ears. Of what had I not been deprived? Things were not so simple as I had pictured them to be. Even the questions of foot binding and concubinage were not so clear-cut and simple as I had imagined. In fact, I was not to appreciate the ethics and esthetics of concubinage and foot binding until I heard Ku Hung-ming's vigorous defense of both. And you will hear much of Ku Hung-ming before we are through.

Here I must mention two matters—opium and ancestor worship—which caused a deep sense of injury and of revulsion against the West in the one case, and a sense of being denationalized on the part of a Chinese Christian in the other.

The Christians kept away from opium, and of course the missionaries condemned it. The dramatic part of it, the tragic part of it, was that it was the missionaries' compatriots who brought it in and forced it on us at the point of a gun. It was the great fearless Chinese mandarin Lin Tseh-shu (of my own illustrious clan) who as the imperial commissioner of Canton burned bales of opium on the jetties of Canton and precipitated the war on the opium brought in by the Christians. Lin Tseh-shu had to die in exile in Hsinkiang (Chinese Turkestan) after China's defeat in the Opium War, and after the defeat the Open Door was thrown wide open. Bales of opium, stacks of them, began to roll in, brazenly. But the point is that the missionaries came in the wake of those stinking bales of opium. And then a third item came into the picture. Both the missionary and the opium were under the benevolent protective shadow of the gunboat. The situation became not only deplorable, but comic and downright ridiculous. The missionaries highly disapproved of the merchants, and the merchants highly disapproved of the missionaries, each thinking the others insane. As far as a Chinese could see, the missionaries had taken care to save our souls so that when the gunboats blew our bodies to bits we were bound to go up to Heaven, and that made it "quits," of course.

As for ancestor worship, it was, now that I look back upon it, so basically a part of being Chinese that, in being forbidden to participate in it, the Chinese Christians virtually excommunicated themselves from the Chinese community and justified the accusation that they were "eating foreign religion." The matter was basic and central, and poses the question of how far an unthinking Church could go to injure its believers. Ancestor worship is the only visible form of Confucianism as a religion; the worship of Confucius at the Confucian Temple was and had always been a matter for the scholars and the successful graduates of imperial examinations. But even so, there was no reason for Chinese Christians not to join in it and no reason whatsoever to cut themselves off from it.

For ancestor worship antedated Confucius, as anybody who reads the Chinese classics should know. Confucius was practically doing antediluvian research when he tried to re-establish the evidences of the forms and rules of ancestor worship of the founders of the Chou Dynasty some seven centuries before him, something more remote than Chaucer and a little nearer Beowulf for a modern scholar. Ancestor worship, for the Chinese, is the embodiment of reverence for the past and continuity with the past, and of the strong and deep family system and therefore of the Chinese motivation for living. It was the basis of all that was good and honorable and of the desire to go forward, to achieve success in society. Practically, the motivation of Chinese conduct is: "Do good so that thou mayest be an honor to thy family, and abstain from evil so that thou mayest not be a disgrace to thy ancestors." It is his reason for being a good son, a good brother, a good uncle, and a good citizen. It is the reason for a Chinese being a Chinese. As for the forms of worship, only by the wildest stretch of imagination could they be called idolatry, as the Christian churches called them. Compared with the riot of images in some Christian cathedrals, especially in Italy and in France, these square tablets inscribed with the names of the particular ancestors look almost like the work of some unimaginative, rationalist spirit. There were fewer words on them than on a Christian tombstone. An ancestral temple had an altar behind which stood a collection of such wooden tablets, looking like oversized foot rulers, marked as the "seat" of the spirits of the different ancestors, men and women. On the altar, at the time of worship, candles and incense were burned. As for kneeling before the tablets at worship, which is the real point of objection of the Christian churches, it was forgotten that Chinese knees were always more flexible than Western knees and that we often knelt before our parents and grandparents on formal occasions when they were living. The bending of the knees was an act of homage. Confucius said: "To gather in the same places where our fathers before us have gathered; to perform the same ceremonies which they before us have performed; to play the same music which they before us have played; to pay respect to those whom they honored; to love those who were dear to them—in fact, to serve those now dead as if they were living, those now departed as if they were still with us: this is the highest achievement of true filial piety." Scratch a Chinaman and you will find an indelible pride in his ancestors.

Now, the non-Christians in Amoy were tolerant toward us. There was no social ostracism. The Christian communities in Amoy and Changchow were close-knit like all members of a parish; they were progressive and successful, and their children had better facilities for schooling for both boys and girls. If there was hostility, I think it was in the matter of ancestor worship. We had not been incarcerated; we had incarcerated ourselves and cut ourselves off from the social community. In a modern city, it would not matter very much, but in a village it could be the most embarrassing personal problem for a Chinese Christian believer. Some Christians had come to my father to ask if they might not, with the best will in the world, contribute to the social fete and the theater on such occasions. What these Christians were really asking was whether they should willfully excommunicate themselves in the eyes of their cousins and uncles and other members of the clan. It was this which the Christian churches forbade while they cheerily celebrated at home Mother's Day and Father's Day when the parents were living and, if they were dead, with something infinitely nearer to idolatry—actual photographs instead of the tablets which resembled foot rulers. "When you drink water, think of its source," says the Chinese proverb. Should Chinese Christians drink only from faucets and stop thinking of the source of the water?

When I was a child I was too young to sense any hostility or to feel the fact that the Chinese Christians had cut themselves off from their own community. Certainly in my school-days we were too happily progressive to sense anything. But

I remember some non-Christian leaders in my village who were hostile to the Church. The incidents were trivial and amusing—there was none of the violence and hatred which broke out in the national explosion called the Boxer Uprising. The year after my father had completed building the new church, an unsuccessful candidate and unemployed opium-smoking scholar decided to solicit contributions to build a Buddhist temple right on the same street, and he did. Poor man, whether he had a wife who refused to wash his clothes or whether he determined to look unwashed and spiritual-looking I could not ascertain; all I can remember is that he had blackened teeth, wore a dirty, half-buttoned gown, and managed to give an eternally unwashed appearance whether he had the desire to wash or not. I am sure he was reserving the pleasure of a sponge bath for his first day in the Buddhist Paradise, and this in spite of the fact that a crystal-clear brook ran right past his temple. But at least the poor man had wit, by which he was making a living. Our church had a bell donated by some Americans, for which a bell tower some fifty feet high had been built at the entrance, and this "unemployed scholar" consequently had a drum installed at his Buddhist temple, which was most unusual. (Buddhist temples also used bells, which he could not afford.) When the church bells rang on Sundays, he took care to have his drum sounded also. As he put it, "When Jesus clanged, Buddha rolled." We boys determined not to be outdone. We would take turns to help pull the ropes, and listen during the intervals for the drum. We kept the competition going until Father thought we were crazy, and stopped us. The following year, after my return from school, the drum was gone. The yellow-toothed man had probably sold it to obtain money for opium. We had won.

Another Chinese leader was more respectable because of his age and his beard. He was a kind of alderman for the entire valley. My father got on friendly terms with "Grandfather Kim," but Grandfather Kim would not come to the church and would prevent others from coming. Now, the river came down from the mountains, and at a bend where the bridge was, on one side stood the one street of shops of Poa-a, high on the bank and constantly threatened with erosion, as it received the full impact of the current when a flood came; on the other side was a pebbly beach where the rotating fairs of the region were held once every five days. At the foot of the bridge on the beach side was the house of Grandfather Kim, so situated that he could properly be said to own the bridge. The bridge was a wooden affair with rounded logs roughly flattened on top, but with no planks across them. As these logs were not perfectly straight, one could see through to the water below, and women with bound feet had to pick their way carefully so that their heels might not get caught in one of the holes. We knew that the bridge was Grandfather Kim's source of income, for he also smoked opium, and needed money to buy it. When there was a big flood, the bridge was either washed away or needed repairs. Every time a flood came, Grandfather Kim would be out collecting money from the villagers for repairs, and a completely washed-away bridge was of course a windfall. Now, autumn floods were fairly frequent in my village, providing a constant source of money for Grandfather Kim. Moreover, by diligent attendance to flaws in the structure and by seeing to it that the bridge had poorly fitted joints, Grandfather Kim made sure that the bridge was sensitive to the slightest changes in water level, the only requirement being co-operation between Grandfather Kim and Grandfather Heaven. Grandfather Kim, as I remember, was a gentle, reasonable man. The only reason for his hostility to the Christian Church was that he ran a gambling den. As my father tried to prevent Christians from gambling, so he had to prevent the gamblers from becoming Christians.

*

There was a natural desire on the part of an intelligent Chinese to join in the national stream of thought of his country, and not to be considered a denationalized Chinese.

I was a graduate of the best college for English in China—so what? I had a fair grounding in the Confucian classics through my father's personal instruction, and I had memorized, as every educated Chinese was expected to have memorized, the sayings of Confucius in the *Analects*. It was a necessary part of conversation among educated men. But my calligraphy was horrible, the first sure mark of an uncultivated man in China. My knowledge of Chinese history and poetry and philosophy and literature was full of gaps. Here I was in Peking, the center of the culture of China. I felt like an English student in the first year at Cambridge talking with his don. The don smokes at him and rattles off about Swinburne and Keats and A. E. Houseman, with whom the student has only a nodding acquaintance. The first thing an intelligent lad would do after such an encounter would be to go to the library and read Swinburne and Keats and A. E. Houseman so that he might not appear so boorish and ignorant the next time. That is the normal process of what we call true college education, by the association of minds, or, as one might say, by contagion. I plunged into the study of Chinese literature and philosophy with a sense of shame. The vast world of pagan wisdom opened before me, and the process of true postgraduate education—the process of unlearning—began. This process was to include jumping the limits of Christian beliefs.

Outwardly I was a success as a teacher. I got on well at Tsinghua, which had been founded with the money refunded from the American portion of the Boxer Indemnity. The college was rapidly coming to the fore as one of the most modern and best-equipped in China, and it was beginning to build a magnificent library. It had a marvelous Chinese college president and a good Chinese and American staff, and it was situated in what was formerly a Manchu prince's garden outside Peking. But mentally I was awkward and ill-adjusted. To this day I am still sometimes amiably referred to by Dr. Hu Shih (see below) as a Puritan. I was a Puritan. I do not have the suavity and good camaraderie expected of a non-Christian

Chinese poet or scholar. By constitution I cannot drink; wine dries up my eyelids. As for the pipe of tobacco, I would defend to eternity this reliable comforter of the spirit. Although I called myself a pagan, such a thing as the feast of Bacchus remained outside my power of comprehension, and still does. At a drinking feast of Roman captains, reclining on couches and eating bunches of grapes served on gold platters, I would forever remain an observer. As for women, there was something good in a Puritan education, in discipline. While some of my colleagues went whoring on Sundays, I conducted a Sunday school in Tsinghua, which was a non-Christian college. A fellow professor called me a virgin, which I was till my marriage. That is why I love so much the nude shows of Parisian nightclubs. No one can properly appreciate nude shows so well as a good Puritan. I was never suave and confident like the rich men's sons at college, and although in later years I learned to be at home in the society of men and women, I still could not learn to slap a fellow violently on the back. That is, I think, because the spirit of the high mountains has never left me, and I am essentially a boy from the country, which the words "pagan" and "heathen" etymologically mean. Even today I still enjoy walking about in my socks over the carpets in my apartment as one of the greatest luxuries of life. I think that human feet as God made them for walking are perfect. There can be no improvement upon them, and wearing shoes is a form of human degeneracy. Thomas Wolfe has written rather intimately in *Look Homeward, Angel* about the warping of his toes as he grew up. Sometimes, while walking in the streets of Manhattan at night, I scandalized my wife by letting out a loud yawn or a sudden deliberate and prolonged scream. I was liberating myself. For though I walked upon the cement sidewalks of Manhattan, mine eyes still saw the untrammeled spaces of mountain peaks and mine ears still heard the sweet laughter and chatter of the mountain streams, and I was unafraid.

I have often wondered what it is like to be born a rich man's son, to be suave, and to know when to keep one's mouth shut, calmly waiting to be promoted as an official. For in China, to be a scholar was to become a member of the ruling class. I have seen a colleague of mine who came from an official family. His origin and his undoubted destiny were officialdom. But I am from Fukien—not from Shanghai or Peking. We produced poets, scholars, and beauties, but no first-rank statesman in all China's history.* During the short period when I was in the Foreign Ministry, I saw this colleague who had learned to keep his mouth shut and who was polite to everyone, and suave and imperturbable. He spent his time in his office drinking tea and reading newspapers. I said to myself, This man will surely one day become a provincial governor. Actually, he did. I have often wondered profoundly at this mystery of the relation between the unspeakable charm of keeping a closed mouth, and official careerism. And I have come to the conclusion that while a soldier gives his blood for his country but never gives up his honor, a real, successful politician gives up his honor for his country but never gives his blood. A soldier's duty is but to do and die; a good politician's is just to do and never talk about it. All he does is love his country.

*

My brief theological studies had shaken my belief in the dogmas. One of the professors tried to convince me of the *theoretical necessity* of the Holy Ghost by saying that if there were A and B, there must be a connecting line C between the two. This arrogance of the scholastic method, plus the dogmatic spirit, hurt my inner consciousness. These dogmas were produced by scholastic minds, treating spiritual things as material things, and even equating God's justice with man's

* Three great Chinese writers of the past generation came from Fukien: Yen Fu, translator of Adam Smith, Montesquieu, and Thomas Huxley; Lin Shu, translator of Scott and Dickens, whom I have mentioned; and Ku Hung-ming (see below).

justice. The theologians were so sure of themselves; they
wanted their conclusions accepted as final, sealed and encased
for all eternity. Of course I rebelled. Many of the dogmas were
irrelevant and obscured the truth of Christ. By a codifying
process, Paul knew more than Peter, and the Church Fathers
of the fourth century knew more than Paul. By comparison of
their teachings, Jesus knew least of all.

I had lost the certainty of belief while still clinging tena-
ciously to the belief in the fatherhood of God. Conducting the
Sunday-school class at Tsinghua at Christmas, I already had
great difficulty in visualizing just how the stars could guide
the Magi to the exact street of the stable. And I enjoyed the
beauty of the symbolism of angels singing upon the midnight
clear in the Santayana sense only. Santa Claus was a dis-
enchanted myth, but still a beautiful myth. Nevertheless,
something had to happen before I could cut myself off from
the Christian Church.

At Peking I came into contact with two first-class minds
which left an indelible influence upon me and which, in different ways, contributed to my further development: one was
Dr. Hu Shih, whose name spells the Chinese Literary Renaissance of 1917. The Literary Renaissance was strictly speaking
anti-Confucianist, among other more important things. Dr. Hu
Shih, then a postgraduate student of Columbia, had fired the
first shot from New York, a shot which changed the entire
tenor of Chinese thinking and Chinese literature of our generation. This was the Literary Revolution, a historical land-
mark in Chinese literature, advocating the change from the
classical language to the vernacular as the normal medium of
literary expression. Meanwhile, the organ *La Jeunesse* was
being edited by Chen Tu-shiu, a Communist professor at
Peking National University. Hu Shih, returned with national
acclaim to join Peking University, and I was at Tsinghua to
greet him. It was an electrifying experience. I felt instinctive
sympathy for the whole progressive attitude of the movement.
The greats of contemporary China were there, Liang Chi-

chao, Tsai Yuan-pei, and Lin Chang-min. Then came Paul Monroe and John Dewey on the invitation of Peking University before I left abroad for study. (Mao Tsetung was there as a librarian when I returned from Germany to join the Peking National University in 1923—but no one took any notice of him, and I never saw him.)

All in all, the Literary Renaissance was a liberating force, a true resolve on the part of intellectual Chinese to make a complete break with the past. While the warlords were fighting, intellectual China was in the grip of its own challenges and controversies. Peking was life. Lin Shu, the great translator whom my sister had read, was also at the Peking University, and he damned the vernacular tongue as the "language of rickshaw pullers and peddlers." There was controversy and there was life, provocative of thought and of study. There was a cause to fight for or against. Young China was shaken to its foundations. Chen Tu-shiu the Communist continued to damn the whole Confucian system in general and the Confucian worship of chastity and widowhood in particular, while Hu Shih, a typical rationalist, grounded in the scientific method of research, was actually more moderate and wrote like a scholar. Chen condemned and denounced other superstitions, like the Chinese planchette in which the mediums wrote out scholarly verse. Of course, the literary organ also took foot binding in its stride, although it was a somewhat belated effort. We were already living in republican days. A zealous student wrote, "We all ought to bear [the responsibility for] all China's women's small feet upon our shoulders"—certainly an unusual task for the new champions of liberty, considering the fact that there were at least fifty million small feet of Chinese women to carry, and that this young man might have weak knees. Inevitably I gravitated toward the Peking National University, which I joined later, after my return from abroad. In the midst of this general *Umwälzung*, or upheaval, I plunged into the study, for my own salvation, of Chinese philosophy and philology—everything I could lay my hands on. I swam—and how I swam—in that vigorous current of Chinese awakening!

There was a man, however, who did not join the hue and cry. He had returned from the universities of Berlin and Edinburgh and Oxford in the year 1885, and was therefore a generation above me. For him, we, the young upstarts of the republican days, were ignoramuses and cads, if not sneaks, who had been corrupted by the modern mob worship, pleasantly called democracy, tarnished souls all, or, as he put it, "the modern queueless, up-to-date Chinamen, the returned students" who "had learned from the people of Europe and America" not to behave themselves but to "misbehave themselves." He was a crank but not a bore, for his was a first-class mind and he had, above all, insight and depth, as no man in my generation had. No man in China wrote English the way he did, because of his challenging ideas and because of his masterly style, a style reminiscent of Matthew Arnold's poised and orderly evolution of ideas and repetition of certain phrases, plus the dramatic bombast of Thomas Carlyle and the witticisms of Heine. This man's name was Ku Hung-ming. Ku Hung-ming was a son of Amoy. Ku acted like a glass of claret before one tackled the feast of Chinese humanism; he played a critical role in the direction of my beliefs by turning everything upside down.

I cannot do better than quote Somerset Maugham's description of him. Maugham never mentioned Ku Hung-ming's name, but used the phrase "the philosopher" in his book *On a Chinese Screen*. Maugham saw him in Szechuen, above the Yangtse Gorges, probably in 1921. Here is a vivid description, very much to the point as revealing the man's character:

> And here lived a philosopher of repute, the desire to see whom had been to me one of the incentives of a somewhat arduous journey. He was the greatest authority in China on the Confucian learning. He was said to speak English and German with facility. He had been for many years secretary to one of the Empress Dowager's greatest viceroys, but he

lived now in retirement. On certain days in the week, however, all through the year he opened his doors to such as
sought after knowledge and discoursed on the teaching of
Confucius. He had a body of disciples, but it was small,
since the students for the most part preferred to his modest
dwelling and his severe exaltations the sumptuous buildings
of the foreign university and the useful science of the bar-
barians: with him this was mentioned only to be scornfully
dismissed. From all I heard of him I concluded that he was
a man of character.

When I announced my wish to meet this distinguished gentleman, my host immediately offered to arrange a meeting;
but the days passed and nothing happened. I made inquiries
and my host shrugged his shoulders.

"I sent him a chit and told him to come along," he said. "I
don't know why he hasn't turned up. He's a cross-grained old
fellow."

I did not think it was proper to approach a philosopher in
so cavalier a fashion and I was hardly surprised that he had
ignored a summons such as this. I caused a letter to be sent
asking in the politest terms I could devise whether he would
allow me to call upon him and within two hours received an
answer making an appointment for the following morning at
ten o'clock. . . .

The philosopher entered. I hastened to express my sense of
the honor he did me in allowing me to visit him. He waved
me to a chair and poured out the tea.

"I am flattered that you wished to see me," he returned.
"Your countrymen deal only with coolies and with compradores; they think every Chinese must be one or the other."

I ventured to protest. But I had not caught his point. He
leaned back in his chair and looked at me with an expression
of mockery.

"They think they have but to beckon and we must come."

I saw then that my friend's unfortunate communication still
rankled. I did not quite know how to reply. I murmured
something complimentary.

He was an old man, tall, with a thin grey queue, and bright
large eyes under which were heavy bags. His teeth were

broken and discolored. He was exceedingly thin, and his hands, fine and small, were withered and claw-like. I had been told that he was an opium-smoker. He was very shabbily dressed in a black gown, a little black cap, both much the worse for wear, and dark grey trousers gartered at the ankle. He was watching. He did not quite know what attitude to take up, and he had the manner of a man who was on his guard. . . . Presently I was conscious of a certain relaxation in his demeanor. He was like a man who was all set and rigid to have his photograph taken, but hearing the shutter click lets himself go and eases into his natural self. He showed me his books.

"I took the Ph.D. in Berlin, you know," he said. "And afterward I studied for some time in Oxford. But the English, if you will allow me to say so, have no great aptitude for philosophy."

Though he put the remark apologetically, it was evident that he was not displeased to say a slightly disagreeable thing.

"We have had philosophers who have not been without influence in the world of thought," I suggested.

"Hume and Berkeley? The philosophers who taught at Oxford when I was there were anxious not to offend their theological colleagues. They would not follow their thought to its logical consequences in case they should jeopardize their position in university society."

"Have you studied the modern developments of philosophy in America?" I asked.

"Are you speaking of Pragmatism? It is the last refuge of those who want to believe the incredible. I have more use for American petroleum than for American philosophy."

And so on, with more of this tartness. I think Maugham's characterization is just (I have sworn not to use the favorite cliché of the critics, the word "perceptive"). "But his study of Western philosophy had only served in the end to satisfy him that wisdom after all was to be found within the limits of the Confucian canon."

Once my friend saw him at the Chenkuang cinema theater, and in front of Ku sat a bald-headed Scotsman. Now, a white man is usually treated with great respect throughout China. But Ku Hung-ming made a point of insulting a white man to show that the Chinese were superior. He wanted to light a foot-long Chinese pipe and had run out of matches. When he spotted the Scotsman in front of him, he lightly tapped the Scot's bald head with his pipe and, with outstretched, tapering fingers, said calmly, "Light, please!" The Scotsman was so taken aback that he obliged in the most Christian manner. Perhaps Ku is best known among the Chinese for his witty defense of concubinage: "You have seen a teapot with four teacups," he said. "But have you ever seen a teacup with four teapots?" It was also said among us that if you wanted to see Ku Hung-ming, the way was not to go to his house but to look for him in the Pata Hutung red-light district. This was not the pose of an old roué, it was a philosophic conviction of some importance. He urged the ignorant Westerners to go to the Pata Hutung district if they wanted to study the true Chinese culture and civilization, and witness for themselves the essential decency, modesty, and virtue of Chinese womanhood in the person of the singsong girls. And Ku was not far wrong, for the singsong artists, like the geishas of Japan, could still blush, whereas the modern college girl had ceased to do so.

Ku Hung-ming had acted as Governor Chang Chih-tung's "secretary-interpreter." (Chang Chih-tung was himself one of the great reformist mandarins toward the end of the nineteenth century, and played an important role in keeping the Boxer Uprising out of the Yangtse valley.) I saw Ku, with very thin hair, walking alone in the central park. One might have taken him for a eunuch fallen upon bad days, or not noticed him at all. What pride of isolation! However, I did not feel equal to approaching this expert on Matthew Arnold and Ruskin and Emerson and Goethe and Schiller. And this, in spite of the fact that I had admired him from a great distance in my college days, when Eugene Chen (later foreign minister of the Nationalist Government in 1928) and Ku Hung-ming were exchanging blows in the *Peking Gazette* (an English daily edited by Chen) in 1915. Ku was a confirmed royalist and a proud supporter of a lost cause, and Chen a republican. Both were past masters of the diatribe, and perfectly at home in English. Chen called Ku a mountebank and a scribe, and Ku called Chen a jackal and a "babu" (a denationalized, half-Anglicized Hindu), for Chen, born in Trinidad, spoke Chinese like a foreigner. When I was studying in Germany, which was just after the close of the first Great War, I found that Ku Hung-ming was quite well known in certain circles in that country. His booklet *Verteidigung Chinas gegen Europa* (so far as I can remember, a German translation of his book *The Spirit of the Chinese Civilization*) was well known among cultured circles. The book was written in 1915, shortly after the outbreak of the Great War, and although he castigated Prussian militarism in no uncertain terms, he placed the first blame for the war on the "bastard British imperialism" and the "Cockney mob worship." He had kind things to say for the German "intense love of righteousness," for order and tidiness (*Zucht und Ordnung*), and for their "moral fiber." At home in Goethe and Schiller, and a great admirer of Frederick the Great and Prince Bismarck, his words have had a good hearing in Germany, although he is totally unknown in the United States.

Ku Hung-ming was strong meat and not for weak stomachs, and for Westerners especially his writings are as full of bristles as a porcupine. But he had depth and insight, which excuse many sins, for the quality of true insight is rare. Not the least of his services was his translation of three of the Confucian *Four Books*. It was more than a faithful translation. It was an act of creative interpretation, a sudden transfusion of light of the old texts through a deep philosophic understanding. He acted, in fact, as the galvanizer of ideas Eastern and Western. His *Discourses and Sayings of Confucius* was studded with illuminating remarks from Goethe, Schiller, Ruskin, and Joubert. His translations of the Confucian books were good because the originals were well understood. Chinese classics had never been well translated. The Sinologues did a poor job of it, and the Chinese themselves had neglected it. The translation from Chinese into English was so difficult. The ideas were so different and, what was worse, the modes of thought were so different, and what was still worse, grammatical relations were expressed solely by syntax in Chinese, without inflections and without the usual connectives and articles and sometimes without the subject of a predicate. Thus the very "sources" of Chinese philosophy were, and still are very much today, clothed in a twilight of hazy likenesses. The result is that Herbert A. Giles, the late professor of Chinese at Cambridge, was able to express his opinion that Confucius was perhaps only a dull, humdrum, platitudinous village schoolmaster. The pitfalls in the translation of philosophic ideas are very great. The very concepts for *ren* (benevolence? mercy? humanity? manhood?), for *yi* (justice? right? righteousness?), for *li* (ritualism? courtesy? good form? social order?) have not been even understood.

In this connection I may perhaps be excused for giving an example of cumbersome circumlocution which passes for translation. This is from James Legge, whose translations of the Confucian classics have been incorporated in the *Sacred Books of the Far East,* edited by Max Müller. Legge made a fetish of literalness, as if a certain air of foreign remoteness, rather than clarity, were the mark of fidelity. What Mencius said was this, in exactly twelve words in Chinese, that when armies were lined up with spears and shields to attack a city, "the weather is less important than the terrain, and the terrain less important than the army morale." Or, more literally, if one preferred: "Sky-times not so good as ground-situation; ground-situation not so good as human harmony." To any Chinese child "sky-times" simply means the weather and can mean nothing else; "ground-situation" means the terrain, and "human harmony" means the army morale. But, according to Legge, Mencius said, "Opportunities of time (vouchsafed by) Heaven are not equal to advantages of situa-

tion (afforded by) the Earth, and advantages of situation
(afforded by) the Earth are not equal to (the union arising
from) the accord of Men." Ku Hung-ming's translations will
forever stand, for they have that happy matching of sense and
expression that can come only through the mastery of both
languages and understanding of their deeper meanings. Ku's
translations are veritable revelations.

Nurtured on Matthew Arnold, Carlyle, Ruskin, Emerson,
Goethe, and Schiller, Ku thought he comprehended Confucianism as no other man ever did before him. His central idea
turned around the question of culture and vulgarity. Culture
meant the Confucian idea of the gentleman, and vulgarity, in
Ruskin's terms, was simply "a dead callousness of the body
and the soul" and "a want of sensation." What put teeth into
all his discussion of culture and anarchy was the spectacle
of white imperialism fighting to grab China's territory while
its apostles, including certainly some Christian missionaries,
pontificated about the "heathen Chinee" and about their civi-
lizing mission to educate them, especially after the Boxer
Uprising. When the open robbery of China's territory in the
name of the Open Door was accompanied by what he called
the "unbearable British cant" about civilization, and when the
white man added insult to injury by abusing "H.I.M. the
Empress Dowager" in the *North China Daily News*, Ku was
enormously nettled. He lashed out at what he called the
"bastard British imperialism" catering to the Cockney instinct
of trade and money-grabbing and "worship of the mob" and
the "man-eating Kolonial Politik" of the Kaiser, and the combination of the cad and the sneak whose own souls were very
much in need of salvation. It was nationalism with a sting and
a vengeance in it, plus a royalist, antidemocratic bias with an
ideal of "kingliness," such as that represented by Frederick the
Great (Carlyle's influence).

For Ku Hung-ming, the Boxer Uprising was the voice of the
people, and it was in his *Papers from a Viceroy's Yamen*, published in 1901, in the wake of the confusion, that he was at

his most caustic and astringent. The plain fact was, of course, that the Boxer Uprising was precipitated by the unholy trinity of missionary, opium, and gunboat. It must be remembered that for the murder of one missionary, China had to pay Kaiser Wilhelm with the port of Tsingtao and the railway rights of the entire province of Shantung. White imperialism *was* rampant. And when the very integrity of China was at stake, Ku Hung-ming flayed and lashed out with all his strength, and all but sank his teeth into the flesh of the British religion of mob worship and of the Kaiser's "Kolonial Politik." He wrote *Defensio Populi ad Populos,* or "The Modern Missionaries Considered in Relation to the Recent Riots." His voice cried to high Heaven. The *Papers from a Viceroy's Yamen* contained, as the longest paper, the *Latter-Day Notes on the Chinese Question* (originally published in the *Japan Mail* in Yokohama), which proved to be a historical examination of culture and its degeneration in England, France, Germany, and the United States. His voice was strident; he had no geniality in his soul, but the wine of his sarcasm was strong. This is the tone of light mockery of the Englishman in China:

> After Lord Beaconsfield's death, the British aristocracy again became helpless, and their doyen, Lord Salisbury, met a Birmingham lad with a Cockney intellect. This Birmingham Cockney has been trying to toady to the pride of the British aristocracy by copying the flag of Lord Beaconsfield's Imperialism and waving it aloft for the self-assertion of the Anglo-Saxon race! . . . Really, were it not so tragic, the picture of the fine old British aristocracy, now hard up for money as well as in ideals and ideas, being led by a small Birmingham Cockney lad with his "Imperial" rag of Anglo-Saxon self-assertion, would be as comical as the picture of the Scotch "pennyless lass with a lang pedigree."*

In swift, impressionistic strokes, Ku traced the intellectual degeneration of Germany and France:

* This and the following quotations are from *Papers from a Viceroy's Yamen,* Kelly & Walsh, Shanghai, 1901.

After Frederick, Germany is Prussia. Germany is the Scotland of Europe. The Prussian is the Lowland Scot who, living in a flat country, is devoid of imagination. Moreover, the climate in Prussia is much more severe. Therefore, the Prussian, besides want of imagination, has—a terrible appetite. "In our family," says Prince Bismarck, "we are all great eaters (*lauter starke Esser*). If many had such an appetite (*Kapacität!*) like us, why! the nation would not be able to exist. I would have to emigrate." . . . Frederick had no imagination. But he had, besides genius, the French culture, *l'ésprit*, the quick movement of mind and lucidity of the French culture. After Frederick, the Prussian Puritan for want of imagination could not continue the Lord Protectorate over Germany. Therefore, Napoleon had to come back with the Glorious Restoration at Jena. . . . Emerson, with great insight, has remarked that what sent Napoleon to St. Helena was not loss of battles, but the vulgarity, the *bourgeois*, the Cockney in him. All the cultivated gentlemen of Europe hailed Napoleon when he came as the bringer of the great Liberal ideas of the Revolution. But when they found out that the Corsican *bourgeois* only wanted to found a dynasty, all the gentlemen of Europe were disgusted. Then the Prussian Puritan in the uniform of Marschal "Vorwärts" arose and joined the gentlemen of Europe in their chase of the Corsican *bourgeois*. . . . When Marschal "Vorwärts" chased Napoleon out of Germany, he wanted to chase also the great Liberal ideas of the French Revolution. Against this the whole of intellectual Germany rose to fight him. That was the beginning of the "Kulturkampf." . . . The true great Liberal ideas of the French Revolution are for "open door," *carrière ouverte aux talents*, in politics and for "expansion" in religion. The inclination to selfishness of the Lowland Scot in Marschal "Vorwärts" made him dislike the "open door" and the want of imagination of the Prussian Puritan hindered him from understanding what "expansion" means in religion.

And so on and on Ku Hung-ming rattles. He skips and romps through the grounds of modern European history. And he arrives at the remarkable conclusion that "the real Anarchy of the world today is not in China, although the Chinese are suffering from its effects—but in Europe and America." And he cried out to the people of Europe, *"Seht zu! Voelker Europas! Wahret eure heiligsten Gueter!"* (Look out! People of Europe! Look after your holy cultural values!)

In respect to true Christianity, Ku Hung-ming did not attack the teachings of Jesus Christ, but he vehemently attacked the active co-operation of the Jesuits with the French Army and that of the German bishops with the German Army during the Boxer Rebellion. Here is an example of his bitterness:

> Christianity was formerly a power that kept down the selfishness of the Lowland Scot and the terrible appetite of the Pomeranian great eater in the German nation. But now Christianity in Germany is as dead as the dodo. In its place they have officially set up the Christianity of Bishop Anser, of Kiaochow fame, or perhaps of that national-socialist and political person who thus writes in the last number of the *Zukunft* on the "No Pardon" speech of the German Kaiser: "What are we to do with 50,000 Chinamen who surrender? To feed them won't do." Therefore, when we meet with 50,000 caterpillars, what are we to do? Crush them with a roller. Disgusting business! But it cannot be helped. We do not know how Jesus might have spoken if He had lived not in a world of peace, but of wars. Jesus Christ, too, according to this parson, would become a carnivorous animal!

And this is what he said about the true Christian and true Christianity. Quoting Confucius, he says:

> It is what you are: that is your religion. It is not your religion which makes you what you are. Be unselfish and merciful, then, no matter whether you are a Jew, Chinese or German, a merchant, missionary, soldier, diplomat or coolie—you are a Christian, a civilized man. But be selfish, be unmerciful, then you are a sneak, a cad, a *Philister*, a heathen, an Amalekite, a savage, a beast, even if you are the emperor of the world.

Then he went on to quote Goethe's conception of Christianity, of progress, and of civilization in *Dichtung und Wahr-*

heit as consisting in mercy and considerateness and being human even to the inhuman. "It will have yet to be seen whether Europe and America, in dealing with the Chinese Problem, will adopt Goethe's conception of civilization or that of the German political person who, with his steam roller, wants to make Jesus Christ a carnivorous animal!"

> The true Christian is one who is a Christian because "it is his nature to be so," because he loves holiness and all that is lovable in Christianity. . . . That is the true Christian. The sneak Christian is one who wants to be a Christian because he is afraid of hell-fire. The cad Christian is one who wants to be a Christian because he wishes to go to Heaven to drink tea and sing hymns with the angels. Now, the true Jesuit is one who does not very much believe in Heaven, angels or hell-fire, but he wants other people to believe in these things—to be a Christian for his benefit! That is the Jesuit.

Such reading was strong wine which easily went to the head of a young Chinese reader. It was good reading, but also reading with a peculiar soul-provoking quality, for one about to ask what was the essence of Christianity and what was, after all, Confucianism. So, relaxed and amused, one could sit back and read more comfortably his rather extraordinary criticism of the different nations:

> The American people, I may be permitted to say here, find it difficult to understand the real Chinaman and the Chinese civilization, because the American people, as a rule, are broad, simple, but not deep. The English cannot understand the real Chinaman and the Chinese civilization because the English, as a rule, are deep, simple, but not broad. The Germans again cannot understand the real Chinaman and the Chinese civilization because the Germans, especially the educated Germans, as a rule, are deep, broad, but not simple. The French,—well, the French are the people, it seems to me, who can understand and have understood the real Chinaman and the Chinese civilization best . . . [because] the French people have to a preëminent degree a quality of mind such as all the people I

have mentioned above as a rule, have not,—a quality of mind which, above all things, is necessary in order to understand the real Chinaman and the Chinese civilization; a quality of mind, namely, *delicacy*.

It will be seen from what I have said above that the American people, if they will study the Chinese civilization, will get depth; the English, broadness; the Germans, simplicity; and all of them, Americans, English and Germans, by the study of the Chinese civilization, of Chinese books and literature, will get a quality of mind which, I take the liberty of saying here that it seems to me, they all of them, as a rule, have not to a preëminent degree, namely delicacy.*

It was all very comfortable and very soothing. I dispute the point that the Chinese had breadth or broadness, although simplicity and delicacy and depth they certainly have. But one was stimulated by such reading to rediscover one's own country, and to make a journey of exploration through the obscure, luxuriant jungle of Chinese thought and try to arrive at some kind of understanding.

* From the Preface to *The Spirit of the Chinese Civilization*, published in Peking, 1915.

CHAPTER 3

The Mansion of Confucius

K U HUNG-MING had helped to cast off my moorings and put me out to a sea of doubts. Perhaps without Ku Hung-ming I would have returned to the national stream of thought anyway; no Chinese could, if he was of a searching mind, remain long satisfied with a half-knowledge of the Chinese intellectual landscape. The call to discover one's own history and national heritage was a call from the deep. There was something in the character of the Chinese language which invisibly but most emphatically changed one's mode of thought. The modes of thinking, the concepts, the images, the very sounds of words are so different between the English language and the Chinese. Speaking English, one thinks in English, and speaking in Chinese one thinks inevitably in Chinese. If I were to write two essays one morning on the same subject with the same ideas, one in English and the other in Chinese, the essays themselves would come out differently because the flow of thought, following different imagery and allusions and associations, would automatically lead into different avenues. Man does not talk because he thinks, but thinks because he talks, because he has words to play with, and thinking is only the tumbling about of words. The ideas themselves come wearing a different dress and complexion when one speaks a different language because the words have a different timbre and different associations. Hence, studying Chinese, I began to think as a Chinese, and thinking as a Chinese I understood and accepted certain truths and imagery almost instinctively. The leap between the two languages so different as the Chinese and the English was somewhat bizarre. The English in me laughed at the smooth, shining pebbles of Chinese monosyllabism, and the Chinese in me recognized the greater definition and exactness of English thought but also ridiculed its jumble of incredible abstractions.

Now the Chinese, I must say, have no aptitude for abstract ideas. In the Chinese language, as in woman's gossip, everything creeps or crawls or gets married or has an in-law. Chinese abstract ideas, following the law of Chinese concrete thinking, are often composites of two concrete qualities: thus *big-small* stands for "size" ("What is the *big-small* of the diamond?"), *long-short* stands for "length," and *light-heavy,* for "weight." What is still more inexplicable is that the ordinary word for "thing" is *east-west* ("Have you got any *east-west* to eat in the icebox?"). Strictly philosophic concepts, "right," "justice," "loyalty," "interests," are cryptic monosyllables which tend constantly to resemble one another. In the case of *shih* and *fei,* merging the two pairs of concepts, true and false and right and wrong, the demarcation of areas is almost obliterated. Furthermore, the separation of the heart and the head becomes impossible when Chinese avow that they think with their stomachs ("In my belly I think," sometimes "In my heart I think"). The word *shin* means both the heart and the mind at the same time, wherefore the Chinese are so emotional in their thinking. The Biblical "bowels" comes nearest to it. Oliver Cromwell in his letter to the General Assembly of the Church of Scotland in 1650, says, "I beseech you, in the bowels of Christ, consider that ye may be mistaken." In Chinese thinking, therefore, having few abstractions or none, one never leaves the periphery of life. There is no danger of being submerged in the process of abstract ratiocinations too long. One is like a whale which must come up to the surface to breathe the free air, incidentally taking a look at the clouds and the sky. One result of such thinking is the absence of academic jargon in Chinese philosophy, of the specialist's code of communication, and the absence of a division between "popular" knowledge and scientific knowledge. It was never a shame to write about philosophy in a language which the common people could understand. The Chinese academicians did not look upon the "popularizers" of knowledge with contempt. It may be true that Plato wrote two versions of his philosophy, one technical and the other "popular," and that the technical version fortunately did not survive, so that the modern reader may enjoy the clarity of Plato's *Dialogues*. If Western philosophers could use the English language with the ease and clarity of Plato, philosophy might yet win a place in the common man's thinking, which it decidedly has not. (I suspect that if they were to write clearly, they would reveal that they haven't anything to say.)

I have sometimes asked myself, Did China ever produce a mind like Kant's? The answer is, obviously, No. Moreover, she could not. A Chinese Kant would laugh at himself the moment he talked of the *Ding-an-sich*, the thing-in-itself: his reasoning—and he could have a powerful reasoning, immediate and intuitive—his reasoning would tell him that he was becoming ridiculous. All knowledge, according to Kant, is derived from sense perceptions: fine. All reasoning is determined by a priori laws of the mind: fine. Thus a blind man would gain knowledge of a pear or a banana by feeling the difference between the texture of the pear skin and of the banana skin through the tactile sense of his fingers. Surely, however, the Chinese philosopher would feel that there must be qualities and differences in the pear skin and the banana skin corresponding to the resulting differences in touch. Isn't this knowledge "real"? What do you want to know the banana-in-itself and the pear-

in-itself for? Granted that a different being, differently constituted and endowed with different psychic powers, say, a
Martian, would by a different kind of sense feel the difference
between the banana skin and the pear skin in a different way.
Would not this difference still correspond to a difference between the banana-in-itself and the pear-in-itself? What profit
is it, then, to talk of the banana-in-itself and pear-in-itself
instead of apprehending the immediate feeling and experience
of the tougher skin of the pear and the smoother, softer skin
of the banana which communicates itself to one immediately,
accurately, and most usefully? And so with the immediate
apprehension of the differences in sound waves by the ear and
of light waves by the eye. These are nature's ways of "knowledge," so subtly developed that a deer can apprehend the
presence of a tiger at a great distance by its smell or sound or
sight. These senses must be extraordinarily accurate and must
correspond to the real environment and therefore must be
"real," or the deer would not be able to survive. It should be
remembered, for instance, that the picture of a changing outside world, such as that of a car two hundred yards away and
moving in one's direction or away from it, is recorded in the
image of the retina within the area of half an inch, and therefore the image of the moving car itself can only be perhaps a
thousandth of an inch, and this slight change in the ten-
thousandths of an inch is registered immediately and usually
infallibly. What did Kant want to talk about the car-in-itself
for? The Western philosopher will answer immediately, "You
Chinamen, you don't understand what Kant is talking about."
"Of course I don't," counters the Chinese. "Now may I eat my
banana?" And so the Occidental and the Oriental must shrug
their shoulders and part company.

And I have also asked myself, Did China ever produce a
mind like Aristotle's? The answer is, again obviously, No.
Moreover, she could not. The capacity for analysis, the sys-
tematic and logical examination of ideas, the objective interest
in the different avenues of thought and fields of knowledge

were not there. For the striking thing about Plato and Aristotle is that their mode of reasoning is so modern, and the
Chinese mode of reasoning is totally different. After all, the
medieval scholastic type of reasoning and the epistemological
witch hunt began with Aristotle. A Chinese is well prepared
to hear about Aristotle's *Ethics* and *Politics* and *Poetics,* and
is amazed and duly impressed at his *breadth,* at his knowledge
of botany and astronomy and meteorology and biology, crude
as his notions often are. The dispassionate inquiry, the curious
objective dissection of life in all its segments in physics and
biology (for Aristotle was a medical doctor), is astounding.
The limited vision of the Chinese compels him to make a
scientific classification of all chicken as either "tough" or
"tender," while its possible relation to other fowl such as the
pheasant or the guinea hen is dismissed at once as idle. Confucius had a disciple, Tseshia, who had a propensity for accumulating facts of information, and who was interested in
the birds and insects mentioned in the *Book of Songs.* Confucius said to him: "Be a gentleman scholar; do not be a petty
scholar. That type of knowledge which consists in memorizing
facts to answer questions is not worthy to make one a teacher."

The Chinese, in fact, are given to the intuitive comprehension of the totality, which Professor F. S. C. Northrop of Yale
calls the "undifferentiated esthetic continuum." What Professor
Northrop means is that the Chinese like to size up things at
a glance and thus preserve a better sense of their totality;
they are forever suspicious of the dissection of the indivisible.
They rely rather on the immediate perceptions. What Egon
Friedell says of Emerson's style of thought is true of the
Chinese philosopher: "His propositions are there, unprepared,
indisputable, like sailors' signals coming out of a misty deep.
. . . He is an absolute Impressionist in his style, his composition and his thought. He never propounds his ideas in a definite logical or artistic form, but always in the natural and often
accidental order which they have in his head. . . . Things like
'order of content,' 'introduction,' 'transitions' do not exist for

him. He begins to develop this or that view, and we think he is going to weave it systematically, elucidate it from all sides and entrench it against all possible attack. But then, suddenly, some alien picture or simile, epigram or *aperçu* strikes him, full in the middle of his chain of thought, and the theme thenceforward revolves on a quite new axis."

So my grand detour began. At first it made no sense to me. Trained in the modern weapon of thought like any college graduate, my mind had to flash across the continents of thought, and found them strange, or uninteresting or jejune. (Confucius always sounds a little jejune at first.) I wrote on my fortieth birthday a couplet to myself: "One mind seeks the learning of ancients and moderns; Two legs straddle the cultures of East and West." I had to interpret the Chinese conscience and intuitive perceptions in the more exact frame of logical thinking, and subject the propositions of Western thinking to the test of Chinese intuitive judgment.

I must therefore pause to describe in separate chapters what I have seen on the way before I came to accept Christianity as a "satisfactory" answer to man's spiritual problems. Some people have expressed surprise, and even regret, that I have returned to Christianity, and found it hard to believe that I should exchange the gay, cheerful, reasonable acceptance of the world, with its joyful realism, for a more questionable and metaphysical entity called the Christian "faith." I think I should make the evolution and the transition clear by detailing both the beauties and the deficiencies of the Chinese systems, by pointing out wherein they have reached heights of their own and wherein they have fallen short of giving a completely satisfactory answer. I should also make it clear that Heaven and Hell have nothing to do with it. I still know, as I have said elsewhere, that if God loves me only half as much as my mother did, He will not send me to Hell—as Christian religion would have it, not for five minutes, not for five days, but for all eternity—a sentence which even a secular court would never find it in its heart to condemn me to. I would not believe such a thing. I have returned to the Christian Church rather by an intuitive perception of my moral being, by one of those "signals out of the deep" at which the Chinese excel. And I must make it clear that the process is not facile or easy, that I do not lightly change what I have always believed, that I have roamed in the pastures of sweet, silent thought and beheld some beautiful valleys. I have dwelt in the mansion of Confucian humanism, and climbed the peaks of Mount Tao and beheld its glories, and have had glimpses of the dissolving mist of Buddhism hanging over a terrifying void, and only after doing so have I ascended the Jungfrau of Christian belief and reached the world of sunlight above the clouds.

I shall discuss only Confucianism and Taoism, the two most important and most influential streams of Chinese thought, and Buddhism, the third great spiritual force in the Orient. There were in ancient Chinese philosophy besides Confucianism and Taoism also the Sophists, the Logicians, the Legalists, the Motians or Motseans (followers of Moti or Motse), and the Yang Chu School (living for oneself), besides a number of other minor schools. I shall not even touch upon the Motseans, because the school completely died out in the third and second centuries B.C. and therefore left no permanent influence on Chinese thought. But Moti and his followers were remarkable for the development of the question-and-answer method and of logic. His was indeed a remarkable religion of asceticism and living for others and self-sacrifice based on the doctrine of "fatherhood of God" and brotherhood of Man ("universal love"). It is said that the Motseans "wore the hair off their calves," that is, worked themselves to the bone, to help others. Moti also definitely taught a monotheistic God which he called Heaven, the regular word in Chinese for God.*

* For some readings in Moti, or Motse, see my selections in *The Wisdom of China and India,* and in regard to the Logicians, or Neo-Motseans, see Hu Shih's *The Development of the Logical Method in Ancient China.* There was an incredible complexity and richness of thought of

In the following three chapters, on Confucianism, Taoism, and Buddhism, my concern is chiefly with man's spiritual problems and how these respective systems of thought bear on a view of the universe and on a philosophy of life. I am concerned chiefly with the ideals of life and human character. The teachings of Jesus are admittedly in a category by themselves, unique and of a strange beauty, teaching something which is not found in other religions. Yet I should like to say here explicitly, first, that it would not do to make a convenient contrast between darkness and light, or to say that, Christianity being "true," Confucianism is therefore "false." It would not do to dismiss the Buddhist religion with the simple phrase "heathen idolatry." And it would not do to say that Jesus' teachings on love and humility are right, therefore Laotse's teachings on the power of love are wrong. Perhaps that is the very reason why I must go into these three systems of thought and these ideals of life, before comparisons can be made. Second, it must be pointed out that systems of thought are rarely mutually exclusive at all points. Even Stoicism and Epicureanism appear to be mutually exclusive on the surface, but approach each other on closer scrutiny. This is particularly true of the Chinese teachings as regarded by the Chinese themselves. It is not Chinese Pyrrhonism; it is merely the Chinese ability to admit truth and beauty wherever they are found. The great Chinese minds like Po Chuyi (eighth century) and Su Tungpo (eleventh) lived Confucian lives, and wrote Buddhist poetry permeated with Taoist sentiments. Especially in the case of Confucianism, it is not possible to say that a Christian cannot be a Confucianist. For Confu-

---

divergent schools in the few centuries following Confucius, and also a great deal of interaction between the different schools. For a glimpse of the complex situation, see the extremely important *Prolegomena*, or *The Main Currents of Ancient Chinese Thought* by Chuangtse in *Wisdom of Laotse* (Modern Library), translated by myself; and further, for a very stimulating discussion of the interrelation of Confucianism and Taoism, see *A Confucian Notebook* and *A Taoist Notebook* by Edward Herbert in the *Wisdom of the East* series.

cianism is the religion of the "gentleman," of "good breeding" and "good manners," and to say that would almost amount to saying that a good Christian does not believe in being a gentleman, in good manners. Taoism reinforces the Christian teachings on love and gentleness more than many people dare to admit. And if the Buddhist formula for salvation is different from the Christian one, its basic starting point, the recognition of sin and deep concern with the fact of human suffering, is akin to Christianity.

The best example of this merging of cultures is found in the poems of Su Tungpo to his mistress Chaoyun. Su Tungpo, one of the greatest of Chinese poets and a great Confucian scholar, was living in exile, in his sixties. His wife had died, and his young mistress chose to follow him to his exile, in A.D. 1094, at Huichow. Now, Chaoyun had become a Buddhist, and Su praised her as a celestial maiden of Vimalakirti in the service of God (*Buddhist*). In one of the poems, Su Tungpo spoke of her throwing aside the long-sleeved dancing dress of the past, and being occupied with Buddhist sutras and the pill furnace (*Taoist*). When the pill of immortality should be formed, she was going to say goodbye to him and enter the fairy mountains (*Taoist*). No longer would she be like the fairy maidens of the Wu Gorges, tied to a mortal union (*Confucianist*). It is this curious mixture of religious emotion and human sentiments which so distinguishes another poem. The imagery of the Buddhist celestial maiden of Vimalakirti ("Name Undefiled") appears again. The celestial maiden, according to Buddhist legend, would scatter flowers from heaven, and the flower petals would slip off the dresses or bodies of the saints, but would cling to those who still had mortal desires. He wrote:

> When time's due course doth age with white hair crown,
> And Vimalakirti so well doth one become,
> Fear not the flower petals that do no harm,
> Though the heavenly maiden scatters them around.
> Thy lips enchant; thy hair glorifies;
> So this eternal cycle of life goes on,

Because this sentient heart of love is fond,
Engenders human gestures and mortal ties.
I see thee sit with a sweetly pensive smile,
Setting thy curls, or archly letting them fall.
Tomorrow is Tuanwu Day! Come, I shall
Pick thee an orchid corsage, and with my wile
    Compose for thee the sweetest poem ever known
    And write it on the girdles of thy gown.

The following summer Chaoyun died. She said a Buddhist verse before she drew her last breath, and was buried, according to her wish, near a Buddhist temple. The poem Su Tungpo wrote on the white plum blossoms upon her grave is one of the most exquisite things I have ever read:

Bones of jade, flesh of snow,
May thy ethereal spirit stand unafraid,
Though the dark mist and the swamp winds blow.
May the sea spirits attend thee,
The paroquets and cockatoos befriend thee!
Thy white face doth powder spurn;
Vermilion must yet from thy lips learn.
Flesh of snow, bones of jade,
Dream thy dreams, peerless one.
Not for this world thou art made.

Such indeed is human life, with its problems of pain and death and loneliness and the relation of the spirit and the flesh, as expressed by a great human spirit. Here the spirit of man is confronted with the problems of human life, with all its pathos and its beauty. It is this very problem of human life which Jesus solved with such clarity and simplicity.

I. Confucius the Man

If I write about the mansion of Confucian philosophy now, I am aware that thousands of Chinese scholars have done so before me; still, I can write only of my own perceptions and

insights and my own evaluations and interpretations. I accept
nothing, take nothing for granted, and am inclined to strip
Confucius and Confucianism of certain notions and beliefs
with which they have been colored. I am more of a Taoist by
instinct than a Confucianist by belief. The Neo-Confucianists
have looked at Confucius' teachings through Buddhist eyes;
why should I not look at Confucius' teachings through Taoist
eyes? Confucianism and Taoism are regarded as the opposite
poles of Chinese thought: Confucius was a positivist, Laotse
a mystic; Confucius' main concern was with man, while Laotse's
main concern was with the mystery and nature of the universe;
Confucius regarded the universe as a part of man, while Laotse
considered man as a part of the universe. And yet the matter
is not so clear-cut and simple at close range. I think a great
deal of Confucius' concern about God and God's will and his
view of the spiritual nature of the universe have been obscured
by the usual notion of Confucian positivism. For Taoism means
depth, and Confucianism is all on the surface, at least decep-
tively so. A Taoist mind can better appreciate certain aspects
of Confucius and his doctrines and save him from the virtue
of mere obviousness and occupation with the practical problems of living. In particular, I wish to examine Confucius'
attitude and feelings toward the larger problems of death and
God and God's will and the spiritual nature of man.

Confucius was born in 551 B.C. out of wedlock. His father
was one of the three famous captains of Lu, and the following story is told of one of his exploits. Once he had led the
Lu army to invade a town. When half of his troops had entered
the gate of the enemy town and half were still outside, the
enemy suddenly let down the gate from above and his troops
were trapped. Confucius' father, sensing treachery, held up
the gate single-handedly until all his troops could beat a retreat.

The father of Confucius was well over sixty when he married the youngest of three sisters, a very young girl who became Confucius' mother. Confucian Puritans have tried their
best to explain away the historical record that he was born

"out of wedlock," but I think there is no necessity to do so. Children born out of wedlock have often been very brilliant, and this is natural. "All children are natural," as a French lady says, but I think illegitimate children are more natural than the others; that is to say, the child is usually the result of a violent romance obeying the law of natural sexual attraction. Other records seem to support the story, for the great historian Szema Chien recorded that Confucius' father died when Confucius was a baby and that his mother would not tell the whereabouts of his father's grave. ("His mother concealed the truth from him.") It was only after Confucius' mother died, and when he was grown up, that he was able to learn from an old village woman who his father was and where his grave was, thereby enabling him to bury both parents together. Confucius himself was described as nine foot six inches tall, an ancient foot being the length of a span, or eight inches, which makes him about six foot four in modern measurements. In any case his nickname was "the tall man."

In his boyhood Confucius herded cattle and sheep for Lord Chi and was thus strictly a cowboy, and learned to do many menial things. But, unschooled and self-taught, he grew up to be the first scholar of his times. At the age of fifty, he was appointed Metropolitan Magistrate of Lu, promoted to Secretary of Public Works, and eventually as Grand Minister of Justice. There he had a chance to put his social and political doctrines into practice, but was disappointed and disillusioned in the nobles of Lu, who held the real power, just as Plato was to be disillusioned and disappointed in Dionysius of Syracuse. Eventually, he resigned and left his country to embark on a long period of travels and wanderings in foreign countries (that is, city-states) for fourteen years. Like Plato, he tried again to enter political life but failed, for in his mind he had his *Republic,* and believed he knew how to order it if given a chance. It was during this period of failure that Confucius was at his best. Very often he was in difficulty, scoffed at and rejected of men, and even arrested and waylaid several times, but he was "mellow and mild and did not know what to do," which a great Confucian scholar has pointed out as the most charming aspect of his character. For in this period he showed his true strength. None of the rulers were willing to take him seriously or give him power, and Confucius, to the dismay of his disciples, was contented and resigned, and even happy. It was his habit to sing or recite poetry to a self-accompaniment on a stringed instrument when arrested or under detention. He went on with his historical studies. After the wanderings of many years, he finally returned to his own country, when several of his disciples were already in the government service. He therefore returned at sixty-seven as the "grand old man," a teacher of ministers, and died at seventy-two. It was during the last four or five years that he did his greatest work. He devoted himself to editing the ancient works embodying a lifetime of historical research, and these were handed down to us as the Five Confucian Classics.

The Neo-Confucian Puritans have always tried to paint Confucius as a punctilious, venerable sage. What they did was to make him into a perfect saint and less charming human person. As a matter of fact, Confucius was a Dr. Samuel Johnson of his days, and was as much feared as he was respected. According to the *Analects*, he did quite a few things which scandalized the orthodox critics. "A sage certainly could not have done that," exclaimed such critics. "Such passages must obviously be later interpolations. Glory be to Confucius!" I need mention only one instance recorded in the *Analects*. Confucius apparently had as strong a sense of revulsion against glib talkers and hypocrites as Jesus had against the Pharisees. One day a scholar of this type came to call on Confucius. He told his servant to tell the visitor that he was not at home. Then, in order to show his stern disapproval of this man, who was called Rupei, Confucius did a rude thing. He took up his stringed instrument and sang when the caller was still at the door, "in order to let him hear it." Repeatedly Confucius said, "The respectable goody-goodies are the thieves of virtue." "The people whom I would not mind not coming in to see me when passing my house are the goody-goodies." Once he described the rulers of his days as "rice baskets," good only for stuffing rice, and once he actually took a cane to strike the shin of a man he highly disapproved of, and called him a "scoundrel." Such is the paragon of Confucian politeness.

The man was as solid as a rock. Born with inexhaustible energy, he was capable of enormous stretches of work, and once described himself as "one who neglects his meals in a spell of work, forgets all his worries when he is overcome with joy, and is unaware that old age is coming on." Sensitive and even emotional, once he "hated himself for shedding tears without reason" when he found himself accidentally at the funeral of a mere acquaintance, and tried to cover it up by sending a funeral present to make it appear as if he had intentionally come to the funeral. Amiable and gentle with his close disciples, he yet wrote a book, the "Spring and Autumn" (*Annals*), which was a terrible indictment of the rulers of his days, and said, "I will stand or fall with this book." It caused quite a flurry among the ruling circles because of his verdicts on the usurpers. In such a situation, when a man was at odds with his generation, Confucius exhibited a combination of stubborn pride and a humorous awareness of his own ridiculous situation. At one point in their wanderings, Confucius and his disciples were forcibly detained by some small-town politicians, and even denied food for several days, so that they were actually reduced to starvation. After several days, many of his followers fell ill, but Confucius continued to make recitals with string music.

Tselu came in and spoke to Confucius, anger on his face, "Does a moral man also find himself in extremities?"

"Yes," said Confucius. "A moral man also does, but he takes it calmly. When an uncultured man finds himself in an extremity, he is apt to commit foolish things."

Confucius knew that there was grumbling in the hearts of his disciples, and called in Tselu and questioned him:

"It is said in the *Book of Songs:*

> *Neither buffaloes, nor tigers,*
> *They wander in the wilds.*

Do you think my teachings are wrong? How is it that I find myself in this situation?"

Tselu replied, "Perhaps we lack the character to win people's confidence. Perhaps we lack the wisdom to make them follow us."

"Is that so?" said Confucius. "Ah-yu, I will tell you. If men of character could always win the people's confidence, why did Poyi and Shuchi have to die of starvation in the mountains? And if wise men could always make the people follow them, why did Prince Pikan have to be sentenced to death?"

Tselu came out and Tsekung went in. Confucius asked him: "It is said in the *Book of Songs:*

> *Neither buffaloes, nor tigers,*
> *They wander in the wilds.*

Are my teachings wrong? How is it that I find myself in this situation?"

And Tsekung replied, "The Master's teachings perhaps set too high a standard for the people. Why don't you come down a little?"

"Ah-sze," said Confucius, "a good farmer plants a field, but cannot guarantee the harvest. A good artisan can do a skillful job, but cannot guarantee to please his customers. You're not thinking of how to improve yourself, but are only interested in being accepted by the people. I am afraid you're not setting the highest standard for yourself."

Tsekung came out and Yenwhei went in. Confucius said, "Ah-whei, it is said in the *Book of Songs:*

> *Neither buffaloes, nor tigers,*
> *They wander in the wilds.*

Are my teachings wrong? How is it that I find myself in this situation?"

And Yenwhei replied, "The Master's teachings have set the highest standards. That is why the world cannot accept them. However, what does it matter if they are not accepted? The very fact that they are not accepted is proof of their greatness. If we have neglected our ideals, the shame is ours. But if we have made clear what those ideals should be and they are not accepted, it is the shame of those in power. What does it matter if they are not accepted?"

Confucius was very pleased, and he said with a smile, "Indeed you have spoken my mind, son of Yen. *If you were a rich man, I would be glad to be your steward.*"

In his private life, Confucius seems not to have got along with women. He divorced his wife and once made a rather derogatory remark about women: "The vulgar people and women are difficult to live with. If you are familiar with them, they take liberties with you, and if you keep aloof from them, they resent it." On the other hand, Confucius could not have been an easy man to live with. For his wife found that he had many strange idiosyncrasies; he would have his right sleeve made shorter than his left sleeve for convenience at work, and he insisted on having his nightgown made longer than his body by half, which must have taken a lot of cloth. This plus his fastidiousness about food must have made it difficult for his wife. In Chapter 20 of the *Analects,* which describes the details of Confucius' habits, we are told that Confucius "refused to eat" this and "refused to eat" that. Serving each meal must have been a nightmare for Mrs. Confucius, I imagine. "Rice could not be white enough," and "minced meat could not be chopped fine enough." These things she could see to if she had the time. But he insisted on home-brewed wine and home-made roasts. One day, when she had run out of meat at home and had to get it in a hurry and found that her husband refused to eat roasts from a delicatessen, she had already partially made up her mind to leave this obstreperous scholar, whose "greatness" was somewhat difficult to perceive. When again she found her husband refused to eat because she had forgotten to place ginger upon the table, it was about time. But when one day she found that this good man of hers refused to eat meat because it was not beautifully and "squarely sliced," it was the last straw. She had no choice but to walk out and leave him to find another woman who could slice the meat squarely every time. What a gourmet! (A gourmet is not only a man who appreciates good food, but who also insists on its being served right.)

Incidentally, Confucius, his son, and his grandson all divorced their wives. We know this indirectly, for both Confucius' only son and his grandson were faced with the highly technical problem of how long a period of mourning one should observe for a divorced mother. The grandson's own children had the same problem. Tsengtse, the great philosopher of filial piety and teacher of Confucius' grandson Tsesze, also divorced his wife because of her disrespect to her mother-in-law over a trivial matter of cooking pears. In any case, for the greater part of his life Confucius led the life of a bachelor philosopher.

Confucius believed in God and God's will. He said of himself that by the age of fifty, he "knew the will of God," and that "the moral man lives out the even tenor of his life, calmly waiting for the appointment of God." The God or Heaven in those days was strictly a monotheistic God as Confucius understood it, but there was a popular belief in many other spirits. Once someone asked him, "Is it true that it is better to pray to the spirit of the kitchen than to the spirit of the southeast?" And Confucius replied, "Nonsense. When you have offended Heaven (God), you have no one to pray to."

Once Confucius was seriously ill. Someone suggested to him, "Why don't you go to a temple and pray?" And Confucius replied, "I have prayed for a long time." In regard to ancestor worship, he said, "Respect the spirits when you pray as if they were present." It is also well known that Confucius seemed to have no concern for the life after death. This is true as far as the main tenor of his teachings goes. On the other hand, the *Analects* repeatedly records his sense of awe and piety in the presence of death. It also records that the things which he "took very seriously" were the occasions of sacrifices and fasting. In other words, Confucius assumed the existence of a God high above which directed the events of men in some subtle, mysterious manner, for he strongly believed in destiny and fate, as he showed by his interest in the *Book of Changes*. His life-long historical research was concerned with the ancient forms of religious worship. We must assume that this subject of religious worship had exerted a fascination for him. As he said, "If one only understood the meaning of these sacrifices to Heaven and Earth, and the significance of the services in ancestral worship in summer and autumn, it would be as easy to bring peace and order to a nation as to point a finger at the palm."

There was also an esthetic side to his character. The sensitivity of his nature is shown in his great love of music. He sang almost every day, and when he liked a song sung by others he would "ask for an encore and join him." Confucius said of himself that when he was studying music in a neighboring country as a young man and heard a certain great musical composition, he "forgot the taste of meat for three months." This may be an exaggeration, but it certainly indicates a passion for music. His very unusual description of the importance of music as the crowning "consummation" of a man's education shows him to be the kind of philosopher that he was, always concerned with the invisible influences affecting man's mind and society's morals.

II. *The Silent Revolution*

Confucius is chiefly known as a speaker of proverbs. This is an impression arising from the miscellaneous sayings of Confucius in the *Analects*. The *Analects* is like a book of familiar quotations. They are not only taken out of their context and narrative background; they are not even edited and put into any kind of order. Therefore, it has been very difficult for Western students and sometimes even for Chinese students to penetrate into the principles of his thought. Yet it is possible to speak of and examine the Confucian system of thought, centering upon two main ideas, the problem of man and the problem of society. For Confucius was essentially an educator, interested in social reform through self-cultivation of the individual, and he was also a social philosopher.

Confucius said, "Among the means for the regeneration of mankind, those made with noise and show are the least important." Confucius had the deep wisdom to try to lay the pattern for man's customs, and left the lawmaking to others. For he repeatedly showed his distrust of laws and law enforcement. There was a curious merging of ethics and politics in his writings. Political order had to be based on social order, and social order had to come from the cultivation of the individual. "From the emperor down to the common man," he said, "the cultivation of the self is the foundation of all." In his theory, he believed that all men were born much alike, but that through habit and customs they grew apart. "The gentleman grows upwards, while the common man grows downwards." The ethical and social problem was clearly, then, how to encourage and establish good habits for individuals and good customs for society. He said once with regard to his distrust of law enforcement that if you regulate people by laws and law enforcement, "people will try to keep out of jail, but will have no sense of honor." If, on the other hand, one regulates the people by morals and moral teachings, "the people will have a sense of honor and will reach out toward the good." This is the very basis of Confucius' teachings.

In other words, Confucius' dealing with the problem of human society was to put the individual approach above the social approach. Social peace and order or social chaos can only come from the individual members who compose that society. Incidentally, in this connection, I may mention that

Confucius and Karl Marx took exactly opposite points of view; Confucius believed that social reforms without personal reform were superficial; Marx, that social environment determined men's moral behavior, and that Utopias were to be brought about by changes in material environment. The course of events in Soviet history in the past forty years has proved how disastrous the latter's assumptions are. Soviet history has been largely determined, in spite of ideological dress-up, by the same human ambitions and greed for power and jealousies and ruthlessness as elsewhere among the leaders, and the personal and very human struggle for comfort and privilege at the expense of equality among the ruling oligarchy. In other words, human nature is still the same, whether man lives in a socialist or in a capitalist state. Utopias where everybody loves and trusts everybody else do not come that easy.

If we examine the Greek philosophies, we can see that Plato was a communist and Aristotle an anti-communist. Aristotle did not believe that *mere socialist reforms could change human nature*. Will Durant in his *The Story of Philosophy* has put together some very appropriate quotations from Aristotle on this point. In regard to the communistic state advocated by Plato, Aristotle says: "That which is common to the greatest number has the least attention bestowed upon it. Everyone thinks chiefly of his own, hardly ever of the public, interest." That is an exact comment on the failure of the agricultural collectives in the Soviet Union, the human explanation of that failure. Again Aristotle says, "Men readily listen" to Utopias, "and are easily induced to believe that in some wonderful manner everybody will become everybody's friend, especially when someone is heard denouncing the evils now existing, . . . which are said to arise out of the possession of private property. These evils, however, arise from quite another source— the wickedness of human nature."

Confucius, like Aristotle, put his bet on human nature and proposed accepting human nature as it is rather than changing it. A better society can be brought about, not by changing the systems of production, but by reforms in the men themselves. The human problem has not been solved by the Marxist society. Today the men and women in the Soviet Union are exactly the same as the men outside it, dominated by the same motives, the same parental care for children, for sending them to better schools than their neighbor's children, the same monetary incentives for work, for higher pay, and the same desires for class and privilege. Private property and inheritance have already been restored. Class and privilege and inequality of pay have grown steadily. It is possible that, given time, this anomalous Russian state will steadily "progress" toward capitalist society, even permitting free labor and liberty of thought and of travel, while still flaunting the flag of "socialism." That is to say, socialism has to make terms with human nature, not human nature with socialism. History has proved that, contrary to the theory of international communism, Russia has grown to be a strictly nationalistic state, based on national glory and expansion, and that the Marxist followers intuitively distrust the "love of the masses" and contradict it by instituting the worst and most terroristic regime. Once more, men determine events; events do not determine men.

The doctrine of silent revolution, of social reform based on individual reform and on education, of self-cultivation, is then the Confucianist's first and foremost occupation. Confucianism may be described as the religion of the gentleman, the *chun-tse*. The gentleman is a cultivated man in various stages of perfection, and may be more appropriately described as a person who constantly tries to improve and cultivate himself. In contrast to this cultivated man, Confucius always used the word *shiao-ren*, literally meaning "the small man." The exact translation for this "small man" is neither the common man nor the mean person. The *shiao-ren* is essentially a "vulgarian," an uncultivated, uncultured man. The *Analects* is full of contrasts between the *chun-tse* and the "small man," such as the saying that "the gentleman understands what is right; the small man understands what will sell."

What makes Confucianism comfortable is that Confucius made no impossible demands on human nature. He was not occupied with the problem of sin, but merely with bad manners and bad breeding and the ignorant smugness of the uncultivated man. He was satisfied if a man had some kind of moral awareness and constantly strove to improve himself. In this sense, Confucianists claim, and claim rightly, that such teachings are easy to practice. Once Confucius said sarcastically, "I do not expect to find a saint today; if I can find a gentleman, I shall be satisfied." The most extraordinary thing was that he set a purely human standard and taught that *the measure of man is man himself.*

> To one who loves to live according to the principle of true manhood without external inducements and who hates all that is contrary to the principles of true manhood without external threats of punishments, all mankind seems but like one man only. Therefore the gentleman discusses all questions of conduct on the basis of *himself as the standard,* and then sets rules for the common people to follow.
>
> Therefore, if the gentleman measures men by the standard of absolute righteousness, then it is difficult to be a true man. But if he *measures men by the standard of man,* then the better people will have some standard to go by.
>
> The *Book of Songs* says: "In hewing an axe handle, the pattern is not far off." Thus, when we take an axe handle in our hand to hew another axe handle and glance from one to the other, some still imagine that the pattern is far off. Wherefore the moral man in dealing with men *appeals to the common human nature and changes the manner of their lives and nothing more.*

What Confucius did hold up as the ideal was the "human best," the best in manhood, or "true manhood." This philosophical idea of *ren,* or true manhood, became, for Confucius, an ideal somewhat difficult to attain. He allowed that his best disciple, Yenwhei, could "maintain *ren* for a whole month," but not the others, and being asked on many occasions whether this or that distinguished person was a true man, his answer was invariably that the person in question was wonderful or excellent in some respects, but he did "not know about his being *ren*, or a true man."

The Chinese word for *ren* sometimes means "kindness," but in Confucius it came to mean the "human best," the ideal complete development of manhood. It is pronounced exactly like the word for "man," also *ren*, so that a *ren* man was a *ren-ren*. It suggests a parallel in the English language in the kindred meanings of *human* and *humane*. The English word *humanity*, like the Chinese *ren*, contains the double meaning of "humaneness" and "manhood" ("the humanity of Christ"), and *ren* developed into the philosophic meaning of "true manhood."

The following example throws light on what Confucius really meant by *ren*. Once when Confucius was traveling in the South and his disciples saw that there was no chance of his entering any government to put his doctrines into practice, they wanted to know how Confucius felt. One of them went in to ask Confucius' opinion of two ancient sages who had retired from government under bad kings and eventually died of starvation. The disciple asked Confucius what he thought of these two men. To his surprise, Confucius said a very unusual thing. He said, "Why, they were true men." Confucius had very seldom allowed the application of this phrase "true men" either to men of the past or to his contemporaries. The disciple asked again, "Do you think that they had regrets?" And Confucius replied in the following manner, "Why, they wanted to seek *ren* [that is, true manhood], and they had realized it. Why should they regret it?" The disciple returned to report that Confucius was happy.

This shows how inadequate it is to translate the word *ren* by "benevolence" or "kindness," in relation to a question as to the two men dying of starvation in the mountains. Confucius did allow that this true manhood was within the reach of everyone: "If I want *ren*, it is right here by me." But to be a "real man," in English as well as in Chinese society, is not easy. I suppose Confucius would say that Abraham Lincoln was a *ren-ren,* a real man, an example of the human best, consistently maintained at a high level. He would probably say of Benjamin Franklin that he was a genius but "would not know of his being a *ren-ren."* Thomas Jefferson would be a man of great intellect and of principles, but Confucius would not know . . . he doubted . . . perhaps . . . Perhaps all three deserved it; I am merely trying to suggest how sparingly Confucius used the word. In the restricted use of the word, the Confucian ideal of *ren-ren,* the human best, was the humanist counterpart of the Roman Catholic "saint." What this *ren,* the realization of the true self, the human best, exactly means will be seen in the following discussion by Tsesze.

III. *Tsesze: the Moral Law Within*

Tsesze* was the grandson of Confucius. He was only thirteen years old when Confucius died, and was taught by the youngest of Confucius' disciples, Tsengtse. He was the author of several chapters in the *Liki,* a Confucian classic, and one of them, the *Chung-yung,* was regarded as so important that it formed one of the Four Books for Chinese schoolchildren. In this book, we see the philosophic basis for Confucianism. It speaks of the spiritual nature of the universe and the moral law governing it. By living in conformity with this moral law, man realizes his true self. Thus a harmony is established between the moral universe without and the laws of true manhood within. In discovering his true self, man finds unity with the universe, and, conversely, in finding unity with the moral laws of the universe, man realizes his true self, or true manhood. In this short book, I find the most complete statement of Confucian philosophy.

* Tsesze (492-431 B.C.). The pronunciation of this word is difficult. The nearest approach to the vowel in English is the unaccented and slurred short "i." Pronounce it like an unclear "tsi-si." The sound is suggested by the last syllable of *tsetse* (fly).

The reason why man sometimes fails to realize the human best in him is because he has not come to a true understanding of the universe. "To arrive at a true understanding by realizing one's true self is called (the way of) nature. To realize one's true self from understanding (of the universe) is called (the way of) culture. Who has realized his true self gains thereby understanding. Who has gained a (complete) understanding finds thereby his true self."

According to Tsesze, the universe is a moral order, and what man needs is to discover that moral order in himself and thus reach the human best which conforms with and "rivals" the moral universe of the universe. "Confucius remarked: 'The life of the gentleman is an exemplification of the universal moral order (*chung-yung*). The life of the uncultivated person is a contradiction of the universal order." *Chung* means "the central," and *yung* means "the constant." The phrase *chung-yung* means "the Central-Constant" or "the Inner-Unchangeable." I therefore follow Ku Hung-ming's translation of *chung-yung* as the "universal moral order," as well as in the following quotations from *Chung-yung*.

Now what is this moral law of the universe and what is the moral law of man and wherein lies that harmony? The author of *Chung-yung* makes it clear that he has a conception of this moral law of the universe which comes very near to the scientific view of the laws governing the universe. This law is universal in its operation and is all-pervasive:

> The moral law [Tao] is a law from whose operation we cannot for one instant in our existence escape. A law from which we may escape is not the moral law.

It comprises the infinite and the infinitesimal:

> The moral law is to be found everywhere, and yet it is a secret. . . . For there is nothing so great but the mind of the moral man can conceive of something still greater which nothing in the world can hold. There is nothing so small but the mind of the moral man can conceive of something still smaller which nothing in the world can split.

This law or these laws are indestructible and self-existent:

> Thus absolute truth is indestructible. Being indestructible, it is eternal. Being eternal, it is self-existent. Being self-existent, it is infinite. Being infinite, it is vast and deep. Being vast and deep, it is transcendent and intelligent. It is because it is vast and deep that it contains all existence. It is because it is transcendent and intelligent that it embraces all existence. It is because it is infinite and eternal that it fulfills all existence. In vastness and depth, it is like the Earth. In transcendent intelligence, it is like Heaven. Infinite and eternal, it is the Infinite itself.

This law is immutable:

> The principle in the course and operation of Nature may be summed up in one word: because it obeys only its own *immutable* law, the way in which it produces the variety of things is unfathomable.

There follows a rhetorical passage about the physical laws governing the universe:

> Nature is vast, deep, high, intelligent, infinite and eternal. The Heaven appearing before us is only this bright, shining mass; but in its immeasurable extent, the sun, the moon, stars and constellations are suspended in it, and all things are embraced under it. The Earth, appearing before us, is but a handful of soil; but in all its breadth and depth it sustains mighty mountains without feeling their weight; rivers and seas dash against it without causing it to leak. The mountain appearing before us is only a mass of rocks; but in all the vastness of its size, grass and vegetation grow upon it, birds and beasts dwell on it, and treasures of precious minerals are found in it. The water appearing before us is but a ladleful of liquid; but in all its unfathomable depths, the largest crustaceans, dragons, fishes and turtles are produced in them, and all useful products abound in them.
>
> In the *Book of Songs* it is said:
>
>> The ordinance of God,
>> How inscrutable it is and goes on for ever!
>
> That is to say, this is the essence of God.

This is then the conception of the moral laws of the universe which led to a conception of the spiritual nature of things. In this matter, Confucius was explicit:

> Confucius remarked: "The power of spiritual forces in the Universe—how active it is everywhere! Invisible to the eyes and impalpable to the senses, it is inherent in all things, and nothing can escape its operation.
> "It is the fact that there are these forces which makes men in all countries fast and purify themselves, and with solemnity of dress institute services of sacrifice and religious worship. Like the rush of mighty waters, the presence of unseen Powers is felt; sometimes above us, sometimes around us."
> In the *Book of Songs* it is said:

> > "The presence of the Spirit:
> > It cannot be surmised,
> > How may it be ignored!"

> Such is the evidence of things invisible that it is impossible to doubt the spiritual nature of things.

The following quotation from Tsesze best sums up the philosophic basis of Confucianism, regarding the nature of the moral law, the spiritual truth behind material existence, and regarding the "fulfillment" of nature by man's dual powers of the moral sense and the intellect:

> Truth means the fulfillment of our self; and moral law means following the law of our being. Truth is the beginning and end of material existence. Without truth there is no material existence. It is for this reason that the gentleman values truth.
> Truth is not only the fulfillment of our own being; it is that by which things outside of us have an existence. The fulfillment of our being is moral sense. The fulfillment of the nature of things outside of us is intellect. These, the moral sense and intellect, are the faculties of our being. They combine the inner or subjective, and outer or objective, use of the powers of the mind. Therefore, with truth, everything done is right.

Ren, or "true manhood," in the form of "the moral sense," is based on a moral harmony of the man within and the universe without. When this "true self" is realized, "the universe then becomes a cosmos and all things attain their full growth and development." This is the philosophic basis of Confucianism.

I find this satisfactory. Human nature is not regarded as contradictory to the moral law, to be variously fought against, overcome, or suppressed. Man has the capacity for goodness in him. Thus, in contrast with the later Neo-Confucianism of the twelfth and thirteenth centuries, which had a tendency to emphasize restraint and fear of human passions owing to Buddhist introduction of "sin," this primitive or classical Confucianism taught "the fulfillment of our nature" as the moral law. And this might surprise many students who do not understand classical Confucian idealism. Moreover, this human nature is "God-given," says Tsesze. Hence the opening three lines of the *Chung-yung,* pregnant with philosophic import:

> What is God-given is called *human nature.*
> To fulfill that nature is called *the moral law* (Tao).
> The cultivation of the moral law is called *culture.*

It is true that even in classical Confucianism, one spoke of "regulating" human desires, but human nature was seen as something to be fulfilled, rather than fought against. The word for "fulfill" here means literally to "follow."

Thus the fulfillment of the God-given nature and the realization of man's true self were Confucian tenets. In this, both Confucianism and Taoism agreed. One of the great concerns of the Taoist Chuangtse was to let animals and men live out the even tenor of their lives, or literally, to "let them fulfill peacefully the dispositions of their original nature." Confucianism tried to bring out the best in man through cultivation of good habits and customs; Taoism was terribly afraid of all interference.

Here we may note some similarities between Confucianism

and Taoism. One need not jump to the conclusion that Confucianism "borrowed" from Taoism because of the use of the word "Tao." In ancient and modern Chinese, the word "Tao" was in general usage, meaning the "truth," the "way," or simply "moral teachings." Thus today we speak of the teachings of Confucius as the "Tao of Confucius." Confucius himself used the word again and again, and in the common parlance of classical times, one constantly contrasted "a world without Tao," or moral chaos, with "a world with Tao," in which moral teachings prevail. In this book by Tsesze, there are certain phrases very characteristic of what are commonly known as Taoist teachings of "inaction." Twice such a statement occurs in *Chung-yung*: "Such being the nature of absolute truth, it manifests itself without being seen; it produces effects without motion; it accomplishes its ends without action." To accomplish ends without action is of course a typically Taoist doctrine. Again there is the statement, "Therefore the moral man, even when he is not doing anything, is serious; and, even when he does not speak, is truthful." A statement like that about not doing anything and about not speaking is of course reminiscent both of Laotse and of his great follower Chuangtse who constantly spoke of "the teachings without words." It must be remembered, however, that an inference of Taoist borrowings is not entirely justifiable. Tsesze lived too close to Confucius himself to justify the view that such a unified view of the moral law of the universe was necessarily a borrowing from Laotse, the Taoist. I think we have no right to assume that Confucian teachings consisted of a jumble and miscellany of Confucius' wisecracks and moral maxims without a central moral philosophy behind it.

IV. *Mencius: Finding the Lost Heart*

The most important development of the Confucian School was in the teachings of Mencius (372–289 B.C.). After the death of Confucius, the teachings were divided into two schools, one of Hsuntse and one of Mencius, the former believing in the wickedness of human nature and the necessity of restraint, and the latter believing in the sheer expansiveness of the good heart of man. Mencius said, "The great man is one who has not lost the heart of a child." He started out from the assumption that man has the innate capacity for good and loves what is good, that it is through corruption that man deteriorates, and that therefore the essence of self-cultivation, of preserving one's moral character, consists merely in "finding the lost heart of the child." This has become the orthodox school. Mencius has been given a place next only to Confucius, and it is common to speak of Confucian doctrines as "the teachings of Kung-Meng," meaning Confucius (*Kung*) and Mencius (*Meng*).

Mencius used the phrase "the expansive spirit," and the following quotation probably best illustrates what Mencius meant:

> There was once a time when the forests of the Niu Mountain were beautiful. But can the mountain any longer be regarded as beautiful, since being situated near a big city, the woodsmen have hewed down the trees? The days and nights gave it rest, and the rains and the dew continued to nourish it, and a new life was continually springing up from the soil, but then the cattle and the sheep began to pasture upon it. That is why the Niu Mountain looks so bald and denuded, and when people see its baldness, they imagine that there was never any timber on the mountain. Is this the true nature of the mountain? And is there not a heart of love and righteousness in man, too? But how can that nature remain beautiful when it is hacked down every day, as the woodsman chops down the trees with his axe? To be sure, the nights and days do the healing, and there is the nourishing air of the early dawn, which tends to keep him sound and normal, but this morning air is faint and is soon destroyed by what he does during the day. With this continuous hacking away of the human spirit, the rest and recuperation obtained

during the night are not sufficient to maintain its level, and when the night's recuperation does not suffice to maintain its level, then the man degrades himself to a state not far from that of a beast. People see that he acts like a beast and imagine that there was never any true character in him. But is this the true nature of man? Therefore with proper nourishment and care, everything grows, and without proper nourishment and care, everything decays. Confucius said, "Keep it carefully and you will have it, let it go and you will lose it. It appears and disappears from time to time in we do not know what direction." He was talking about the human soul.

It was this faith in the innate goodness of human nature which the later Confucian scholars so loved and which has been incorporated into the body of Confucian humanism. When the Sung Neo-Confucianists came, they saw the tremendous import of Mencius, and consequently included his books in the Confucian Four Books to be learned by schoolchildren.

Mencius spoke of the "great man," rather than of the *chun-tse* or the "gentleman." He developed the theory of man's higher self and his lower self.

Kungtutse asked Mencius, "We are all human beings. Why is it that some are great men and some are small men?" Mencius replied, "Those who attend to their greater selves become great men, and those who attend to their smaller selves become small men."

This "air of the early dawn," this "expansive spirit," was something like the *élan vital* of Bergson. Certainly Mencius had a lot of *élan*. He was concerned with the seeping out and gradual depletion of this expansive spirit of man which he said could "fill up the whole universe." And he asked: Why is it that some men who have a deformed finger would feel ashamed of it and go hundreds of miles to have it fixed by a good doctor? Why is it, then, when men have lost this original heart of goodness, they do not feel ashamed of themselves? Mencius went on to speak of the "nobility of God" as dis-

tinguished from the "nobility of man." I remember that my
father loved to preach on this topic, and his eyes shone when
he spoke of the nobility of the God of Mencius from the Christian pulpit.

Mencius said, "There is the nobility of God, and there is
the nobility of man. The people who are kind, righteous,
faithful and love virtue without fail belong to the nobility of
God, and the dukes, ministers and lords belong to the nobility
of man. The ancient people cultivated what belonged to God's
noblemen and they obtained without conscious effort the ranks
of man-made nobility. People today, on the other hand, cultivate what belongs to this nobility of God in order to secure
man-made honors, and after they have secured the man-made
honors, they forsake the things that make for the nobility of
God. Thus they are led grievously astray and must soon perish
after all."

Mencius said, "All people have the common desire to be
elevated in honor, but all people have something still more
elevated in themselves without knowing it. What people
usually consider as rank or honor is not true honor, for he
whom Chao Meng [a powerful lord] has honored, Chao
Meng can also disgrace."

This cheerful and noble optimism enabled Mencius to teach
the capacity for greatness *in all men*. For he said, "All men
can become like Yao and Shun" (the idealized sage-emperors
of Confucius). He proved this by saying that in plants and
animals, those of the same species are essentially alike, and that
"the sages and ourselves are of the same species" and therefore are also essentially alike. He asked, If all mankind had
not the same taste for flavor, why should the world unite in
acknowledging the famous chef Yiya as the best cook? And if
men had not the same taste for music, why should the world
unite in acclaiming the great music master Kuang? And if men
had not the same eye for beauty, why should the world agree
in calling Tsetu the handsomest man? "Therefore I say there
is a common love for flavors in our mouths, a common sense

for sounds in our ears, and a common sense for beauty in our eyes. Why then do we refuse to admit that there is something common in our souls also? What is that thing which we have in common in our souls? It is reason and the sense of right. The Sage is the man who has first discovered what is common to men's souls. Therefore, reason and the sense of right please our minds as beef and mutton and pork please our palate." Mencius assumed that reason and the sense of right are inborn in us.

Mencius always spoke about this sense of right with a kind of moral enthusiasm. Once he visited a king, and the king asked him, "Old teacher, how can my country profit from your presence?" Mencius immediately replied, "Why do you speak of profit, sire? Isn't there also the sense of mercy and the sense of right?" And Mencius once said: "I love fish and I also love the bear's paw. If I cannot have both, I would sacrifice fish and have the bear's paw. I love life, but I also love righteousness. If I cannot have both, I would sacrifice life to do what is right." This is the kind of lofty idealism which has nourished the Confucianists' pride and high sense of honor. It is, we must say, a rather high standard. The Mandarinate has often been corrupt, as we know that officialdom in all countries has often been corrupt. But the true Confucian scholars always looked askance at the doings of the corrupt officials and held for themselves the strict moral standard set up by Confucius.

One example of this is the method of *sze-chien*, or sending of a "death memorandum" to the emperor. In the times of tyrants, scholars who wanted the emperor to do what was right and who sent him a memorandum crossing his will knew that they were courting death. In the seventh century, in the time of the megalomaniac Empress Wu, for instance, there was a great imperial secretary. A number of high officials, including the Prime Minister, the Lord Chancellor, and the President of the imperial secretariat, had all already been sentenced to death for opposing the empress. This official by the name of Liu carried on the fight. He sent up a *sze-chien* to the reception office of the palace, where a drum would be beaten to make sure that it could not be ignored. This official knew what was coming. He therefore had his last supper with his family, gave them his final instructions and his will, and dressed himself in the proper official robes with great calm and dignity. He then committed suicide.

V. The Family as a Social Unit

If Confucius had been only a moral philosopher teaching the ideal of a gentleman or a cultivated moral person, he could never have the influence which he has had over Chinese society as a whole. But Confucius was also a social philosopher. By the permanent results he achieved, he was probably the most successful social philosopher in all history. He had a dream of a social order, and that social order was accepted by the Chinese people for almost two thousand five hundred years, affecting their manners, customs, family life, and social habits and religious worship. Confucius stood for the moral China; he was the moral China, giving form to Chinese society and to Chinese social institutions, from government down to the relationship between husband and wife and man and child. There have been many social philosophers from the Greeks down, and many socialist schemes for a better society, like those of Saint-Simon and Fourier, to the present day. None has succeeded. A few have within a few years become ridiculous*; and one at least has come to stay, but, by stubbornly ignoring human psychology it has become a disastrous return to tyranny and autocracy, that is, the denial of the goal

---

* See the extremely amusing account of the Brook Farm in Emerson's "Historic Notes of Life and Letters in New England." Emerson described it as "a perpetual picnic, a French Revolution in small, an age of Reason in a patty-pan." "The ladies took cold on washing day, as it was ordained that the gentlemen-shepherds should wring and hang out clothes; which they punctually did. And it would sometimes occur that when they danced in the evening, clothes-pins dropped plentifully

of socialism. On the other hand, Confucius' dream of a social order kept clear of economics but laid a tight hold on human psychology, particularly on the love of man for woman and of parent for child. Whoever flouts these laws must perish soon, despite bayonets and prison walls. Even today, Confucius is still the most terrible underground leader in Red China, for the sentiments nourishing revolt are Confucian. Whoever says that Confucianism is dead in China is saying that a mother's love for her child can be dead. And when, in the course of time, the flood of underground human sentiments bursts and explodes, it will not come bearing political or economic slogans, but the simple one: "We return to every man his wife, and to every mother her child. We give you back your homes."

No doubt Confucius dreamed a social dream. His recurrent dream was that of Choukung, for in his old age, he said, "My! I must be really getting old! Choukung [Duke Chou] has not appeared in my dream for a long time!" Choukung was the elder brother of Emperor Wu, and was responsible for laying down the social and religious institutions of the Chou civilization, its songs and sacrifices, its ranks and ceremonies, its village festivals, and its manners and rules of social intercourse. Choukung, of course, did not do all these things; but in the mind of Confucius he stood as a symbol of the social order, glamorized by dances and music, robes and carriages, and temples of worship. This period of Choukung was Confucius' "Golden Age," the dream of a social order in which society was stabilized and everybody knew his rights and responsibilities. It was this social order that he wished to see restored as against the terrible social disintegration of his days. Confucius said: "I do not create; I only tell of the past."

Confucianism was always described by its exponents as the

from their pockets." In a Fourier society where everybody did what he could and took what he needed, the most serious sociological problem was, who was going to clean up the table and wash the dishes? Emerson is seldom as easy to read, nor does he elsewhere show at the same time such a continuous sparkle as in these "Notes."

teachings on human relations (*jen-lun*), and of the "basic" (*ta-tuan*) human relationships in particular. Of these "basic" relationships there were five, each with a particular moral quality to be taught: loyalty between rulers and ruled; love and respect between father and child; affection between husband and wife; humility between juniors and elders; and honesty between friends. All these come under the grand, all-inclusive concept of *li*, or "good form," the principle of social order in China. This may be summed up by saying that Confucianism taught "good breeding" in personal conduct and good form in social intercourse. In this broad sense, it may be said that Confucianism was successful. Chinese may be liars, thieves, corrupt officials, but it will be rare to find a Chinese common laborer or farmer who does not place first emphasis upon good personal relations and good manners, or who can be called rude or ill-bred. I maintain that the frictions of society can best be smoothed by the oil of good manners, and that however you dislike to be robbed, it would make one feel better if the robber would say, "I beg your pardon, but I must borrow this carpet from you." In the story, the rich carpet owner referred to the thief as "the gentleman on the roof."

The Confucianists constantly claim that they have possession of the eternal truth because Confucius had laid hold of certain inescapable psychological truths about human nature. Insofar as the human psychology, or human sentiments, will not change and cannot change, these truths are eternal. Let all the other schools teach what they like, sooner or later one must come back to those common human truths of the family. Hence the family system became the core of Confucian teachings. Social action follows naturally from a good family breeding. Learn to be a good child at home, a good son, and a good brother, and all the other goods will be added unto you.

I think it is always more desirable for the reader to have firsthand acquaintance with the original than to rely on any paraphrase of mine. For this reason, I am giving here extracts from a lengthy conversation between Confucius and the king of his country, Duke Ai (in Chapter 27 of the *Liki,* a Confucian classic), concerning this very broad principle of *li,* the principle of good form in society. Confucianism is usually referred to as the "religion (or teachings) of *li*" (*li-chiao*).

Duke Ai asked Confucius, "What is this great *li?* Why is it that you talk about *li* as though it were such an important thing?"

Confucius replied, "Your humble servant is really not worthy to understand *li.*"

"But you do constantly speak about it," said Duke Ai.

Confucius: "What I have learned is this, that of all the things that the people live by, *li* is the greatest. Without *li,* we do not know how to conduct a proper worship of the spirits of the universe; or how to establish the proper status of the kings and ministers, the rulers and the ruled, and the elders and the juniors; or how to establish the moral relationship between the sexes, between parents and children and between brothers; or how to distinguish the different degrees of relationships in the family. That is why a gentleman holds *li* in such high regard, and proceeds to teach its principles to the people and regulate the forms of their social life. When these are established, then he institutes different insignia and ceremonial robes as symbols of authority to perpetuate the institutions. When everything is in order, then he proceeds to fix the periods of burial and mourning, provide the sacrificial vessels and the proper offerings, and beautify the ancestral temples. Every year sacrifices are made in their proper seasons, in order to bring about social order in the clans and tribes. Then he retires to his private dwelling where he lives in simple contentment, dressed simply and housed simply, without carved carriages and without carved vessels, sharing the same food and the same joys with the people. That was how the ancient princes lived in accordance with *li.*"

Duke Ai: "Why don't the princes of today do the same?"

Confucius: "The princes of today are greedy in their search after material goods. They indulge themselves in pleasure and neglect their duties and carry themselves with a proud air. They take all they can from the people, and invade the territory of good rulers against the will of the people, and they go out to get what they want without regard for what is right. This is the way of the modern rulers, while that was the way of the ancient rulers whom I just spoke of. The rulers of today do not follow *li*."

Confucius was sitting in the company of Duke Ai, and the Duke asked: "What, in your opinion, is the highest principle of human civilization?" Confucius looked very grave, and replied: "It is the good fortune of the people that Your Highness has asked this question. I must do my best to answer it. The highest principle of human civilization is government."

The Duke: "May I ask what is the art of government?"

Confucius: "The art of government simply consists in making things right, or putting things in their right places."

Here follows a most unexpected but most characteristically Confucian connection between government and sexual relations.

The Duke: "Tell me more in detail about this art of government."

Confucius: "The husband and wife should have different duties. The parents and children should be affectionate toward each other. The king and his subjects should have rigid discipline. When these three things are right, then everything else follows."

The Duke: "Can you enlighten me a little more on the method to carry out these three things, unworthy as I am?"

Confucius: "The ancient rulers regarded loving the people as the chief principle of their government, and *li* as the chief principle by which they ruled the people they loved. In the cultivation of *li*, the sense of respect is the most important, and as the ultimate symbol of this respect, the ceremony of royal marriage is the most important. The ceremony of royal marriage is the ultimate symbol of respect, and as it is the ultimate symbol of respect, the king goes with his crown to welcome the princess from her own home personally because he regards the bride as so close in relationship to him. He goes personally because the relationship is regarded as personal. Therefore the sovereign cultivates the sense of respect and personal relationship. Without love, there will be no *personal* relationship, and without respect, there will be no *right* relationship. So love and respect are the foundations of government."

Duke Ai: "I want to say something. Isn't it making the royal marriage a little too serious by requiring a king to wear his crown and welcome the princess from her own home?"

Confucius looked very grave, and replied: "Why do you say so? A royal marriage means the union of two ruling houses for the purpose of carrying on the royal lineage and producing offspring to preside over the worship of Heaven and Earth, of the ancestral spirits, and of the gods of land and grain."

Duke Ai: "Excuse me for pressing the question, for if I do not persist, I shall not be able to hear your opinions on this point. I want to ask you something, but do not know how to put it. Will you please proceed further?"

Confucius: "You see, if Heaven and Earth (representing *yin* and *yang*) do not come together, there is no life in this world. A royal marriage is for the purpose of perpetuating the ruling house for thousands of generations. How can one take it too seriously?"

Confucius then said: "In the art of government, *li* comes first. It is the means by which we establish the forms of worship, enabling the ruler to appear before the spirits of Heaven and Earth at sacrifices on the one hand; and on the other, it is the means by which we establish the forms of intercourse at the court and a sense of piety or respect between the ruler and the ruled. It restores the social or political life from a condition of disgraceful confusion. Therefore *li* is the foundation of government."

Confucius then went on to say: "The ancient great kings always showed respect to their wives and children in accordance with a proper principle. How can one show disregard toward one's wife since she is the center of the home? And how can one be lacking in regard for one's children, since the children perpetuate the family? A gentleman always shows regard for everything. First of all he shows a pious regard toward himself. How dare he have no pious regard for himself since the self is a branch of the family line? Not to show regard for one's self is to injure the family, and to injure the family is to injure the root. When the root is injured, the branches die off. These three things, the relationship toward one's wife, toward one's children and toward one's self, are symbols of the human relationships among the people. . . ."

Duke Ai: "What do you mean by 'glorifying one's ancestors'?"

Confucius: "When a man is distinguished, we call him 'a princely man' [*chun-tse*], and the people gladly follow him and honor him, saying that he is 'a prince's son' (or 'son of a gentleman'). Thus his own father is called a prince through him and his name is glorified."

Duke Ai: "May I ask what you mean by 'living a full life'?"

Confucius: "Just follow the natural law of things."

Duke Ai: "May I ask why the gentleman lays such stress on the laws of God?"*

Confucius: "The gentleman lays such stress upon God's law, because it is eternal. For instance, you see the sun and the moon eternally following one another in their courses—that is God's law. Life in this universe never stops and continues forever—that is God's law. Things are created or produced without any effort—that is God's law."*

Duke Ai: "I'm stupid. Will you make it clearer and simplify it so that I can remember?"

A change came over Confucius' countenance. He rose from his seat and said: "A great man simply follows the natural law of things. A good son simply follows the natural law of things. Therefore a great man feels he is serving God when he serves his parents, and feels he is serving his parents when he serves God. Therefore a good son lives a full life."

Duke Ai: "I am extremely fortunate to have heard these words from you, and I crave your pardon if I fail to live up to them hereafter."

Confucius: "The pleasure is mine."

Psychologically, the family is satisfying as a social unit. It is satisfying even in a semireligious sense. For no man lives

* See section above, on Tsesze.

alone in this world, and all religions have to cope with the problem of the loneliness of the human soul. That the human soul is individual and lonely is the reason for all religions and for all organizations such as clubs, societies, the church, and the state. When Yang Chu taught "self-love" or egotism on the one hand, and Moti taught "universal love" on the other, Mencius challenged them both and said that human love had its natural "gradations" or points of emphasis, and that love, to be real, must be based on natural ties of respect and affection. The Confucianists therefore avowed that if man must live in a social unit and learn good form in conduct, the best and the most natural unit is the family, for it is a social unit which is biologically natural.

Of course, the basis of family life is biological. The family is founded upon the basic relation between man and woman, as Confucius said—in other words, upon sexuality. Sexuality, or the love of man for woman and of woman for man, is a beautiful thing. This is the way I look at it. For when a man is born, he is dependent upon his parents, but as he grows older, in his teens, he develops a sense of individuality, and feels that he is complete in himself. Boys of twelve or thirteen normally show almost complete indifference to girls, and vice versa. Then, in the period of maturity, man and woman suddenly feel themselves incomplete and lonely. Then follows the courtship which is but the act of one soul looking for a soul of the opposite sex. Marriage comes, and man finds his fulfillment in woman and woman finds her fulfillment in man. Then a curious thing happens. Both man and woman are persons or individuals with separate wills of their own. And yet, though physically separate, in a happy marriage they grow to complement each other as one complete being. This is what I call *sexuality*. In a happy marriage, there is a fusing of personalities, the merging of two wills, so that in having each other and by complementing each other the two beings become one and become complete. There is a complementing of each other's defects, as if man were born with an extra head and an extra pair of eyes—where one fails, the other sees—and this process goes on every day in tastes, in likes and dislikes, in changing the direction of one's thoughts and opening up new frontiers of feeling and of vision, not so much because they think alike as because they think differently. Thus man—and woman—in marriage is like one who has an extra window to his soul, an augmentation of his psychic powers, for sensing dangers as well as for profiting from life's gifts and joys.

Man and woman think differently, and that is the whole value of this intersexual thinking. What man desires in woman is the totality of her womanliness, and what woman desires in man is the totality of his manliness. As seen in many old couples, there is a sense of complete merging and complete belonging. And in woman, even in a young woman, I feel that the sense of complete belonging is more closely associated with "love" than in man, which means that she has a better, because more intuitive, grasp of the total meaning of sexuality. Thus one achieves solace in sorrow and shares happiness in success. Where this complete, or even partial, merging does not take place, there are inevitable disharmonies and conflicts, as when one partner is resistant to such merging, or tends to impose his or her will on the other, or simply has not got what it takes to be worth the merging. Still, the law of loneliness of the human soul and of seeking fulfillment in the complementing of the other sex is a law from whose operation, as Confucius would say, "there is no escape"; hence this inborn loneliness, this need for escape from one's own incompleteness, takes other forms. This is what I mean by the totality of man's and woman's sexuality. To read some of the current books on marriage, one might suppose that the physical gratification of love were the whole content of sexuality. And this is the danger of the Western method, of cutting life up into separate segments and looking at one segment only (such as the "isolating" of mother love, pinning it down to the action of mammary hormones and even "proving" it), the inability to

size up the totality of any subject in its indivisible and indeterminate essence.

The family system, as it developed in China, therefore became the social group in which man grew up and learned his
first lessons in life and continued to operate throughout his
life. The family provided the sense of security. If a woman
became a widow, the family took care of her; if a child became
an orphan, the family brought him up; and if a man was unemployed, the family gave him food and shelter; and above
all, when a man grew old he could comfortably look forward
to a life of ease and leisure and respect without ever having
to trouble about economic support.

Hence the overwhelming importance which Confucianism
attached to "filial piety." I do not know why the notion *shiao*
is translated in this cumbersome fashion. To be *shiao* simply
means to be a good son or a good daughter. Confucianism
provides for the motivation of living, not for a man to become
a good man in the abstract, but rather in concrete terms to
be a good son, a good brother, a good uncle, or a good grandfather. But above all, one begins life as a child, and therefore
the matter of being a good son in the family is all-important.
For it is in one's childhood that a man's habits are formed
and his general attitude toward his fellow men is established.
He is either rebellious and inconsiderate of others and has no
regard for good form in social conduct, or he has learned to
consider others and to give respect and affection to those
to whom respect and affection are due. The Confucian theory
is that a good son at home automatically becomes a good citizen in the state, because the sense of order and discipline and
sense of duty and loyalty are already established in his childhood. The extension of these habits and attitudes at home to
society in general is repeatedly emphasized in Confucian
philosophy. "Respect old age in your home and then extend it
to cover respect for old age in society; love your own child
and you will learn to love the children of others" (Mencius).
In simple English, filial piety simply means "good breeding."

Good breeding in the young, good form in social intercourse, the formation of habits and customs, emphasis on certain basic human relationships—these are the threads that form the warp and woof of Confucian social philosophy from the beginning to the end.

VI. *The Ruling Class*

The Confucianists became the aristocracy of intellect in ancient China, and, by reason of the imperial system of examinations for selection of talent for civil service, the ruling class of China. The Confucianists became a class by themselves, with the class consciousness of an aristocracy of learning. And there was much to be said for this system of imperial examinations. It was a system open to all, except the children of barbers and butchers, and rewarded its members with imperial government honors and national recognition. It was a distinctive institution of the empire and involved a series of competitions for championship in literary honors, with very rigid controls against favoritism or corruption. First there was a district examination. Those who qualified had a double-checked examination under a provincial commissioner, on the lookout for those who had got in by accident and for real talents who might have failed. Every form of encouragement and search for possible talent, like scholarships, was given to the young scholars. Those who made Grades *A* and *B* (say, like college graduates, or more precisely like a French licentiate or a graduate of a German gymnasium) had the right to join the provincial examinations, which were also held once in three years. Here the chief examiner was an official directly appointed from the capital to supervise the competition with the assistance of eighteen other judges carefully selected. The descent of the imperial examiner from the capital was like that of one holding the power of life and death over the candidates. The successful candidates of the pro-

vincial competition (like M.A.) then qualified to enter the
national examinations at the capital, which was called also
huei-shih, or the "final series," and also *ta-pi,* or the "great
competition," meaning a competition of all the talents of the
nation. This was held at the capital in the autumn once every
three years and was followed by the "palace examinations" in
the following spring under the supervision of the emperor
himself. The successful ones became *chin-shih,* or Ph.D.'s,
graded A, B, and C. All *chin-shih* were established for life.
Even the M.A.'s and B.A.'s acquired a definite standing in the
Confucian hierarchy of scholarship. It was the most important
date in a man's life. In Chinese biographies, the dates of birth
and death are often missing, but the year one took an M.A. or
a Ph.D. is always mentioned.

The Number One in the palace examinations among the
chin-shih became the "National Champion in Letters," the
chuangyuan. It was the hope of every brilliant scholar to cap-
ture that great honor, as expressed in the lively phrase "a dead
chin-shih but a living *chu-ren*" (or M.A.), for while a *chu-ren,*
there was still hope of becoming the national champion, but
for a *chin-shih* the chance had already been lost. The controls
were very strict. At all levels the candidates' bodies were
physically searched. They were shut up in cubbyholes for
about three days in the district exams while passing the tests,
bringing their own food but given hot drinks, and going to the
toilet under supervision. At the national examinations, even
the examiners themselves were shut up in the palace, for the
palace examinations were held in the front throne hall, and
the examiners were forbidden to communicate with the outside world until the grading was over and the results announced. This meant a complete isolation from the world for
a minimum of a few weeks. There were four bureaus in charge
of the papers, one for reception and register of the examination papers, another for the replacing of the names of the
candidates with serial numbers and properly sealing them, a
third for recopying the papers in red ink to avoid favoritism

through recognition of a person's handwriting, and a fourth for checking between the copied papers in red and the originals in black ink. The chief examiner was usually the minister of education or the president of the Hanlin Academy, assisted by vice ministers and other prominent officials selected personally by the emperor himself. Finally, the judges agreed on a list of successful candidates who were thus admitted to the "golden register." The first ten papers were selected, from among whom the "National Champion in Letters" was to come, the names of their authors revealed, and submitted to the emperor. The emperor then had an oral interview with the first ten and made notes of their personal appearance and their intelligence, their character and their ability to answer questions, and made his own grading of the first three. Finally, the results were announced and His Majesty personally decorated the National Champion in Letters, sometimes also presenting him with a princess for a wife. He was crowned, put on a white horse, and paraded through the streets of the capital.

All this had to do with the formation of the ruling class, the aristocracy of intellect, and the high respect for learning in ancient China. (The imperial examinations began in Tang dynasty, in the eighth century, with modifications in the successive dynasties.) The ruling class were of course all Confucianists, and they were required to follow the Confucian code of honor more strictly than others, and were also exempt from corporeal punishments at court. On the whole, the social structure was that of an aristocracy of intellect believing in the supremacy of learning and of reason, and conscious of its powers and responsibilities.

It was this fact which, as reported by the Jesuits, so aroused the enthusiasm of the eighteenth-century rationalists of Europe, like Leibnitz, Voltaire, and Diderot. Confucian humanism had considerable influence upon the philosophers of the Enlightenment in Europe. These men believed in the advance of the sciences and the ordering of human society on a pattern of reason. Confucianist China seemed to them to stand for such an example. Leibnitz' concepts of the monad and of "pre-established harmony" were similar to the Neo-Confucian ideas, if not directly inspired by them. He admired the Confucian emphasis on practical life and on education for socially useful action. Leibnitz, in fact, went into raptures over this Confucian system of thought. In his preface to the *Novissima Sinica,* he said: "The condition of affairs among ourselves seems to me to be such that, in view of the inordinate length to which the corruption of morals has advanced, I almost think it necessary that Chinese missionaries should be sent to us to teach us the aim and practice of natural theology, as we send missionaries to them to instruct them in revealed theology. For I believe that if a wise man were to be appointed judge— not of the beauty of goddesses but of the goodness of peoples —he would award the golden apple to the Chinese—unless, indeed, we should outdo them in nobility by conferring on them that which is, indeed, a superhuman good—the divine gift of the Christian religion."

Likewise Voltaire, who was anticlerical and against supernatural theology and believed in reason, wrote extensively about China in his *Essais sûr les mœurs et l'ésprit des nations* and in the *Philosophical Dictionary.* Among other things, he says, "One need not be obsessed with the merits of the Chinese to recognize at least that the organization of their empire is in truth the best that the world has ever seen, and moreover the only one founded on paternal authority." Voltaire, I think, imagined China to be better than she really was, although it is true that he lived at a time when China was under the glamorous reigns of Kangshi and Chienlung. He asked, "What should our European princes do when they hear of such examples? Admire and blush, but above all imitate."

Diderot in his *Encyclopédie* says: "These people, gifted with a *consentiment unanime,* are superior to all other Asiatics in antiquity, in intellect, art, wisdom, policy, and in their taste for philosophy; nay, in the judgment of certain authors, they dispute the palm in these matters with the most enlightened peoples of Europe." That was true enough in the period of peace and blossoming of the arts under Emperor Chienlung.

In the rococo period China was held up as the land of reason, and there was a cult for things Chinese. In 1701, Leibnitz' Berlin Society of Sciences obtained a grant for planting mulberry trees for the feeding of silkworms. Chinese gardening as seen in the English garden of the eighteenth century became a cult. Socially, men wore queues (as George Washington did) and colored silk brocades, and some courtiers and their ladies were carried about in sedan chairs.*

I cannot conjecture what the course of development in European thought would have been if the Age of Reason had not been followed and largely superseded by the upsurge of a mechanical materialism in the following century. The Chinese heritage and the European heritage (Greek philosophy, scholastic theology, Galileo, Bacon, and Descartes, and so on) were different and therefore led to different developments. Western men were born "with knives in their brains"; the weapon of logic was too sharp; it cut up almost everything which came into contact with it, and offended the truth which was always whole. Supernatural religion lost ground, but the scholastic habits of mind remained. Man began to study himself by dissecting himself. He produced some monsters of puerile, quasi-scientific materialism, and pushed himself overboard. But at least in one thing the East and the West behaved alike: Rationalism was followed by Romanticism. In China this Romantic reaction against Confucian Rationalism and decorum and "propriety" came in the form of the Taoism of Laotse and Chuangtse. Romanticism was a necessary psychological reaction against barren reason. One could be terribly tired of Reason; a properly rational society in which man always acted according to reason could be very boring to a

* See Adolph Reichwein, *China and Europe* (Kegan Paul, London, 1925).

grownup, just as a mansion, well scrubbed and well dusted and well ordered by a staff of efficient butlers and matrons could be to a normal child. Man has feelings, and sometimes not unreasonable dreams. Therefore Romanticism had to follow Rationalism.

What is true of Chinese Rationalism is true of any rationalist philosophy and of any scheme for a future society of the world. Let's organize life and society; but a wise man would see to it that life and society are not too well organized. The Chinese nation could not have survived two thousand years if every man performed his Confucianist duties and every step that was taken was taken according to the light of reason. Any materialistic philosophy which is mechanistic in its method, as Confucianism was not, would necessarily go further than Confucian rationalism, and proceed to regard both the producer and the product in terms of units of work done. A mechanical mind would produce a mechanical universe and proceed to organize human life on the model of the completely rational society of the ants or bees. It must produce a Marxist society in which production alone is god, and wherein human individuals are necessarily sacrificed before it. In the Red Chinese communes, man is already heading for the society of bees. I see mechanical minds galore in Western society. I shall deal with this in the chapter on Materialism. Fortunately for China, the Chinese were half of the time Taoists.

CHAPTER 4

The Peak of Mount Tao

EMERSON SAYS, "Aristotle and Plato are reckoned the respective heads of two schools. A wise man will see that Aristotle platonizes. . . . We can never go so far back as to preclude a still higher vision." I may be said to have "platonized" Confucius in the preceding chapter, showing that the Confucianists were not entirely devoid of a higher vision. In the case of the Neo-Confucianist school of Lu Chiu-yuan (A.D. 1139–1192), they even developed a strictly "transcendental idealism" which antedated Kant and Hegel by about seven centuries. "Even if the Heaven and Earth were destroyed, the Universal Reason would still be there."

Every time I want to write or talk about Laotse of *Tao-teh-ching* fame, I read Emerson a little to put myself in the proper frame of mind. It is not that their expressions or style are similar. Laotse, or the "Old Boy" (which is a literal translation), was full of paradoxes; Emerson is only occasionally so. Emerson's nuggets are strewn over long paragraphs, among stones with less sparkle; Laotse packs his oracular wisdom into five thousand words of concentrated brilliance. No thinker ever wrote fewer words to embody a whole phi-

losophy and had as much influence upon the thought of a
nation. Nor is it because there is some similarity in the contents of their thoughts, though there is much Taoism in Emerson's essays "On Circles" and "On Compensation." Rather it
is that Emerson, like Laotse, communicates that excitement
of the soul which every American college youth must have
experienced. Always that line of Emerson's comes back to
me: "I am the doubter and the doubt." Somewhere a mind
was groping for something beyond the realm of the usual
positive knowledge. It is like the feeling of landing in moon-
light upon a subtropical coral reef with the hot, suffocating
winds of the unknown. Reading Emerson is not like standing
by watching a farmer plowing a straight furrow in the distance, but rather like standing close by the great sculptor,
watching him chisel his sentences out of granite, sending out
sparks. Reading Montaigne is more like watching a plowman
at work in the distance, for he never hurts you. But when
you get too close to Emerson, a chip sometimes flies into
your face and causes you to smart—you have a sense of par-
taking in the creative process itself. You've got to be careful
to watch where he is going to strike next. Unexpectedly, you
find your mind traveling off in some new direction. John Jay
Chapman has something of the same quality. Emerson excites, but does not soothe, which is why you cannot read
Emerson for long. For reading which excites as well as
soothes, I prefer Santayana's *Soliloquies in England*.

All this is by way of saying what reading Laotse is like.
That was the kind of impact Laotse had on me, and particularly the impact of Chuangtse, the greatest exponent of
the Taoist school of thought. What we have here is a system
of thought which knocks us out of our propriety of thoughts
and ideas. Confucius had been very "proper," concerned with
all the duties of human relationships, of being a good father
and a good son, and with all the virtues likely to ensnare one
into becoming a good citizen. All good sense: admitted. But
there is a danger that our solid citizens may become too solid,

and then goodbye to all thinking, to all fanciful imaginings, and glimpses of truth. Breathes there a soul so dead that he never wants to be something more than a good father or a good child? After all debts are paid and one's children are sent to the best school in town, does one never ask, Who am I and what have I become? Is one truly satisfied, or does somewhere from the unknown depths of man a doubt arise? I am the doubter and the doubt. Who am I? How did the universe begin? What lies beyond? Surely, despite that solid good sense of duty, one has sometimes a lurking desire to explore the beyond, to take a daring leap into the dark void and ask a question or two of God Himself. Confucius kept the spirits and God Himself at an arm's length. It is good sense to say: "We do not know how to live. How can we know about death?" as Confucius did. It is always good sense to say, "When you know, hold that which you know, and when you do not know, admit that you do not know—that is knowledge." To one who none the less may be forced to jump the limits of this "knowable" knowledge and pursue the unknowable at the risk of pain and anguish and perhaps of frustration, such a statement cannot be satisfactory. It did not satisfy me.

"Give a ceremonial bath to your mind!" Laotse is said to have advised Confucius, supposedly a younger man coming to him for advice. That is what Laotse gave to the Chinese nation, the thinking part of it, and how they needed it! Scrub heartily and purge yourself of all your virtues of benevolence and righteousness; then you may be saved. Jesus said practically the same thing, "Unless your righteousness be greater than that of the Pharisees and the Sadducees, ye cannot enter the kingdom of God." Once in a while one can stand such a ceremonial bath, a purging away of all the self-righteous virtues of good citizenship, and have a general cleansing of the soul and start all over again. Emerson says, "I unsettle all things," and further, "People wish to be settled; only as far as they are unsettled is there hope for them." There was never a greater thinker in the world who did not have that "unset-tling" effect on one's mind and who did not more or less compel a total reversal of values. The more a teacher unsettles a man's smug, complacent notions and self-satisfactions, the greater usually is his influence.

Laotse's influence is great because he filled a void left by Confucian positivism and common sense. Judged as a human spirit, as an intelligence, Laotse has greater depth than Confucius, and I would be ashamed of Chinese thought if it had produced only a Confucius without his spiritual counterpart, Laotse; just as I am happy for Athens that it produced not only an Aristotle, but also a Plato. As a philosopher, Plato was more dangerous, more speculative, and Aristotle more solid and rational, but a nation can use both, in fact needs both. You have to have a Martha and you have to have a Mary in the family, although I know that Mary was less of a cook and less tidily dressed.

Taoism and Confucianism are thus but two facets of the Chinese soul, and that may explain why, although the Chinese are good merchants, they are *never* a nation of shopkeepers. What made the Chinese people philosophic? Not Confucius, but Laotse. Who made the best proverbs that circulate in the currency of Chinese popular thinking? Not Confucius, but Laotse. I know the Chinese people have a reputation for being philosophical, for taking life airily, *sans souci*. Confucius never taught man to take life airily, but rather to live with an intense German seriousness and earnestness of purpose. There is, however, in the Chinese soul always that wistfulness, arising from Laotse, that terrible, unspoken strength of endurance, that tongue-in-cheek submission to authority, that mighty nonresistance which determines to suffer and sit it out and outlive any tyrant, however powerful he may seem. For Laotse, as the world's first philosopher of camouflage, taught the strength of that soft substance water. The wistful look, the half-closed eye, the apathetic quiet-spoken appearance of a true philosopher—all this has been associated with the

"Chinaman," and all this is true. All this is Taoism, although I must point out that the apathetic, lackadaisical look associated with the "Chinaman" is not necessarily the true philosophical look. Sometimes one sees listless people standing on a corner of Chinatown who give the impression that time has suddenly stood still, and one believes that he is seeing a nation of philosophers stoically watching the hustle and bustle of the world go by. It is not that at all. That look may quite well be the look of plain malnutrition. Mere sluggishness of mind or body does not make one a philosopher.

For Taoism and Confucianism are, as I have said, only two facets of the Chinese soul, one of action, of doing and believing; the other of being, of doubting, and wondering, which invests life with a dreamlike quality. It is good that it is so. Mencius said, "The sense of mercy is in all men; the sense of right is in all men." But surely the sense of wonder is also in all men. Besides the right to think, one has a right to wonder, though nothing may ever come of this wonderment and one may not understand all that lies beyond. But the very exercise of this sense of wonder is already an emancipation. Even a puppy has that definite sense of wonderment at his master's doings, and may not man himself wonder at the blue beyond? Better to have come to no conclusions than not to have wondered at all.

Taoism answers that need for wonder and that need for emancipation, and confers on man that right, in Chuangtse's words, to set his mind free and "wander in the realm of Nowhere." Oliver Cromwell says a great thing: "A man never rises so high as when he knows not whither he is going." That saying of Cromwell's is Chuangtseasque.

Taoism and Confucianism are but two alternating moods in the nation's soul. Every Chinese is a good Confucianist when he is a success, but a Taoist when he is in trouble or frustrated and beset by difficulties and failures. As men more often fail than succeed, and even those who apparently succeed have secret doubts of their own in the middle of the

night, the Taoist influence is more often at work than the
Confucian. The official who has been kicked out of office immediately goes to a hot spring and plays with his children,
and says to himself: "I am a free man once more! It is wonderful. That is how God intended man to live all along." This
official probably used to suffer from insomnia when he was
an important secretary at some ministry; now he sleeps well
because he is sleeping in the bosom of the Taoist universe.
So it happens, as I have said elsewhere: "Officials liked Confucius and writers and poets liked Chuangtse and Laotse, and
when the writers and poets became officials, they liked Confucius openly and Laotse and Chuangtse secretly."

*

Laotse was according to tradition a contemporary of Confucius, probably some twenty years older. But Confucius was
also a contemporary of Buddha. Thus:

Laotse	570(?)–(?) B.C.
Buddha	c. 563–483 B.C.
Confucius	551–479 B.C.

The three great founders of Oriental thought were born in the
same sixth century and almost in the same decade. While we
are dealing with dates, it should also be mentioned that
Chuangtse was a contemporary of Mencius and Plato. Chuangtse was to Laotse what Mencius was to Confucius, Plato
to Socrates, and St. Paul to Jesus. In each case, the master
wrote very little or nothing at all, and there came a disciple
who wrote voluminously and sometimes brilliantly, and who
did not mind writing at all. The comparative dates are:

Moti	c. 501–416 B.C.
Socrates	469–399 B.C.
Plato	427(?)–347(?) B.C.
Aristotle	384–322 B.C.
Mencius	372–289 B.C.
Chuangtse	c. 335–275 B. C.

Chuangtse and Mencius both had interviews with the same kings of Liang and Chi, but neither mentions the other in his works. Very roughly, the sequence is as follows in terms of centuries:

Laotse, Buddha, Confucius	Sixth Century B.C.
Moti, Socrates	Fifth Century B.C.
Plato, Aristotle, Mencius, Chuangtse	Fourth Century B.C.

Very little is known about Laotse and Chuangtse. Laotse apparently came from a family of officials, and was keeper of official archives of the Chou Imperial House. Sometime in his middle life, he resigned his post. When passing the important pass which led into northwest China on his journey to retirement, he was asked, so the tradition says, by the officer of the pass, who was one of his admirers, to leave his wisdom for posterity. The book which resulted was the famous *Tao-teh-ching*. He may have lived to a hundred, or to a hundred and sixty, as one record says, or may have bodily ascended to Heaven to become an "immortal," as the later Taoist believers in occultism will have it. As far as we know, the last that was seen of him was when he was riding on the back of a black buffalo across the pass. His descendants, however, were carefully traced from generation to generation in *Shiki*.

Chuangtse also came of the same country as Laotse, Chu, in modern Honan and Hupei, north of the Yangtse, then regarded as the "South" of ancient China, while Confucius and Mencius came from Shantung. We know that he had several brilliant debates with the famous sophist Hueishih, a great speculator about the physical universe, and that he had interviews with several kings. And we know too that he was once "an officer of the Lacquer Orchard." He was reported to have been offered a high post by the King of Chu, but declined by asking if he was to be fed and fattened like a pig in order to be offered up on the altar for the gods' sacrifices. If one understands Chuangtse's caliber and temperament, one is not surprised. There is an anecdote about him. He was married, and

when his wife died and her coffin was still lying in one corner
of the hall, his disciples came to condole with him, but found
him sitting on the ground beating a basin and singing. To the
disciples' question, Chuangtse's reply was an occasion for one
of his great discourses on the subject of death. The question
of life and death fascinated Chuangtse and became an important part of his philosophy, as we shall see presently.

I should like to say a few words here about the critical
research of the Chinese scholars in connection with Laotse
and Chuangtse. Some recent scholars have avowed that Laotse
was not a contemporary of Confucius but probably lived
several centuries later, perhaps in the third or second century
B.C. There is also an unestablished but "floating suspicion" that
only the first seven of the thirty-three chapters of the works of
Chuangtse are undoubtedly genuine, while the rest, the "outside chapters," are suspect of forgery for some unclear reason.
Over three hundred thousand words have been written in the
last two decades, discussing the subject of when Laotse lived,
and the volume of scholarly nonsense is impressive.

I have considered it necessary to mention this point because
in discussing the authenticity of texts in general there has been
a lot of loose talk which cannot measure up to the standards
of true criticism, and which may mislead Western Sinologists.
It has been the fashion to cry forgery on the slightest pretext,
and some scholars have not even distinguished between interpolation of sentences and forgery of a whole chapter. Some
were moved by pietistic feelings about Confucius. Others
indulged in tendentious reasoning buttressed by a parade of
pedantry. Above all, this fashion for "criticism" happened to
be associated with the narrow sectarianism of the "Han
School." It became then a sectarian bias and a fashionable
thing among scholars to look for inconsistencies, inaccuracies,
and perhaps anachronisms in a certain text, which are common
in all ancient texts copied by hand, and announce another
"forgery." These efforts culminated in the nonsense of Kang
Yu-wei, the great reformist around 1900, who wrote two books

claiming that all of Confucian texts were forgeries and that
Confucius was the greatest forger of all. His disciple, the
distinguished scholar Liang Chi-chao, carried the tradition
right up to the Republican days, for it was he who first
proposed the very original and attractive theory that Laotse
lived long after Confucius and therefore also after Chuangtse.
It startled people, and it made "good talk." How, if that was
the case, Chuangtse could talk in his own works again and
again about a man who was born after him was not made
plain. Oh, then, Laotse could have been created by Chuangtse;
or Chuangtse's works themselves could have been forged in
the third century B.C. There follows a parade of pedantry.
Such loose talk carries one nowhere. Now the thing about this
cry of forgery was that it always sounded superior to dismiss
a thing as spurious; one became an "expert" by doing so. It
became the "fashionable" thing, and therefore the accepted
thing. Everyone wanted to be "up to date." Professor Fung
Yu-lan, for example, would not discuss Chuangtse's theory
except on the basis of the first seven chapters, which sounded
very much like scientific caution, and very "professorial."

I will sum up this situation by saying that in regard to
Laotse, there is no positive proof of Laotse living in the third
century but a great deal of tendentious surmise only; that the
weight of evidence seems to incline toward the tradition that
he was a contemporary of Confucius, for the interviews between Confucius and Laotse are recorded not only in the
books of Chuangtse, but at least once also in *Liki*, a Confucian
text itself. Little as we know about the authors of Laotse's and
Chuangtse's works, the critics' surmises are vaguer and airier
still. There is and has been no strict philological evidence one
way or the other. I will mention merely the example of how
speculative and unsound such arguments are. A contemporary
professor of today accepts the theory that Laotse must have
come after Chuangtse on the purely theoretical argument
which runs as follows: The Tao of Confucius was a Tao solely
concerned with man; later in Chuangtse the Tao was the Tao

both of man and of heaven, and therefore the Tao of Laotse, being entirely the Tao of heaven, can only be a culmination of the gradual "evolution" of the idea of Tao and must come last. Why the century which could produce such fresh fountains of thought as Moti and Confucius could not produce a Laotse, or where Confucius or Moti suddenly "evolved" from, has not been made plain. Liang Chi-chao hazarded the opinion that Laotse came in the later centuries because the social and political conditions in the third century had so steadily worsened that it would "justify" and "provoke" such a theory of return to nature as advocated by Laotse. Liang forgot the fact that in Confucius' own time the world was chaotic enough, so much so that it very much provoked Confucius, and one of the unknown sages in the *Analects* remarked that "the world was full of those people going about gabbling" new doctrines.

In regard to the so-called "outside chapters" of Chuangtse, which Professor Fung fights shy of touching, there is *only one anachronism* in the entire "outside chapters" which could have been due to the mistake of an amanuensis. (At the time of Chuangtse, a certain event was "nine generations" old; at the time of the copier of the text, it was put down as "twelve generations" old.) And even an interpolation is not a basis for throwing out all the chapters as a forgery. Who else wrote those famous essays like "Autumn Floods" and "Horses' Hoofs"? No one has even offered an opinion. It is easy and tantalizing enough for a young student to advance an original theory and parade it with footnotes and references and data. I have seen one such work devoted to proving the forgery of Chuangtse's "outside chapters." How did he prove it? Not by philological evidence, and not by discrepancies in style or content, and not by external evidence, either. This man went on the basis of accepting the first seven chapters of Chuangtse as the solid ground to go upon, and whenever a phrase occurred that was not found in the first chapters it was immediately regarded as evidence of forgery; if Chuangtse spoke only of "doing nothing" in the first chapters, but used the basic Taoist phrase "by doing nothing everything was accomplished" in an "outside chapter," it was pointed out as evidence of being "not Chuangtse." In other words, the evidence was not any contradiction of ideas, but rather anything supplementary or complementary; anything beyond what was already said in the first seven chapters could not be accepted as from the pen of Chuangtse. In other words, Schopenhauer could have written only *The World as Will and Idea;* he could not possibly have written the *Parerga et Paralipomena* (the "Essays"), because things were said therein that had not already been said in his main work! Obviously, such a puerile argument could not be accepted in a sophomore paper.

I. *Laotse*

Laotse is one of the greatest epigram makers of the world. He is full of paradoxes which are crisp and clear and unforgettable: "He who knows others is learned; he who knows himself is wise"; "He who knows does not speak; he who speaks does not know." A paradox is not merely a witticism or the unexpected turning of a phrase to amuse and make a striking effect, as in the witticisms of Oscar Wilde. A paradox proceeds naturally from a fundamental point of view, and if this point of view is different from the commonly accepted views of men, it is at once regarded as a paradox. It implies a reversal of the scale of values. Such is Jesus' paradox "He who loses his life shall find it." Such is the paradox of Isaiah that "all our righteousness is as filthy rags." Such is the paradox of St. Paul: "If any man among you seems to be wise in this world, let him become a fool, that he may be wise." All the paradoxes of Laotse stem from a philosophy, and a point of view of his own. His epigrams are well coined and well written:

> To yield is to be preserved whole.
> To be bent is to become straight.

> To be hollow is to be filled.
> To be tattered is to be renewed.
> To be in want is to possess.
> To have plenty is to be confused.*

But behind such paradoxes, there was a different scale of values:

> Therefore the Sage embraces the One,
> And becomes the model of the world.
> He does not reveal himself,
>   And is therefore luminous.
> He does not justify himself,
>   And is therefore far-famed.
> He does not boast himself,
>   And therefore people give him credit.
> He does not pride himself,
>   And is therefore the ruler among men.
>
> It is because he does not contend
> That no one in the world can contend against him.

Laotse's epigrams always give one the impression of saying something important and beautiful and of a religious nature:

> He who embraces this Tao
> Guards against being over-full.
> Because he guards against being over-full
> He is beyond wearing out and renewal.

And here we begin to see the subtlety, the cunning wisdom of the mystic Laotse. For Laotse is, as I have said, the world's first philosopher of camouflage:

> The greatest cleverness appears like stupidity;
> The greatest eloquence seems like stuttering.
> Movement overcomes cold,
> [But] keeping still overcomes heat.
> Who is calm and quiet becomes the guide for the universe.

* This and following translations from Laotse are from *The Wisdom of Laotse* (Modern Library), translated by myself.

And there is always a gentle message, which gives it great
charm, and makes it a pleasure to read:

> The universe is lasting.
> The reason the universe is everlasting
> > Is that it does not live for Self.
> Therefore it can long endure.
>
> Therefore the Sage puts himself last,
> And finds himself in the foremost place;
> Regards his body as accidental,
> > And his body is thereby preserved.
> Is it not because he does not live for Self
> That his Self achieves perfection?

As the first philosopher of camouflage, Laotse describes himself as follows:

> The vulgar are knowing, luminous;
> > I alone am dull, confused.
> The vulgar are clever, self-assured;
> > I alone, depressed.
> Patient as the sea,
> > Adrift, seemingly aimless.

And again:

> The people of the world are merry-making,
> > As if eating of the sacrificial offerings,
> > As if mounting the terrace in spring;
> I alone am mild, like one unemployed,
> > Like a new-born babe that cannot yet smile,
> > Unattached, like one without a home.

Whence arise all these paradoxical statements? Supporting
them is the philosophy of Tao. Laotse puts it in the following manner:

My teachings are very easy to understand and very easy to prac-
> tice,
But no one can understand them and no one can practice them.
> In my words there is a principle.
> In the affairs of men there is a system.

Because they know not these,
They also know me not.
    Since there are few that know me,
    Therefore I am distinguished.

The great central principle of Laotse's thought is of course the Tao. Laotse's Tao is the great active principle behind all phenomena, the abstract principle which gives rise to all forms of life, and which, like the great water which flows everywhere, benefits all things and takes no credit for itself. The Tao is silent, all-pervasive, and described as "evasive, elusive," unseen and invisible, but all-powerful. Being the origin of all things, it is also the principle to which all manifested forms of life eventually return:

> Before the Heaven and Earth existed
> There was something nebulous:
>   Silent, isolated,
>   Standing alone, changing not,
>   Eternally revolving without fail,
>   Worthy to be the Mother of All Things.
> I do not know its name
>   And address it as Tao.
> If forced to give it a name, I shall call it "Great."
> Being great implies reaching out in space,
> Reaching out in space implies far-reaching,
> Far-reaching implies reversion to the original point.

Laotse's book is known as *Tao-teh-ching*. The second word, Teh, literally means virtue, but denotes the active principle of Tao when Tao manifests itself in the physical world. Arthur Waley has translated the title as "The Way and Its Power," and this is correct enough in the sense that this word Teh (Waley's "power") originally meant "virtue," and can have the ancient connotation of the "virtue" of medicinal herbs. The clearest indication of the meaning of these two words is perhaps in the following quote:

> Therefore Tao gives them birth,
> Teh fosters them,

Makes them grow, develops them,
Gives them a harbor, a place to dwell in peace,
Feeds them and shelters them.

It is clear from the above that Teh is merely Tao manifested
in action. This Tao is invisible, inaudible, and intangible:

Looked at, but cannot be seen—that is called the invisible [*yi*].
Listened to, but cannot be heard—that is called the inaudible
[*shi*]. Grasped at, but cannot be touched—that is called the
intangible [*wei*]. These three elude all our inquiries and
hence blend and become One.

Not by its rising, is there light,
Nor by its sinking, is there darkness.
Unceasing, continuous,
It cannot be defined,
And reverts again to the realm of nothingness.

I think the best summary of the concept of Tao is in the following four lines which emphasize the *Principle of Reversion*
and the gentleness of the function of Tao:

Reversion is the action of Tao.
Gentleness is the function of Tao.
The things of this world come from Being,
And Being from Non-Being.

And thus we see Tao as lying in the natural state of quiescence, unseen, unheard, and permeating everywhere and then
"rising to activity," giving rise to various forms, as Laotse
describes it in the following:

Attain the utmost in Humility;
Hold firm to the basis of Quietude.

The myriad things take shape and rise to activity,
But I watch them fall back to their repose.
Like vegetation that luxuriantly grows
But returns to the root from which it springs.

Nature is therefore seen as moving continually in a circle,
changing its forms but always coming back to the central

principle of Tao which in Western philosophy might be called a "substance." The Tao in another place is described by Laotse as like a bellows, which draws and supplies air continually and is never exhausted itself. But with this principle of universal reversion to opposites, nothing ever lasts long and the tendency of the thought is that everything is equalized, and all opposites become merged and almost identical.

> Nature says few words: Hence it is that a squall lasts not a whole morning. A windstorm continues not a whole day. Where do they come from? From nature. Even nature does not last long [in its utterances], how much less should human beings?

Because nature equalizes everything and restores everything to its original form, therefore all opposites are alike and are interdependent upon each other. "It is the Way of Heaven to take away from those that have too much and give to those that have not enough." Hence arise all the paradoxes of Laotse:

> He who is to be made to dwindle
> Must first be caused to expand.
> He who is to be weakened
> Must first be made strong.
> He who is to be laid low
> Must first be exalted to power.
> He who is to be taken away from
> Must first be given,
> —This is the Subtle Light.

And here is one which I like very much:

> Therefore: He who loves most spends most,
> He who hoards much loses much.

In regard to the relativity of all qualities, Laotse says, "Being and Non-Being interdepend in growth; difficult and easy interdepend in completion; long and short interdepend in contrast; high and low interdepend in position; tones and voice interdepend in harmony; front and behind interdepend in company." From Laotse's point of view, human folly begins from the cutting up of the original unity of the universe and making the distinction of good and evil and ugliness and beauty:

> Banish learning, and vexations end.
> Between "Ah!" and "Ough!"
> How much difference is there?
> Between "good" and "evil"
> How much difference is there?
> That which men fear
> Is indeed to be feared;
> But, alas, distant yet is the dawn!

Therefore Laotse comes up with the annihilation of opposites, of concern with the temporary and transitory forms of life. The great moral principle therefore is to keep to the original simplicity of man, of which the uncarved block of wood, or the newborn baby, is repeatedly used as a symbol. The moral lesson is therefore to "keep to the core," to hug close to man's primeval simplicity and innocence. And in this matter, the principle of the Female stands for the principle of quiescence, while the principle of the Male stands for the principle of activity. "The Female overcomes the Male by quietude, and achieves the lowly position by quietude." The principle of the Female, the principle of *yin*, as opposed to *yang*, is the symbol of Tao in its natural quiescent state. So Laotse spoke of Tao as the "Mother of Universe," rather than the "Father":

> From the Mother we may know her sons.
> After knowing the sons, keep to the Mother.
> Thus one's whole life may be preserved from harm.

Sometimes the hollow valley, or the ravine, is used equally with the Female as a symbol of the receptive principle:

> He who is aware of the Male
> But keeps to the Female
>   Becomes the ravine of the world.
> Being the ravine of the world,

He has the eternal power which never fails,
And returns again to the [innocence of] the babe.

This idea of preserving the original nature leads to the tenet of noninterference. This noninterference is sometimes translated as "doing nothing," or again as "inaction"; the philosophic meaning is perfectly clear from an understanding of the principle of preserving the simplicity of man's nature:

There are those who will conquer the world
And make of it (what they conceive or desire).
I see that they will not succeed.
(For) the world is God's own Vessel,
It cannot be made (by human interference).
He who makes it spoils it.
He who holds it loses it.

From this doctrine of keeping to the core, variously expressed as imitating the "uncarved wood" and the baby, or as "guarding the pristine innocence and simplicity" and "keeping whole the soul"—from all these expressions and phrases arose the later associations of Taoism with magic and the occult arts.

We have therefore reached a point to understand why Laotse preached a return to nature, like Rousseau. He was hostile to the doctrines of Confucianism, the doctrines of benevolence and justice and kindness and loyalty, and so on, for he traced these virtues to the "thinning out" of the original heart of man. "Therefore: after Tao is lost, then arises the doctrine of kindness; after kindness is lost, then arises the doctrine of justice; after justice is lost, then arises the doctrine of *li* (good form). Now *li* is the thinning out of loyalty and honesty of heart, and the beginning of chaos."

The prophets are the flowering* of Tao
And the origin of folly.

Hence Laotse's cry against wisdom and knowledge of the Confucian type, which Chuangtse echoed vociferously:

* "Flowering" already implies dissipation of energy, and beginning of wilting of the flower.

> Banish wisdom, discard knowledge,
>> And the people shall profit a hundredfold;
> Banish "love," discard "justice,"
>> And the people shall recover love of their kin;
> Banish cunning, discard "utility,"
>> And the thieves and brigands shall disappear.

From all this distrust of contention, of interference, this eschewing of pride and extravagance, Laotse began to preach the doctrine of gentleness, which sounds to me very much like a rationalization of Jesus' Sermon on the Mount. Jesus said, "Blessed are the meek, for they shall inherit the earth," as a categorical statement. No one has quite examined why the meek shall inherit the earth, but Laotse's whole philosophy is based upon the doctrine of gentleness:

> That weakness overcomes strength
> And gentleness overcomes rigidity
> No one does not know;
> No one can put into practice.

> He who can see the small is clear-sighted;
> He who stays by gentility is strong.

And Laotse proved it by constantly using water as an illustration. "The softest substance of the world goes through the hardest. That-which-is-without-form penetrates that-which-has-no-crevice." Laotse, using water as a symbol of humility, asks abruptly:

How did the great rivers and seas become the Lords of the Ravines?
By being good at keeping low.
That was how they became the Lords of the Ravines.

Therefore in order to be the chief among the people,
One must speak like their inferiors.
In order to be foremost among the people,
One must walk behind them.

Here speaks a pagan teacher of meekness and humility,

from an observation of the natural laws of the universe, and not from catechism or creed. Laotse came to believe in noninterference, noncontention, and nonresistance because he believed in the strength of softness, such as the softness of water. He warned against the use of force, not only because he did not believe in it but also because he believed that the use of force represented a symptom of weakness. He warned:

> Stretch a bow to the very full,
> And you will wish you had stopped in time.
> Temper a sword edge to its very sharpest,
> And the edge will not last long.

Disbelief in force is not just a moral injunction but is found to be in consonance with the true laws of human life and of the universe.

Jesus was a friend of the poor and the lowly. Not only did Laotse's teachings on the power of love and of humility agree in spirit with the teachings of Jesus by his intuitive flashes of insight; sometimes the verbal resemblances are startling:

> But he that is greatest among you shall be your servant. And whosoever shall exalt himself shall be abased; and he that shall humble himself shall be exalted. (Matt. 23:11-12)

> But many that are first shall be last; and the last shall be first. (Matt. 19:30)

> Except ye be converted, and become as little children, ye shall not enter into the kingdom of heaven. Whosoever therefore shall humble himself as this little child, the same is greatest in the kingdom of heaven. (Matt. 18:3-4)

I find Laotse arriving at some of the crookedest and yet some of the most charming epigrams, which in spirit rise to the austere heights of Jesus himself:

> The good ones I declare good;
> The bad ones I also declare good.
> That is the goodness of Virtue.
> The honest ones I believe;

> The liars I also believe;
>   That is the faith of Virtue.

Why did Laotse say that? Because he believed that no one should be rejected, however bad he might be.

> Therefore the Sage is good at helping men;
>   For that reason there is no rejected person.
> He is good at saving things;
>   For that reason there is nothing rejected.
> —This is called Stealing the Light.

Laotse says, "Though there be bad people, why reject them?" It is therefore not difficult to move on from there to Laotse's teaching, "Requite hatred with Virtue." And it is almost hard to credit the resemblance to the Christian teaching expressed in the following verse by Laotse:

> Who receives unto himself the calumny of the world
>   Is the preserver of the state.
> Who bears himself the sins of the world
>   Is the king of the world
>   —Straight words seem crooked.

In the latter part of his book, Laotse dealt with some practical problems of government. He was against war, against government interference of all kinds, and against punishment. In regard to noninterference with the life of the people, he made the famous saying, "Govern a country as you would fry small fish," that is, one should not continually turn it over, when the fish might become paste. The great art of government was to leave the people alone. However, it is in his views against war that Laotse was most striking, emphatic, and made some of his greatest pronouncements:

> He who by Tao purposes to help the ruler of men
> Will oppose all conquest by force of arms.
> For such things are wont to rebound.
> Where armies are, thorns and brambles grow.
> The raising of a great host
> Is followed by a year of dearth.

Therefore a good general effects his purpose, and stops.
He dares not rely upon the strength of arms;
Effects his purpose and does not glory in it;
Effects his purpose and does not boast of it;
Effects his purpose and does not take pride in it;
Effects his purpose as a regrettable necessity;
Effects his purpose but does not love violence.
(For) things age after reaching their prime.
That violence would be against the Tao.
And he who is against the Tao perishes young.

Of all things, soldiers are instruments of evil,
Hated by men.
Therefore the religious man avoids them.

Soldiers are weapons of evil.
They are not the weapons of the gentleman.
When the use of soldiers cannot be helped,
The best policy is calm restraint.*

And then Laotse comes out with what I regard as one of his greatest sayings:

Even in victory, there is no beauty,
And who calls it beautiful
Is one who delights in slaughter.
He who delights in slaughter
Will not succeed in his ambition to rule the world.

The slaying of multitudes should be mourned with sorrow.
A *victory should be celebrated with the Funeral Rite.*

I have used many quotations from Laotse because I think the reader would like to savor his words, and above all because Laotse can say it so much better and more effectively than any paraphrase of mine. I should like to conclude with a verse which may be regarded as Laotse's summing up of his moral doctrines:

I have Three Treasures;
Guard them and keep them safe:

* In this translation I follow Arthur Waley.

The first is Love.
The second is, Never too much.
The third is, Never be the first in the world.
Through love, one has no fear;
Through not doing too much, one has amplitude of power;
Through not presuming to be the first in the world,
  One can develop one's talent and let it mature.

If one forsakes love and fearlessness,
  Forsakes restraint and reserve power,
  Forsakes following behind and rushes in front,
He is dead!

For love is victorious in attack,
  And invulnerable in defense.
Heaven arms with love
  Those it would not see destroyed.

I once tried to summarize Laotse's teachings as follows:

I teach the wisdom of the foolish,
  The weakness of the strong;
The strength of softness which is water,
  The untarnished newly-born.

I teach the lesson of humility—
  O'erstretched snaps the bow;
The usefulness of futility;
  The advantage of lying low.

How come the king of rivers, the sea,
  But from lowly ravines?
Even in clash and clang of battles,
  The Man of Sorrow wins.

II. *Chuangtse*

Chuangtse is my favorite, and we may linger for some time over him. That is so by reason of both the charm of his style and the depth of his thought. Indubitably, he was the greatest prose master of Classical China; at the same time, he

was, in my estimate, the greatest and most profound philosopher China has produced. He wrestled with problems of
the soul and immortality, the nature of being, the nature
of knowledge which others did not even touch. He dealt
with metaphysics; he penetrated the problems of reality; he
advocated relativity of standards; he was a strict monist;
he anticipated Shan (Zen) Buddhism completely; he had a
theory of eternal flux and "transformation of things" of the
universe; he taught letting men and animals "fulfill their
nature" and he had reverence for life and was deeply religious. He was the first writer in China to have felt and
expressed the inner restlessness over the poignancy of human
life and to have wrestled with the problems of the spiritual
universe. "The style is the man," says Buffon. Chuangtse's
was that of a giant intellect, combined with playful wit, ever-
ready gift of the imagination, and a writer's facility for expression. In other words, Chuangtse was a writer of the first
magnitude; some fourteen hundred years were to elapse before China was to have a comparable genius in the person of
Su Tungpo, with his equal brilliance of intellect and grace
and humor of expression, sweeping Buddhism, Taoism, and
Confucianism into his orbit and commanding both formal and
familiar prose and all forms of poetry. There are many who
can write charming nonsense, but writing *charming sense* is
altogether a different gift, rare as the nectar of the gods.

When I speak of Chuangtse's style, therefore, I am speaking
of his personality. There are vigor in his thought and fancy
in his innumerable fables. Chuangtse described his own work
as consisting of three classes of words: (1) *serious words*—
those of truth and wisdom; (2) *ladle words,* or ladlefuls of
words—those which were poured out of his mind and imagination, without stint and without effort and apparently
inexhaustible, like the widow's jar of oil; and (3) *allegories*
or fables created to make a point, or to lambaste the great of
his days.

His "serious words" are like the following: "Our mind is

finite, but knowledge is infinite. To pursue the infinite with our finite intelligence—alas! what a dangerous occupation!" Or this: "The Great (Universe) gives me this form, this toil in manhood, this repose in old age, this rest in death." Or this: "Those who dream of the banquet wake to lamentation and sorrow. Those who dream of lamentation and sorrow wake to join the hunt." Such lines stand by themselves.

The best-known example of his "ladle words" is perhaps where he compares himself to a butterfly dreaming of being a human being:

> Once upon a time, I, Chuang Chou, dreamt that I was a butterfly, fluttering hither and thither, to all intents and purposes a butterfly. I was conscious only of my happiness as a butterfly, unaware that I was Chou. Soon I awaked, and there I was, veritably myself again. Now I do not know whether I was then a man dreaming that I was a butterfly, or whether I am now a butterfly, dreaming that I am a man.*

An example of his "allegories" is a parable showing the superiority of the invisible over the visible mechanisms of the universe:

> The k'uei [a one-legged hopping animal] envies the centipede, the centipede envies the snake, the snake envies the wind, the wind envies the eye, and the eye envies the mind.
>
> "I hop about with one leg," said the k'uei to the centipede. "There is no one who moves about more simply than I do. Now you have so many legs. How do you manage?"
>
> "How do I manage?" replied the centipede. "Haven't you seen a man spitting? The spittle comes in big drops like beads and small driplets like mist, and they all fall together without number. When I move my natural mechanism, I really don't know how I manage my legs."
>
> "I move about with so many legs," said the centipede to the snake. "How is it that I do not go so fast as you do without legs at all?"

* This and the following quotations are from The Wisdom of Laotse.

"Each one," replied the snake, "moves in his own way by his natural mechanism. What need do I have for legs?"

"I move about with my spine," said the snake to the wind. "Now, at least I have something like a leg. But you come booming up from the North Sea and booming down to the South Sea, and you seem to have no body. How is that?"

"Indeed," replied the wind, "I go booming up from the North Sea and booming down to the South Sea. Yet whoever sticks his finger into me overcomes me, and whoever kicks me also overcomes me. However, only I can tear up big trees and blow off big houses. Therefore, from a great number of small defeats I achieve the great victory. Achieving the great victory belongs to the Sage alone."

Another illustration of his graphic style may be seen in the conversation between General Clouds and the Great Nebula:

When General Clouds was going eastward, he passed through the branches of Fuyao [a magic tree] and happened to meet Great Nebula. The latter was slapping his thighs and hopping about. When General Clouds saw him, he stopped like one lost and stood still, saying, "Who are you, old man, and what are you doing here?"

"Strolling!" replied Great Nebula, still slapping his thighs and hopping about.

"I want to ask about something," said General Clouds.

"Ough!" uttered Great Nebula. . . .

From there on, the two spirits engaged in a discussion on the virtue of silence and inaction.

Chuangtse was the greatest maker of libelous fables about Confucius, for he found the intense seriousness of purpose of the Sage a ready mark for his wit. For if Laotse was gentle, Chuangtse was not. His was a more robust spirit. Laotse's message was meekness of spirit, Chuangtse's was emancipation of the spirit to "roam in the realm of Nowhere." For the strangest thing is that while Chuangtse's works elucidate practically all of Laotse's teachings point by point, he was absolutely silent on the virtue of meekness, or on "keeping to the Female." He was a man's man, and could not quite bring himself to say the word "humility" or "meekness." Thus, while water was for Laotse the symbol of the strength of softness and of the virtue of seeking the lowly, for Chuangtse it was the symbol of enormous latent power in quiescence. Laotse smiles, but Chuangtse roars. Laotse is pithy, Chuangtse eloquent. Both have pity for human stupidity, but Chuangtse is capable of caustic wit. Once he told of the story of a woman's "faithfulness" which matches the story of the virtuous "Widow of Ephesus" by Petronius. Chuangtse once came back from a walk, and his disciples found him wearing a woebegone countenance. On being asked, he explained: "I was taking a walk and saw a woman bending on the ground waving a fan over a new grave. 'What are you doing, and whose grave is it?' I asked. 'It is my husband's,' the widow replied. 'Why are you fanning it?' I asked again, and the woman replied, 'I promised my husband that I would not marry again until his grave was dry. But it rained, and we have such abominable weather these days.'"

Yet Chuangtse was no cynic, but an intensely religious mystic. He was essentially a Pascal. Chuangtse, like Pascal, felt the despair of man to know the infinite by his finite intelligence, but his clear recognition of the limitations of reason did not prevent him, or Pascal, from rising to the certainty of a great spirit informing the entire universe. Therefore reading Chuangtse is like reading a great mystic:

> There is great beauty in the silent universe. There are manifest laws governing the four seasons without words. There is an intrinsic principle in the created things which is not expressed. The Sage looks back to the beauty of the universe and penetrates into the intrinsic principle of created things. Therefore the perfect man does nothing, the great Sage takes no action. In doing this, he follows the pattern of the universe. The spirit of the universe is subtle and informs all life. Things live and die and change their forms, without knowing the root from which they come. Abundantly it multiplies;

eternally it stands by itself. The greatest reaches of space do not leave its confines, and the smallest down of a bird in autumn awaits its power to assume form. The things emerge and submerge, but it remains for ever without change. The *yin* and *yang* and the four seasons move in orderly procession. Darkly and without visible form it seems not to exist and yet exists. The things of the creation are nourished by it, without knowing it. This is the core, from which one may survey the universe.

The *Prolegomena,* the last chapter of Chuangtse's works, is one of the most important sources on ancient Chinese philosophy, giving the main currents of ancient Chinese thought. The opening gives the best expression of the scope of his examinations and the breadth of his point of view:

Many are the professors of philosophies of order and government in the world today. Each school regards itself as having found the best. It may be asked: In what school is to be found the philosophy of the ancients? The answer is that it is to be found in every system. Questions are asked: Whence comes the spirit and how did consciousness arise? The Sage's wisdom must have a source, and the king's power must derive from something. The source of both is the One [of the universe].

Chuangtse goes on to deplore the loss of a unified view of the universe in the hand of the "one-alley scholars":

(Now) the world is in universal chaos. The ways of the wise and the sage are not understood, and Tao and Teh are taught in different ways. Many philosophers emphasize one particular aspect and hold on to it. It is like a person whose senses function properly each in its own field, but do not cooperate with one another, or again like the artisans of different trades who are good each in his own line and are often needed. However, without an adequate comprehension of the whole, these are but one-alley scholars. In their appreciation of the beauty of the universe, their analysis of the principles of the creation, and in their study of the entirety of the ancient men's thoughts, they seldom comprehend adequately the

beauty of the universe and the ways of the spirit. Hence
the principles of the authorities of thought and of government
are hidden in the dark and find no proper expression. Each
man thinks what he likes and creates his own system. Alas,
gone astray are the various schools of philosophy, unable to
find their way back. They shall never find the truth. The
scholars of posterity, unfortunately, shall not be able to see
the original simplicity of the universe and the main foundation of thought of the ancients. Philosophy is thus cut up and
falls apart.

And thus Chuangtse summarizes his own philosophy:

Some of the teachings of the ancients lay in this: reality is
ever elusive and formless, and all life is constant change.
What are life and death? Am I one with the universe? Where
do the spirits move? Whither do they go, and where do they
disappear, so mysteriously and suddenly? The creation lies
spread before me, but in none of these things can be found
the true source. Chuang Chou heard of such teachings and
loved them. With unbridled fancies, facetious language and
sweet romantic nonsense, he gives free play to his spirit without restraint. He cannot be understood from any detached
sayings of his. He regards the world as hopelessly sunk in a
muddle, unworthy to talk with Chou [himself]. His "ladle
words" are a continual pouring forth, his "serious words" are
true, and his "allegories" are broad in implications. Alone he
stands with the heaven and earth and wanders as a companion
of the spirits. But he does not despise the things of the universe, or quarrel about what others regard as right and
wrong, and he mingles with conventional society. Although
his books dazzle and spin out lengthy discourses, this is a
minor blemish. Though his language is uneven [shifting from
the serious to the facetious], it is lively and good reading, for
it overflows from the fullness of his thoughts and he cannot
stop himself. Above, his spirit wanders with the Creator, and
below he makes friends with those who transcend life and
death and beginning and end. The foundation of his thought
is big and wide, deep and unconfined. The core of his teachings can encompass all phenomena and reach up to the divine

order. However, in its adjustment to the changing life and understanding of physical things, its principle is inexhaustible, traceless, dark and formless, and it is difficult to get hold of.

Chuangtse expounded in essays what Laotse said in a few epigrams. He elucidated in eloquent philosophic prose what Laotse said about the character of Tao and inaction and non-interference. In addition to writing some brilliant essays on letting men and animals "fulfill the laws of their being," and besides attacking Confucian virtues, Chuangtse's philosophy occupies itself with three main points: (1) his theory of knowledge, the impossibility of knowing the Infinite by finite intelligence; (2) the leveling of all things in their eternal aspect, in the infinite Tao; and as a corollary, (3) the meaning of life and death.

Chuangtse, like Pascal, began with a searching inquiry into the cause of life, with something like despair. No man felt more the pathos of human life, subject to flux and change, the poignancy of the daily wear and tear in a transitory existence, harrowed by worries and fears:

> For whether the soul is locked in sleep or whether in waking hours the body moves, we are striving and struggling with the immediate circumstances. Some are easy-going and lei-surely, some are deep and cunning, and some are secretive. Now we are frightened over petty fears, now disheartened and dismayed over some terrible mistake. Now the mind flies forth like a swift arrow from a cross-bow, to be the arbiter of right and wrong. Now it stays behind as if sworn to an oath, to cling to what it has secured. Then, as under autumn and win-ter's blight, comes gradual decay, and submerged in its own occupations, it keeps on running its course, never to return. Finally, worn out and imprisoned, it is choked up like an old drain, and the failing mind shall not see light again.
>
> Joy and anger, sorrow and happiness, worries and regrets, hesitation and fears, come upon us by turns, with ever-chang-ing moods, like music from the hollows, or like mushrooms in the swamp. Day and night they alternate within us, but we

cannot tell whence they spring. Alas! Alas! Could we for a moment lay our finger upon their very Cause?

But for these emotions I should not be. Yet but for me, there would be no one to feel them. So far we can go; but we do not know by whose order they come into play. It would seem there was a soul; but the clue to its existence is wanting. That it functions is credible enough, though we cannot see its form. Perhaps it has inner reality without outward form.

Take the human body with all its hundred bones, nine external cavities and six internal organs, all complete. Which part of it should I love best? Do you not cherish all equally, or have you a preference? Do these organs serve as servants of someone else? Since servants cannot govern themselves, do they serve as master and servants by turn? Surely there is some soul which controls them all.

But whether or not we ascertain what is the true nature of this soul, it matters but little to the soul itself. For once coming into this material shape, it runs its course until it is exhausted. To be harassed by the wear and tear of life, and to be driven along without possibility of arresting one's course—is not this pitiful indeed? To labor without cease all life, and then, without living to enjoy the fruit, worn out with labor, to depart, one knows not whither—is not this a just cause for grief?

Men say there is no death—of what avail? The body decomposes, and the mind goes with it. Is this not a great cause for sorrow? Is human life indeed such a puzzle? Or is it I alone who am puzzled, and others not so?

Pascal, too, feels the mystery of the inexplicable relation between the body and the soul. He, too, has that restlessness: "This resting in ignorance is a monstrous thing." He, too, feels the pathos of this human mind, sustained between Nothing and the Infinite, being necessarily incapable of knowing the two extremes.

Limited as we are in every way, this state which holds the mean between two extremes is present in all our impotence. . . . This is our true state; this is what makes us incapable of certain knowledge and of absolute ignorance. We sail within a vast sphere, ever drifting in uncertainty, driven from end to end. When we think to attach ourselves to any point and to fasten to it, it wavers and leaves us; and if we follow it, it eludes our grasp, slips past us, and vanishes for ever. Nothing stays for us. This is our natural condition, and yet most contrary to our inclination; we burn with desire to find solid ground and an ultimate sure foundation whereon to build a tower reaching to the Infinite. But our whole ground-work cracks, and the earth opens to abysses.

1. *Theory of Knowledge.* Chuangtse begins with the inadequacy of language to express the Absolute, for every time we try to express by words some aspect of life or of Tao, we inevitably cut it up, and in cutting it up, lose grasp of the truth, the Infinite, the inexpressible. It is interesting to see this point, so closely allied to the development of Zen Buddhism, which I shall touch upon in the next chapter.

Suppose here is a statement. We do not know whether it belongs to one category or another. But if we put the different categories in one, then the differences of category cease to exist. However, I must explain. If there was a beginning, then there was a time before that beginning, and a time before the time which was before the time of that beginning. If there is existence, there must have been non-existence. And if there was a time when nothing existed, then there must have been a time when even nothing did not exist. All of a sudden, nothing came into existence. Could one then really say whether it belongs to the category of existence or of non-existence? Even the very words I have just now uttered—I cannot say whether they say something or not. . . .

If then all things are One, what room is there for speech? On the other hand, since I can say the word "one" how can speech not exist? If it does exist, we have one and speech—two; and two and one—three, from which point on even the best mathematicians will fail to reach [the ultimate]; how much more then should ordinary people fail?

Hence, if from nothing you can proceed to something, and subsequently reach three, it follows that it would be still

easier if you started from something. Since you cannot proceed, take your rest.

Perfect Tao cannot be given a name. A perfect argument
does not employ words. . . . Who knows the argument which
can be argued without words, and the Tao which does not
declare itself as Tao? He who knows this may be said to have
entered the realm of the spirit.

Chuangtse's methodology is so like Pascal's. Hence Pascal's
dictum is easily understood from the Chuangtsean point of
view. So says Pascal:

True eloquence makes light of eloquence, true morality makes
light of morality; that is to say, the morality of the judgment,
which has no rules, makes light of the morality of the intellect.

For it is to judgment that perception belongs, as science belongs to intellect. Intuition is the part of judgment, mathematics of intellect.

To make light of philosophy is to be a true philosopher.

But Chuangtse's theory of the limitation of knowledge does
not apply only to the sphere of the metaphysical; it applies to
the world itself. It comes from his theory of impossibility of
objective judgment, the futility of words themselves. The following is a good preparation for understanding Zen.

Granting that you and I argue. If you get the better of me,
and not I of you, are you necessarily right and I wrong? Or
if I get the better of you and not you of me, am I necessarily
right and you wrong? Or are we both partly right and partly
wrong? Or are we both wholly right and wholly wrong? Since
you and I cannot know, we all live in darkness.

Whom shall I ask to judge between us? If I ask someone
who takes your view, he will side with you. How can such
a one arbitrate between us? If I ask someone who takes my
view, he will side with me. How can such a one arbitrate
between us? If I ask someone who differs from both of us, he
will be equally unable to decide between us, since he differs
from both of us. And if I ask someone who agrees with both

of us, he will be equally unable to decide between us, since he agrees with both of us. Since you and I and other men cannot decide, how can we depend upon another? The words of arguments are all relative; if we wish to reach the absolute, we must harmonize them by means of the unity of God, and follow its natural evolution to the end of our days.

But what is to harmonize them by means of the unity of God? It is this. The right may not be really right. What appears so may not be really so. Even if what is right is really right, wherein it differs from wrong cannot be made plain by argument. Even if what appears so is really so, wherein it differs from what is not so also cannot be made plain by argument.

Take no heed of time nor of right and wrong. Passing into the realm of the Infinite, take your final rest therein.

2. *Relativity of Standards and Leveling of All Things.* What led Chuangtse to the belief in the futility of arguments was really his basic concept of Tao, the constant Tao which manifests itself in change and flux and contradictory appearances which we know as life and death, beauty and ugliness, big and small, and even the contrast between being and nonbeing. All of these are temporary appearances only, by which men, in the ignorance of Tao (like the Greek *logos*), are constantly being deceived. Tao absorbs them all, annihilates them all.

Therefore take, for instance, a twig and a pillar, or an ugly person and a great beauty, and all the strange and monstrous transformations. These are all leveled together by Tao. Division is the same as creation; creation is the same as destruction. There is no such thing as creation or destruction, for these conditions are again leveled together into One.

Only the truly intelligent understand this principle of the leveling of all things into One.

More explicitly Chuangtse develops the relativity of standards and interdependence of opposites:

There is nothing which is not *this;* there is nothing which is not *that.* What cannot be seen by *that* [the other person] can be known by myself. Hence I say, *this* emanates from *that; that* also derives from *this*. This is the theory of the interdependence of *this* and *that* [relativity of standards].

Nevertheless, life arises from death, and *vice versa*. Possibility arises from impossibility, and *vice versa*. Affirmation is based upon denial, and *vice versa*. Which being the case, the true Sage rejects all distinctions and takes his refuge in Heaven. For one may base it on *this*, yet *this* is also *that* and *that* is also *this*. *This* also has its "right" and "wrong," and *that* also has its "right" and "wrong." Does then the distinction between *this* and *that* really exist or not? When *this* (subjective) and *that* (objective) are both without their correlates, that is the very "Axis of Tao." And when that Axis passes through the center at which all infinities converge, affirmations and denials alike blend into the infinite One. Hence it is said that there is nothing like using the Light.

One might think one was reading the French mathematician. In fact, the meaning of the Chuangtsean phrase the "Axis of Tao" (Tao-ch'u), might elude many a Chinese reader until he read Pascal. The two are so strikingly similar in their approach, and even in the tone of their voice. Read the following, for instance:

> What will he do then, but perceive the appearance of the middle of things, in an eternal despair of knowing either their beginning or their end. All things proceed from the Nothing, and are borne towards the Infinite. Who will follow these marvellous processes? The Author of these wonders understands them. None other can do so.

Is this Chuangtse talking or Pascal? And who is talking about the "ultimate principles of being" resolving in the unity of God?

> The visible extent of the world visibly exceeds us; but as we exceed little things, we think ourselves more capable of knowing them. . . . It seems to me that whoever shall have understood the ultimate principles of being might also attain to the knowledge of the Infinite. The one depends on the other, and one leads to the other. These extremes meet and

reunite by force of distance, and find each other in God, and in God alone.

Let us then take our compass; we are something, and we are not everything. The nature of our existence hides from us the knowledge of first beginnings which are born of the Nothing; and the littleness of our being conceals from us the sight of the Infinite.

With such help from Pascal, therefore, it is easier to understand the passage in Chaungtse's famous "Autumn Floods," in which Chaungtse further develops his ideas of the infinite and the infinitesimal, the *macrocosmos* and the *microcosmos*. Pascal, too, was fascinated by this, and spoke of "nature's immensity in the womb of this abridged atom." But Chuangtse's facetious wit develops this conception of the infinitestimal in a weird story about the battle of the Mans around the tip of a snail's feeler—on the whole, a piece of daring imagination equaled only by the modern discoveries of bacteria. There was a king of Wei who thought himself and his kingdom very big and very important, and this was the allegory told to enlighten him:

> Tai Chinjen said to the King, "Have you ever heard of a thing called the snail?"
> "Yes."
> "There is a kingdom at the tip of the left feeler of the snail. Its people are called the Ch'us. And there is a kingdom at the tip of the right feeler of the snail, and its people are called the Mans. The Ch'us and the Mans have constant wars with one another, fighting about their territories. When a battle takes place, the dead lie about the field in tens of thousands. The defeated army runs for fifteen days before it returns to its own territory."
> "Indeed," said the King. "Are you telling me a tall tale?"
> "It isn't a tall tale at all. Let me ask you, do you think there is a limit to space in the universe?"
> "No limit," replied the King.
> "If you could let your mind roam about in infinity, and

arrive in the Country of Understanding, would not your country seem to exist and yet not to exist?"

"It seems so," replied the King.

"In the center of the Country of Understanding, there is your country, Wei, and in the country of Wei there is the city of Liang, and in the center of the city of Liang, there is the king. Do you think there is any difference between that king and the king of the Mans?"

"No difference," replied the King.

The interviewer withdrew and the King felt lost.

Chuangtse's escape from all this flux and uncertainty was to retreat, on the one hand, to the ordinary common experience, and on the other, to stop talking and speculating as soon as one reached the border of Tao.

(The truly intelligent) discard the distinctions and take refuge in the common and ordinary things. The common and ordinary things serve certain functions and therefore retain the wholeness of nature. From this wholeness, one comprehends, and from comprehension, one comes near to Tao. There one stops. To stop without knowing how one stops— this is Tao.

This is a characteristically Zen position, as we shall see later. In fact, it is Zen itself without being called Zen.

3. *Life and Death.* Some of the most beautiful things Chuangtse said are about the subject of death. It is clear from the above discussion of the identity of opposites, that life and death could only be different aspects of the same thing, and Chuangtse was forced to the conclusion that the soul leaving the body upon death is perhaps on the "great journey home." Why fear death? Why regret this living?

How do I know that love of life is not a delusion after all? How do I know but that he who dreads death is not as a child who has lost his way and does not know his way home?

The lady Li Chi was the daughter of the frontier officer of Ai. When the Duke of Chin first got her, she wept until the bosom of her dress was drenched with tears. But when she

came to the royal residence, shared with the Duke his lux-
urious couch, and ate rich food, she repented of having wept.
How then do I know but that the dead may repent of having
previously clung to life?

*Those who dream of the banquet, wake to lamentation and
sorrow. Those who dream of lamentation and sorrow wake to
join the hunt.* While they dream, they do not know that they
are dreaming. Some will even interpret the very dream they
are dreaming; and only when they awake do they know it
was a dream. By and by comes the great awakening, and
then we find out that this life is really a great dream. Fools
think they are awake now, and flatter themselves they know
—this one is a prince, and that one is a shepherd. What
bigotry of mind! Confucius and you are both dreams; and I
who say you are dreams—I am but a dream myself. This is
a paradox. Tomorrow a Sage may arise to explain it; but that
tomorrow will not be until ten thousand generations have
gone by. Yet you may meet him around the corner.

Again, life and death are "companions" to each other:

Who can appreciate the connection between the two? When a
man is born, it is but the embodiment of a spirit. When the
spirit is embodied, there is life, and when the spirit dis-
perses, there is death. But if life and death are companions
to each other, why should I be concerned? Therefore, all
things are one. *What we love is this mysterious life. What we
hate is corruption in death. But the corruptible in its turn
becomes mysterious life, and this mysterious life once more
becomes corruptible.*

The last line sounds like St. Paul, but is in fact a quite literal
translation. But what beauty of expression!

Behind this is of course Chuangtse's idea of eternal flux,
"the transformation of material things" (*wu-hua*). In a parable, Chuangtse makes Confucius expound his own ideas. How
could that which is changing say that it will not change, and
how could that which regards itself as permanent realize that
it is changing already? . . . Resign yourself to the sequence of

things, forgetting the changes of life, and you shall enter into the pure, the divine, the One." Here we see a note of religious resignation. In a story, Chuangtse told of four friends who had achieved the unified view of the universe, making "Not-being the head, Life the backbone, and Death the tail." One of them suffered from a horrible disease so that his backbone was doubled up.

"Do you dislike it?" asked Tsesze.

"No, why should I?" replied Tseyu. "If my left arm should become a cock, I should be able to herald the dawn with it. If my right arm should become a sling, I should be able to use it to shoot down a bird for broiling. If my buttocks should become wheels, and my spirit become a horse, I should be able to ride in it—what need would I have of a chariot? I came to life because it was my time, and I am now parting with it in the natural course of things. Content with the coming of things in their time and living in accord with Tao, joy and sorrow touch me not. This is, according to the ancients, to be freed from bondage. Those who cannot be freed from bondage are so because they are bound by the trammels of material existence. But man has ever given away before God; why, then, should I dislike it?"

These were four extraordinary philosophers, as Chuangtse portrayed them. I think in the episode of the third friend's illness, Chuangtse reached an attitude of what Christians would call "acceptance of God's will."

By and by, Tselai fell ill and lay gasping for breath, while his family stood weeping around. Tseli went to see him, and cried to the wife and children: "Go away! You are impeding his dissolution!" Then, leaning against the door, he said, "Verily, God is great! I wonder what He will make of you now, and whither He will send you. Do you think He will make you into a rat's liver or into an insect leg?"

"A son," answered Tselai, "must go whithersoever his parents bid him, East, West, North, or South. Yin and yang are no other than a man's parents. If yin and yang bid me die quickly and I demur, then the fault is mine, not theirs. The

Great [universe] gives me this form, this toil in manhood, this repose in old age, this rest in death. Surely that which is such a kind arbiter of my life is the best arbiter of my death.

"Suppose that the boiling metal in a smelting pot were to bubble up and say, 'Make of me a Moyeh (a famous sword)!' The master caster would reject that metal as uncanny. And if simply because I am cast into a human form, I were to say, 'Only a man! only a man!' the Creator too would reject me as uncanny. If I regard the universe as the smelting pot, and the Creator as the Master Caster, how should I worry wherever I am sent?" Then he sank into a peaceful sleep and waked up very much alive.

Isn't this like what St. Paul said about the clay and the potter?

Chuangtse, in fact, believed in the immanence of God, again expressed most facetiously:

"Where is this so-called Tao?" asked Tungkuotse of Chuangtse.

"Tao is everywhere," replied Chuangtse.

"But you must specify."

"It is in the ants," was the reply.

"Why, is it so low?"

"It is in the tare-seeds," said Chuangtse again.

"It is getting lower still," exclaimed Tungkuotse.

"Tao is in the jars and bricks."

"It is getting worse and worse!"

"It is in the excrements," said Chuangtse.

Tungkuotse did not speak any more, and Chuangtse said, "What you asked just now is a question which is a difficult one for me to answer and substantiate with examples. When Corporal Huo went to the head of the market to buy pigs, he looked for the pig's hoofs (as the best place to judge a pig). *You should not have asked me to specify, for thus you cannot get away from the material.* Great truths are [elusive] like this, and so are great teachings."

Chuangtse was fully aware, as he said of himself, that his teachings were "traceless, dark and fathomless, and difficult to get hold of." But that is neither more nor less than what Eddington says of the doings of the electron inside the atom: "Something unknown is doing we don't know what." Chuangtse is rightly called a "mystic," but anybody who dares to communicate with Divinity and says "Thou" in a prayer is *ipso facto* a mystic, and that includes all Christians. As if there ever were or could be a "rationalist" religion!

The beauty of Chuangtse's wisdom was to know where and when to "stop and take your rest" when he reached the borderline of Tao. The folly of Christian theology was in not knowing when and where to stop, but in proceeding with finite logic to define God like a triangle, and to decide for one's own intellectual satisfaction, how *B* was "born" of *A*, and how *C* merely "proceedeth" from *B* and not directly from *A*. Chuangtse says rightly, "You should not have asked me to specify." To which Pascal adds the warning: "Hence it comes that almost all philosophers have confused ideas of things, and speak of material things in spiritual terms, and of spiritual things in material terms."

The history of Taoism is a curious thing. Never was there greater degeneracy from the height of Laotse's wisdom to the occultism, the magic, and the frightful spirits and demons of "popular" Taoism. Taoist priests nowadays are mostly useful for "exorcising" of demons. Popular imagination always created the necessary gods if the philosophers refused to do so. The most persistent strain of Chinese native thought was belief in the *yin* and the *yang* and the five cosmic elements (metal, wood, water, fire, and earth) and their mutual attraction and repulsion. This belief antedated and permeated both Confucianism and Taoism. However, there are explicit references in Laotse, and especially in Chuangtse, to "mental hygiene," "nourishing of the spirit," and "control of breathing," "contemplation" and "seeing the Solitary (One)" which opened the door for all believers in occultism and mental hygiene to fasten the label of Taoism upon themselves.

CHAPTER 5

The Dissolving Mist of Buddhism

So FAR as the popular conception of the word "religion" goes, the Chinese people may be said on the whole to be Buddhists. Buddhism is a popular religion, and by popular religion I mean a church and a system of beliefs which includes temples and monasteries, a priesthood, a Heaven and Hell, prayers and worship, a way of "salvation" from the "misery" and "transitoriness" of the present life, a complete hierarchy of saints and angels (bodhisattvas and arahats) and a number of gods and goddesses ("Buddhas" and the Goddess of Mercy); I mean furthermore a system of beliefs which teaches kindness and mercy and selflessness, denial of worldly values, asceticism, suppression of sinful desires, and tremendous self-conquest and self-discipline. Buddhism has all these in its present form.

In competition with Buddhism, the Taoist cult which grew up tried to outdo it by providing equally numerous gods and spirits and demons and a Taoist heaven of immortals, and even went so far as to include some Hindu deities. But whereas the Chinese scholars as a class look down upon both the Taoist and Buddhist cults as sheer superstitions, Buddhist philosophy,

148

possessing a basic system of fine and elaborate metaphysics, commanded the respect of the Chinese scholars, leaving the Taoist cult to sink lower and lower in its magic incantations and the exorcism of demons. The cheapest form I saw in my village was the cure of stomach-ache by drinking a bowl of "charm water," which was plain water with a piece of paper with occult signs scribbled on it. The only important contribution of the Taoist cult was the development of alchemy in the third century A.D., in search of the philosopher's stone, for the double purpose of finding the elixir of immortality and something of a more practical or commercial value, the transmutation of base metal into gold. It was this "science" which was later passed into Europe by the Arabs.

Unlike the Christian churches or sects, the practice of religion in China is not exclusive. Most Chinese would be puzzled and would not know how to answer if asked what their religion was. There are no parishes and no parish registers, and there were not even birth registers until recent times through civil offices. No family is exclusively Buddhist or Taoist or Confucian. The line of faith cuts across a family somewhat as the political parties in an American family do. Perhaps the wife is a devout Buddhist who pledges vegetarian fasts for a month or a year for the granting of some wish before the Buddha, while the husband, being a Confucian scholar, tolerates her; or the reverse may be the case.

Buddhism was the only foreign intellectual influence on Chinese thought in ancient China, and for a good reason; as I have said, it had a definite, sometimes too elaborate, system of metaphysics which appealed to the Chinese scholars. Now, whatever the scholar class thought about it, the people of China wanted a popular religion, wanted gods to pray to and a paradise to look forward to; in a better sense, they also wanted repentance from sin, and "salvation" from pain, disease, hatred, poverty, and death. Buddhism came to China through the common people and sometimes through men or

women at the court. It did not invade the Chinese scholar
class until the latter had to face it and reckon with it.

Briefly, Buddhism came to China by way of central Asia
over the Pamir Plateau into China's Northwest. Every Chinese
tyrant wanted to live forever, beginning with Chin Shih-huang,
the builder of the Great Wall. Having reached the summit of
earthly power, they wanted to become immortal. Some tried
to obtain the elixir of immortality from across the China Seas,
and others from Chinese Turkestan across the Pamir Plateau.
When Buddhism was introduced into China in the first century (almost exactly A.D. 1, according to some Chinese records,
though there is of course no exact date), Buddhism was already flourishing in a great part of India and in central Asia,
especially under King Asoka (272–231 B.C., emperor of the
Maurya Empire). A Chinese emperor officially sent an emis-
sary to bring back the Buddhist teachings in A.D. 65, but it was
the overrunning of North China by separate Tartar rulers
in the fourth, fifth, and sixth centuries that opened the way for
the great spread of Buddhism among the people. Some of the
great sculptures of Lungmen and Yunkang dated from this
period. By the year 400 A.D., most Chinese families in North
China had become Buddhists. The Chinese monk Fa Hsien
went to India in A.D. 399 and returned with Buddhist texts
fifteen years later. The Indian monk Kumarajiva, the first great
translator of Buddhist texts, was made imperial master by a
ruler in a Northwest kingdom, in A.D. 405, and his work was to
bear permanent fruit in Chinese popular religion. By the sixth
century Buddhism had spread all over China, in spite of short
periods of persecutions, from Confucian scholars or from certain rulers. It had shown itself to be a tremendous force which,
starting from India, had overrun Ceylon, Burma, Siam,
Afghanistan, Turkestan, Tibet, and China and as far as Korea.
In the space of one hundred years, from 517 to 618, five edi-
tions of the Buddhist *Tripitaka* (collection of sacred texts)
had been published. And in the first decades of the sixth century, when the almost legendary Bodhidharma came to China

by way of Canton and became the father of the Shan (Zen) Sect, a famous emperor, Liang Wu-ti, twice entered a monastery to become a monk and was reluctantly persuaded by his courtiers to leave it later.

Translations and studies of Buddhism steadily gained ground in the sixth century. The famous Tientai sect, a school which tried to embody the Mahayana and the Hinayana (Greater and Lesser Vehicles) was formulated in this century. Then in the seventh century, the Huayen (Idealistic) school of philosophy was founded. (The currently used edition of the Huayen Sutra was a third translation completed in A.D. 699 by the decree of the megalomaniac Empress Wu, who pretended that she was an incarnation of Buddha Maitreya, and forged a Buddhist text to support it.) Meanwhile, the most famous Chinese translator, Hsuan Chuang, had gone to Afghanistan and India for a sixteen-year stay and returned in A.D. 645 with 657 Buddhist texts which he devoted his life to translating with fellow workers under the sponsorship of the imperial court. Also in this century, a great number of Japanese students came to study Buddhism at the Tang capital, Chang-an, and brought home with them the Buddhist teachings. (Buddhism had already penetrated Japan from Korea.) By the year 800, the ten Buddhist sects were complete, eight of them belonging to the Mahayana and two to the Hinayana school. The Hinayana sect (based on Pali), or the primitive or classical Buddhism, died out completely by the tenth century, unable to compete with the popular appeal of the Mahayana, especially the appeal of the "Paradise Sect" dating back to Kumarajiva.

As a result of this evolution, there existed, on the philosophic side, the Tientai School, which I may call the historical school, trying to accommodate the various interpretations of the Greater and the Lesser Vehicles, as expressing the same truth of Buddhist teachings; the Huayen School, which did have a great number of *gathas* and prayers, but which in its basic doctrine of the merging of all things and qualities in the

Primeval One, shows the clear influence of Laotse and Chuangtse; and, most important of all, the Shan (Japanese Zen) School, whose principles could be traced directly to Chuangtse and which was essentially the product of the Chinese spirit, particularly of Chuangtsean humor and denial of logic, acting upon Buddhist philosophy. On the "popular" side there was the Paradise Sect already mentioned, very much in demand. In particular, popular imagination was caught by one of the male bodhisattvas, Avalokitesvara, who, touched by the misery of human life, refrained voluntarily from entering the bliss of Nirvana and swore not to return to it until he had saved all mankind. He then became transformed into a female deity, the Kuanyin, "Goddess of Mercy, Savior of the Afflicted and the Distressed," who became the most popular goddess in China. (Compare a study of the growth of similar cults in the eleventh, twelfth, and thirteenth centuries in Europe by Henry Adams in *Mont-Saint-Michel and Chartres*.) From then on, Kuanyin's hold on the popular imagination became irresistible because of her mercy and her compassion. Mention must also be made of the Tantric School of magic formulas and spiritual or near-spiritistic exercises, which has its firm foothold in Tibet and Koko Nor (Panchen and Dalai Lama!), which cannot be despised because it is a living force, kept intact with monastic education and discipline—in general in a much better preserved condition than popular Buddhism in the rest of China.

In all these things I am not talking about the Buddhist influence on Chinese art or sculpture, but on Chinese philosophy, and in return about the way in which the Chinese mind shaped Buddhism to its own practical instinct. I have mentioned previously the influence of Buddhist metaphysics upon the Neo-Confucianist sect of the Sung Dynasty (A.D. 960–1276), and Buddhist philosophy went on leavening the Chinese mind until the Confucianists had to reckon with it and make terms with it in order to survive. While Confucian orthodoxy always frowned upon Buddhism as a "foreign" imported religion,

Buddhism deepened Chinese philosophy and directed its emphasis to the problems of the consciousness and reality and the mind.

The first thing, in fact, which the Neo-Confucianist school did was to take the writings of Mencius and two essays from *Liki*, "Great Learning" and "Central Harmony," because of their great philosophic import, and make them, together with the *Analects* and *Mencius*, the Confucian Four Books for every Chinese schoolboy to learn. Now the first book, the "Great Learning," opened with these words: "The principles of great learning consist in refurbishing the (originally) clear character of man, in renewing the people, and in coming to rest in the ultimate good. Having a point of *rest* comes before *stability* of mind, stability enables one to have *tranquillity*, tranquillity enables one to have *peace* of mind, and peace of mind enables one to *think* discriminately." All this has, or is capable of having, a surprisingly Buddhist connotation. The word "rest" is the same word with which the Tientai School summarizes its chief doctrine. The ultimate good is interpreted by Chu Shi in Buddhist fashion as "arriving at the ultimate good, beyond further change. One must realize the ultimate of the Universal Reason and strip oneself of the slightest human desire." Further in the discussion of the pursuance of knowledge, Chu Shi took the occasion of an apparent lacuna in the text to put in a bit of twelfth-century Sung metaphysics: "By the sentence 'Achieving knowledge depends on the investigation of the material world' is meant the application of our knowledge to explore the Reason in the material things. For there is that knowledge (the German *Wissen* is nearer in meaning) in the consciousness of all human minds, and there is Reason behind all material things. If knowledge fails, it is because the Reason has not been exhaustively explored. . . ." It is evident that the Chinese Confucianist was both repelled by Buddhist philosophy, and stimulated to find something similar to it. In both the prefaces to "Great Learning" and to "Central Harmony," written in February and March, 1189, Chu Shi made reference specifically to the presence of Buddhist thought: *"The heretical doctrines of Nihilism and Nirvana are higher than the Great Learning,* but not practical," and again: "Heresies arose and grew from year to year, until the followers of Laotse and Buddha appeared, when *they seemed to approach Reason,* but only helped to confuse it. . . . Some disciples [of the Cheng brothers] have turned their backs on their teacher and indulged in Laotse's and Buddha's doctrines. . . ." This is what Buddhism had done to Confucianism.

But what is it in the Buddhist metaphysics that so compelled the respect and opened the eyes of the Chinese intellectuals? What happened was that Gautama had ruthlessly carried out the examination of consciousness and reality where Descartes and Kant later stopped. If Descartes had said, "I feel, therefore I exist," he would have been a Chuangtse ("But for me, there would be no one to feel them," that is, the emotions) or a Whitman ("I am as I am"). But why did Descartes want to believe or to prove that he existed at all? If he had questioned even that perceiving mind or "cognitive reason," and pushed it further, he would have landed where Buddha did. Descartes trusted the perceiving mind; Buddha strongly suspected it

The *Suragama Sutra* is a philosophical masterpiece, a lengthy work developing pre-Kantian idealism, in which the category of space itself was annihilated by the Higher Mind, or the Mind Essence, or the "Buddha Mind" (*Buddhahridaya*). Readers who are interested are referred to the very lengthy extract of over fifty thousand words which I have incorporated in *The Wisdom of China and India.* Here is a summary in Buddha's words of the whole argument. The *Suragama Sutra* is extremely charming reading, not difficult like Kant, and it is always good to go back to the original sources and make direct acquaintance with this philosophic masterpiece (essentially Shan). I am giving a few brief extracts (not included in *The Wisdom of China and India*) for their bearing on Buddhist idealism and to permit a clearer understanding of the teachings of Shan:

Then the Blessed One in order to emphasize his teaching summed it up as follows:—

In comparison with Mind-Essence, all conditioned things are as empty as space. Existing as they do under conditions, they are false and fantastic; unconditioned things, having neither appearance nor disappearance, are as imaginary as blossoms seen in the air. As we are obliged to use false expressions to interpret the essence of things, so both the false expressions and the essence of things as thus interpreted by the false expressions become a pair of falsities. It is clear to see that the intrinsic Essence is neither the essence as interpreted, nor the non-essence of the interpretation. How can it be asserted that there is trueness in either the thing as perceived, or in the phenomena of perceiving?

Therefore, as there is no reality at the heart either of the sense-organs and of the objects seen, or of the perceiving consciousness, they must all be as empty as the heart of reeds. As all the knots of the mind and all unloosening of knots have the same basis of unreality, it matters not whether we think of them as sacred or vulgar; there is but one path to emancipation and that is to escape from their bondage altogether.

If you are considering the nature of the center of reeds, it matters not whether you interpret the center as emptiness or as non-emptiness—either would be a misinterpretation. If anyone is puzzled by the saying that both are false, it is because of his ignorance. If one is not puzzled, it is because he has attained emancipation. The unloosening of knots is a gradual process; one must begin with the knots of the five sense-organs, after which the knots of the sixth sense—the perceiving and discriminating mind—will loosen of themselves. Therefore, it is wise to begin with the sense organ that is most yielding and accommodating and by means of it, it will be easier to enter the true Stream of Life that flows into highest perfect Wisdom (*anuttara-samyak-sambodhi*). [Here Buddha refers to the sense of hearing, as leading most easily to a feeling of spirituality, as music certainly does.]

Although the Alaya-vijnana (the universal or "storage" Mind) is immaculate in its self-nature, as it receives the seed of the false thinking, it becomes contaminated and becomes as wild and unmanageable as the current of a torrent. Because one easily falls into attachment to arbitrary conceptions, such as reality interpreted by false expressions and illusions of non-reality, I have not always interpreted things in this way. Since all conceptions of phenomena are nothing but activities of the mind, so, speaking truly, the mind is not a fantastic thing but it becomes a fantastic thing. If you are not in bondage to these contaminations of your own mind, there will be neither arbitrary conceptions of fantastic things, or of things that are not fantastic.

As there is no rising in your Essential Mind of such arbitrary conceptions as non-fantastic things, why should they be raised at all? This teaching is the wonderful "Lotus Flower." It is as gloriously enlightening as the diamond (Vajra-raja), as mysteriously potent as highest Samadhi. This is the Incomparable Teaching! Anyone practicing it with sincerity and earnestness will outdo the graduate disciples in a single moment, as suddenly as a rap on the door. Such a one will become Honored of all the World! Indeed! This Teaching is the only path to Nirvana. [The phrase "in a single moment, as suddenly as a rap on the door," became the warrant from Buddha's words for the development of Shan, as will be seen later.]

What Buddha might have said to Descartes if Descartes were one of the arahats was this: "If you do not trust your own existence, why do you trust the perceiving mind itself?" For the perceiving mind is only one of the six sense organs with the other five (the eye, the ear, the nose, the tongue, and the finger) which contaminate our knowledge of the truth. Buddha's own effort and that of the Buddhists was to eliminate that normal contaminated and conditioned perceiving mind, with its loads of memories and sense impressions, and arrive at complete freedom and a higher mind, the mystical Mind Essence. This is beautifully told in the following illustration by Buddha with six knots in a silk handkerchief. Buddha was talking before a great assembly of disciples, who all became bodhisattvas.

When the Lord Tathagata ("the Perfect One") had finished this supreme instruction, whose profound and comprehensive thoughts had been expressed in well chosen words and beautiful style, Ananda and the whole assembly were enlightened and they praised the Lord Buddha for his sacred teachings.

But Ananda* was not yet satisfied. In reverential manner and spirit, he addressed the Lord Buddha, saying:—Noble Lord! Though I have listened carefully to my Lord's noble and compassionate teaching about the exclusive unity and oneness of the pure, mysterious and eternal Essence, I do not yet fully realize its meaning. It seems to teach that as soon as the six sense-organs have become emancipated from their contaminations and attachments that the remaining arbitrary conceptions of the thinking mind will fall away of themselves leaving only the one intrinsic Essence, and that this process of emancipation will proceed in an orderly and spontaneous fashion. Pray, my Lord, have great forbearance with us less advanced disciples and, for the sake of all future disciples, repeat this instruction in more detail, so that it may purify our minds and the minds of all future disciples.

The Lord Tathagata arranged his garments and taking a silk handkerchief proceeded to tie a knot in it and showed it to the assembly, saying, What is this?

With one accord, they replied:—It is a silk handkerchief in which you have tied a knot.

The Lord Tathagata tied another knot in the handkerchief and said:—What is this?

They replied:—It is another knot, Blessed Lord.

Again the Lord tied other knots until there were six. Then showing the handkerchief to the assembly, and indicating the knots one by one, he asked what is this? And what is this? And to each question Ananda and the others answered as before:—It is a knot.

* The positions of Ananda and Manjusri in the Buddhist Pantheon are comparable to those of St. Paul and St. Peter in the Christian Church. Their images usually stand on the right and on the left of Buddha in a Chinese Buddhist temple.

Then the Lord Buddha said:—Ananda! When I showed you the first knot, you called it a knot, and when I showed you the second and third and so on, you still insisted they were all knots.

Ananda replied:—Noble Lord! The handkerchief is made of silk threads of different colors and is woven into a single piece, but when it is tied into a knot, it is right to call it a knot, also, and if the Lord were to tie it into a hundred knots, each one would be a knot. However, my Lord has only tied it six times—not seven or five—so there are only six knots. Why does my Lord seem to recognize only the first tying as a knot?

The Lord Buddha replied:—Ananda, you are right in saying that this beautiful handkerchief is one piece and that when I tied it six times there were six knots. Now look at it closely. The silk handkerchief is the same piece of woven silk, the tying has not changed it in the slightest, except in appearance —it is still a handkerchief. Now think, Ananda. When the handkerchief was tied the first time, the first knot appeared; and then later and successively, the second knot and the third to the sixth. If I now take this sixth knot and begin to count them backward, the sixth knot becomes the first, does it not?

Ananda replied:—No, my Lord, when the handkerchief was tied six times, the last tying was the sixth knot; it can by no means be called the first knot. No matter what you say, there is no possibility of confusing the order of the knots—it is and always will be the sixth knot.

The Lord Buddha agreed to this, saying:—So it is, Ananda. The six knots may not all be exactly alike, but when you seek the root of their different forms, they are all arrangements of the single handkerchief. You can not confuse the single handkerchief; you may confuse the knots, their differences and order, but you can not confuse the handkerchief because it is a single whole. The same is true of your six sense-organs— they are knots tied in the essential unity of your mind and out of its unity there appears the variety.

The Lord Buddha continued:—Ananda, if you do not like to have knots tied in the handkerchief but prefer its original state, what would you do?

Ananda replied:—Noble Lord! As long as the knots exist in the handkerchief there will be the possibility of a discussion about them—which is first and which second—but when the knots are all untied, there can be no further discussion about them because they will all have disappeared and only the beautiful handkerchief will remain in its original state of oneness.

The Lord Buddha was pleased with this reply and said:— That is true, Ananda. The same is true about the relation of the six organs of sense to the Essential Mind. As the six sense-organs become freed from their contaminations, the remaining arbitrary conceptions of the discriminating mind will disappear also. It is because your mind, having become diseased and bewildered because of the false sense-conceptions accumulated since beginningless time, has developed many desires, attachments and habits. From these there have arisen, incident to the ever changing processes of life, arbitrary conceptions concerning self and not-self and as to what is true and what is not true. These arbitrary conceptions have not developed in a normal way from your pure Mind Essence, but in an abnormal way because of the prior false conceptions that had their origin in the sense-organs, like the sight of blossoms in the air that come to diseased minds. They falsely appear to have had their origin in the enlightening and Essential Mind but, in truth, they have arisen because of diseased conditions.

The same is true, also, of all conceptions, objective and component—universes, mountains, rivers, trees, sentient beings, and deaths and rebirths. Even discriminating thoughts of Mind-Essence and Nirvana, everything, all of which are nothing but phenomena analogous to blossoms seen in the air by diseased eyes and all of which have been manifested by the enslaved, bewildered and ever active, topsy-turvy mind.

Ananda then said to the Lord Buddha:—Noble Lord! If these ever-rising, changing, arbitrary conceptions of phenomena are like knots tied in a handkerchief, how can the knots be unloosed?

The Lord Tathagata took the handkerchief with the knots still tied in it and tugged at it in a blind, foolish way that only served to tighten the knots and asked Ananda if the knots could be unloosened in that way.

Ananda replied:—No, my Lord.

Then the Lord tugged at the knots in another wrong way and again asked if the knots could be unloosed in that way.

Ananda replied:—No, my Lord.

The Lord Buddha said:—I have tried now that way and now this way, but with no success in unloosening the knots. How would you untie them, Ananda?

Ananda replied:—My Lord, I would first study the knot and find out how it was tied, then it could easily be untied.

The Lord Buddha was pleased with this reply and said:— Right you are, Ananda! If you wish to untie a knot, you must first understand how it was tied. The lesson which I have been teaching you—that all things are manifested by causes and conditions—does not refer to these crude terrestrial phenomena of conformity and combination alone, but is the principle that the Tathagata has discovered from the Dharma of Emancipation which applies to both the terrestrial and transcendental worlds. For he knows the originality of all phenomena and accordingly he can make any manifestation he pleases to meet any situation or condition. He even knows each single drop of rain that falls on the sands of the River Ganges. For instance, in our presence there are all sorts of conditions—the straightness of pine trees, the crookedness of shrubs, the whiteness of storks, the blackness of magpies, etc.—the Tathagata knows the cause of each.

Therefore, Ananda, you may select any one of your six sense organs that you please, and if the bondage to that sense organ is destroyed, the arbitrary conceptions of all objects in the discriminating mind will be destroyed at the same time. Once being convinced that any single sense conception, or a thought based upon one, is unreal and fantastic, one's dependence upon sense conceptions in general is destroyed. After all the delusions of sense conceptions have been thus destroyed, there will remain only the true Essence of Mind.

Ananda! Let me ask you another question. This handkerchief has six knots tied in it. If I untie them can they all be untied at once?

No, my Lord. The knots were originally tied one by one in a certain order, so when we come to untie them we must follow the reverse order. For although the knots were made in one handkerchief, they were not made at one time and cannot be untied at one time.

Again the Lord Buddha was pleased at the reply and said:— It is the same with the disentanglements of the conceptions of the six senses. The first knot of false conceptions that must be untied is the one relating to the false conception of an ego-personality; one must first of all attain a realization of its utter non-reality. When this realization of the unreality of one's own ego-personality is perfectly attained it becomes enlightening, then the next knot to be untied is the one relating to personal attainments of any kind. This arbitrary conception must be untangled and its unreality fully realized. These two entanglements—belief in an ego-personality and the conception of personal attainment—must be utterly destroyed and never again permitted to rise to defile the true Essential Mind. This accomplishment may be called the Bodhisattva-Mahasattva's attainment of the Perseverance in the Dharma of non-rebirth through the Practice of their Samadhi.

With regard to the Kantian category of space, Buddha explained it as a "fantastic" addition of the mind:

As soon as this original and perfectly limpid and all-embracing Enlightening Intuition becomes reflected upon objects, it becomes illusive and loses its true Nature. Then as differentiations are manifested, space fantastically appears and by means of space, whole universes come into manifestation. Arbitrary conceptions seem to corroborate the existence of the universes and finally, that which becomes perceptive and sensible of the universe becomes regarded as a sentient being having an ego-personality. . . .

The conception of empty space as existing in the Enlightening Nature of Mind Essence is but foam tossed about by the waves of a great sea. As it is under the conditions of this transient foam that the innumerable conceptions of universes and all that appertains to them which belongs to the intoxicant nature of sentient beings exists, as soon as this foam disappears, there is no more space and hence no more universes and all the three realms of sentient life, body, mind and ego-personality, vanish into nothingness.

Now we are getting closer to the Shan approach, which is, in brief, intuitive grasp of the true reality in a flash. It is difficult to arrive at the liberation of the Mind Essence from any one of the senses:

> The phenomena of fragrance and the smelling sensation are perceived by means of the conception of smelling so that when the sensation and the perception are separated there can be no conception of fragrance. Since the novice does not realize the permanency of his intrinsic smelling nature, it will be difficult for him to attain the essential nature of perfect accommodation through the sense of smelling.

Or from fixing one's contemplation on an object, such as the tip of one's nose:

> In the practice of Dhyana, many novices seek concentration of mind by fixing attention on the tip of the nose, but as this is only a temporary means that is useful to some drifting and confused minds, it can never be relied upon as a permanent means for attaining the nature of perfect accommodation.

It is especially difficult to arrive at true understanding and realization by words of exposition:

> There are sermons that are given without the sounds of words (Chuangtse!) that are enlightening to those advanced disciples whose minds have been disciplined in previous lives, but which are useless to novices who are dependent upon words and definitions and style to keep up their interest; the novice cannot depend upon them for his attaining the essential nature of perfect accommodation.

Lastly, one of the disciples, Manjusri, addressed the other great disciple Ananda and cautioned him against memory, even the memory of Buddha's words which he had just heard:

Notwithstanding Ananda's wonderful memory, he was not able to avoid falling into an evil way. He has been adrift on a merciless sea. But if he will only turn his mind away from the drifting current of thoughts, he may soon recover the sober wiseness of Essential Mind. Ananda! Listen to me! I have ever relied upon the teaching of the Lord Buddha to bring me to the indescribable Dharma Sound of the Diamond Samadhi. Ananda! You have sought the secret lore from all the Buddha-lands without first attaining emancipation from the desires and intoxications of your own contaminations and attachments, with the result that you have stored in your memory a vast accumulation of worldly knowledge and built up a tower of faults and mistakes. . . . Ananda! As you return to the phenomenal world, it will seem like a vision in a dream. And your experience with the maiden Pchiti will seem like a dream, and your own body will lose its solidity and permanency. It will seem as though every human being, male and female, was simply a manifestation by some skillful magician of a manikin all of whose activities were under his control. Or each human being will seem like an automatic machine that once started goes on by itself, but as soon as the automatic machine loses its motive power, all its activities not only cease but their very existence disappears. . . . All the Brothers in this Great Assembly, and you too, Ananda, should reverse your outward perception of hearing and listen inwardly for the perfectly unified and intrinsic sound of your own Mind-Essence, for as soon as you have attained perfect accommodation, you will have attained to Supreme Enlightenment. . . .*

I. Shan (Zen)

When Maha-Kasyapa smiled at one point of Buddha's discourse, it was a smile of understanding to which the Shan School traces its origin. One of the most peculiar sects of Bud-

* The above translations of Buddha's discourse are by Wai-Tao, in *A Buddhist Bible,* edited and published by Dwight Goddard (Thetford, Vermont, 2nd. ed., 1938).

dhism then began, for Kasyapa is regarded as the first teacher of the doctrine of Shan. Twenty-eight generations passed, and Bodhidharma came to China, bringing the message of the Buddha heart and the method of heart assent (literally "heart seal" fitting to a seal print exactly), and became known as the father of the Shan School. This occurred in the sixth century. The Chinese people and some rulers had already taken to Buddhism, and this Shan teaching found a ready echo in Chinese minds. The sect grew rapidly, passing through six generations of masters and pupils, ending in the great Sixth Master Huei-neng,* from which point on it had a rich and varied development in South and North China.

A few dozen more generations passed, and Professor Suzuki came to Columbia University to lecture on Zen (Japanese for Shan). It was quite a feat to teach by words a doctrine denying the use of words, and to explain the futility of the logical approach to a logically minded Western audience. To be sure, one has to use certain words even if only to explain that words are useless for expounding certain infinite truths beyond ordinary human understanding. What Shan tries to achieve is to attain an "indeterminate" mind-state beyond the perceiving mind, and the more one uses words which are determinate in character, naturally the more one tends to confuse. Hence the Chinese masters developed a method of pantomimes and conundrums which are mystifying to outsiders. One master used to slap the inquirer's face for an answer when he was asked what Shan was. Another just lifted his finger. Another might spit. All this is by way of teaching a doctrine which denied all doctrines, a way of conveying a truth, which in itself is shy of all words and all logical approach, by means of a gesture

* In 1944, I saw at the Shan Temple in Kukong, near the northern border of Kwangtung Province, what was said to be the mummy of the Sixth Master. There were two mummies in a sitting position, their bodies and faces preserved by a heavy coating of red lacquer, and retaining a lifelike expression. Their bodies were robed and placed in a niche in a position for worship. I mention this because it is so little known.

or a movement, indicating the awful mystery and the transcendental nature of a simple act of common everyday living. Professor Suzuki, I understand, did not slap Columbia students' faces as a means of communicating divine wisdom. He should have!

For Shan is all intuition. As such, it developed a distinctive technique and a different end result. Shan is short for *Shanna,** which is the Chinese translation for the Sanskrit word *dhyana,* or meditation, originally one of the six methods of Buddhist discipline. But it went far beyond mere "meditation." Buddha is supposed to have passed this "special teaching beyond the church" to Kasyapa, based on the Buddha-heart doctrine. And since all men have this Buddha heart or Buddha mind in them, the business of restoring that heart to its original state merely involves wiping it clean of all contaminations due to the sense impressions and the perceiving, discriminating mind, the mind which is usually cluttered up with words and logical analysis and doctrines. Hence it is said: "Lay down the butcher's knife, and you will become a Buddha on the spot."

Of course, it is straight mysticism, but of a very special kind. What Buddha was trying to teach, by Shan or by any other method, was to knock out the a priori categories of thought themselves, to destroy all discriminations by hearing, sight, sound, and all the other senses of perception. In other words, the goal of Buddhist effort in achieving the *satori* of Shan is to become a kind of gentle superman, if this contradiction in terms can be understood. For a man is a superman if he has annihilated his own perceiving mind and therefore annihilated the notions of space and time; he has risen to a position of freedom from all mental bondage to this sentient existence, and to a view of the universe and of all human life from a supersentient mind-essence which is Buddhahood itself. One must admit that the human notion of time and God's own no-

---

* The Japanese *Zen* is not a corruption of the Chinese *Shan,* but an ancient Chinese pronunciation of the same word. In modern Shanghai dialect, *Shan* is read as *Zen.* The development was *dyna>dzianna>zen>shan.*

tion of time are not the same, and that it is possible to achieve a super-Olympian view and see through all transient existence, all distinctions and all qualities and all individualities as merely the limited or distorted views of things. Now if by such a superhuman effort one does do that, that is, if one can dehumanize all human experience, what does one get? A godlike stability, tranquillity, peace, a "purple-golden brightness within my body," as Maha-Kasyapa expressed it. It is Buddhahood itself. All men can become Buddhas, of course. To do so is victory. For one has overcome the ego (the bugaboo of Schopenhauer and of Freud) and therefore overcome all fears, all worries, all desires, all distinctions. When this ego feeling is annihilated, there is a "sublimation" and a "transference" of the self to the greater self, which includes all fellow men and dogs and cats and all other animals in this wonderful cavalcade of creation. One obtains cosmic pity. That explains the "gentleness," the mercy and compassion of Kuanyin. As Kuanyin described herself, or rather himself, in the story of his personal spiritual emancipation, he said, as Bodhisattva-Mahasattva Avalokitesvara, that "as soon as all arbitrary conceptions of rising and disappearing of thoughts were completely discarded, the state of Nirvana was clearly realized . . . and in this state I acquired two wonderful Transcendencies. . . . The second Transcendency was that my mind was in perfect conformity with the minds of all sentient beings of the Six Realms and felt with them the same earnestness and longing for deliverance."

Now a Hindu Mahasattva could remain a Mahasattva, analyzing his own eighteen "spheres of mentation," eighty-one states of consciousness, thirty-two transformations, fourteen states of fearlessness, and so on. But to a Chinese, it was speculative, complicated, and highly unreal. Did not the Lord Tathagata teach that it was all a flash of intuition? Did he not also say that while some attained to this state of perfect enlightenment by gradual steps of training extending over long periods of years and perhaps *kalpas* (Sanskrit for "ages"), one could also attain it by a sudden flash of insight? That insight says, "I've got it." It may be lost again when the mind (also regarded as a sense organ) gets involved again in distinctions, but in another moment of insight, he may cry again, "I've got it!"

Now, for the Chinese that single sentence of Buddha or that single smile of Maha-Kasyapa is enough. Why all those words to destroy words? Why all those speculative systems of analysis of the emptiness of phenomena? To be sure, Buddha's own ruthless analysis of all perceptions and all elements of the universe is an impressive piece of original thinking. The Chinese scholars had never heard of such a thing as Buddha's statement in his reprimand of Ananda's confusion, that "the sound of the gong, the hearing of the sound, and the perception of the hearing are three different things." That was why all the disciples, the great company of bodhisattvas, adored his superior wisdom and his clear answers to questions, his piece-by-piece destruction of all confusions of the mind. Of course the Great Master was impressive. But the Great Master had also taught that mental speculation is profitless, that it is as vain as to "bite one's own navel." Then why all the Tientai School and the Huayen School? Chuangtse had already said, "One lays a bamboo trap to catch fish; after you have caught the fish, throw away the trap. One reads books to catch truth (Tao); after you have caught the truth, throw away the books."

Shan therefore developed into a revolutionary doctrine. It became impatient with all the sutras, all the systems of speculation, all logical analysis, all idols made of wood or stone, all priesthood, all theology, and all indirect methods of training. It was a doctrine to destroy all doctrines. As Professor Suzuki expresses it, "All the Buddhist teachings as propounded in the sutras and sastras are treated by Zen as mere waste paper whose utility consists in wiping off the dirt of intellect and nothing more." And what does Zen teach? "It teaches nothing," answers Suzuki, but merely shows a point of view. How can intuition be taught, anyway? The kingdom of *satori* is within you. In a highly "destructive" sense, a believer in Shan cares not for God, nor for Heaven or Hell, nor for the abstract soul. He lives and feels and perceives; he does not abstract or meditate.

Actually, this spirit of Shan, this peculiar method and even the very phraseology of Shan is Chungtsean. Shan's fundamental distrust of the use of words, which are determinate in meaning, to explain and propound indeterminate truths is repeatedly stated by Chuangtse. "Now Tao by its very nature can never be defined. Speech by its very nature cannot express the absolute." "Who knows the argument which can be argued without words, and the Tao which does not declare itself as Tao? He who knows this may be said to have entered the realm of spirit." If we follow Professor Suzuki as a student of Chuangtse, it will be quite evident that Chuangtse was the precursor of Shan. We read in his *Introduction to Zen Buddhism:* "When I say there is no God in Zen, the pious reader may be shocked, but this does not mean that Zen denies the existence of God; neither denial nor affirmation concerns Zen. When a thing is denied, the very denial involves something that is not denied. The same can be said of affirmation. This is inevitable in logic. Zen wants to rise above logic, Zen wants to find a higher affirmation where there are no antitheses" (page 14). This easily recalls Chuangtse's statement: "Affirmation is based upon denial, and vice versa. Which being the case, the true sage rejects all distinctions and takes his refuge in heaven." Chuangtse was very impatient with the "affirmations and denials of the Confucian and Motsean schools." Chuangtse believed that affirmations and denials alike blend into the infinite One. The denial of logic and the leveling of all things and all antitheses is exactly the core and the basis of all Chuangtse's teachings. Again we read from Professor Suzuki, apropos of the uselessness of meditation: "Meditation is something artificially put on; it does not belong to the native

activity of the mind. Upon what do the fowl of the air meditate? Upon what do the fish in the water meditate? They fly;
they swim. Is that not enough?" (page 16). Again we are reminded of Chuangtse's emphasis on the following of Tao as
the *unconscious* fulfilling of nature's ways. Chuangtse said that
as fish forget themselves in water, so should men forget themselves in Tao. This following of Tao should be, in Emersonian
terms, a natural flow of goodness without conscious effort. In
a rather striking statement, Chuangtse says, "Unawareness of
one's feet is the mark of a pair of shoes that fit; unawareness
of the waist is the sign of a belt that fits; unawareness of right
and wrong is the mark of a mind that is at ease." One remem-
bers also Chuangtse's parable of the centipede. The centipede
moves his legs without knowing how he moves them; the moment a centipede becomes conscious of his seventeenth or
nineteenth or twenty-third pair of legs, he cannot move any
more. Again one reads in Professor Suzuki: "Zen is neither
monotheistic nor pantheistic; Zen defies all such designations.
. . . Zen is a wafting cloud in the sky." Now, what Professor
Suzuki is afraid of are words like "monotheism" or "panthe-
ism" which mean so many things with so many people, and
the more you define or argue, the more you bring confusion
into the mind. We recall the same question asked of Chuangtse
about the immanence of Tao. If Tao was immanent in the universe, was it in this thing, was it in that thing? And Chuangtse
replied by saying, "It is your mistake. *You should not have
asked me to specify in the first place.*" Finally, in regard to
the end result of all this technique, Professor Suzuki writes:
"Zen reveals itself in the most uninteresting, uneventful life of
a plain man of the street, recognizing the fact of living in the
midst of life as it is lived. Zen systematically trains the mind
to see this; it opens a man's eyes to the greatest mystery as it
is daily and hourly performed. . . ." Curiously, and this is
most important, Chuangtse arrives at exactly the same solution. "[The truly intelligent] discard the distinctions and take

refuge in the common and ordinary things. The common and
ordinary things serve certain functions and therefore retain
the wholeness of nature. From this wholeness, one comprehends, and from comprehension, one comes near to Tao."

This brings us to the most peculiar end product of Shan.
Shan claims that its method is direct and simple and practical.
All Shan training, including meditation, is preparation for that
direct experience. Shan is a "sudden" mystical experience
closely associated with everyday life and everyday living. So
Shan comes to "rest" in the simple, everyday living, regarding
it as a blessed gift, and enjoying every moment of it. I would
call it gratitude for living, a form of Oriental existentialism.
There is a sense of the mystery of the mere act of living. A
Shan monk enjoys the humble chores. The Sixth Master spent
a great part of his life pounding rice (to make it white),
as a kitchen helper. One famous Shan poet, Hanshan,
worked as a kitchen helper bringing fuel from the mountains and scribbling his poems on the kitchen walls. (His
astoundingly simple spiritual verses are still in existence.)
A Chinese Shan poet exclaims, "It is a miracle—I am drawing water from a well!" This is typical of the Shan life
as it ought to be lived. It is a miracle that a cowboy sits
on a buffalo's back at sunset on his way home. It is a miracle that flies swarm and weeds grow and a man drinks a
cup of water. Is it not a wonderful thing, a miracle, that a man
drinks a cup of water, knowing not what water is, nor what
a cup is, and not even what he himself is? All life and all living
are miracles. One becomes a poet as the plowman wipes the
sweat off his brow and feels the cooling breeze upon his head,
or, as Tao Yuan-ming records almost with ecstasy about a walk
in the field at dawn, "The morning dew wets the skirts of my
gown!" That pleasure and tranquillity in merging oneself with
all sentient existence is Buddhahood itself. It accounts for a
great deal of the spiritual quality of Chinese landscape painting.

II. Sin and Karma

This is the burden of Buddha's message: that this life is a bondage and full of suffering, subject to worries (*fan-nao*), fears, pains, and death; that this world is illusion (*maya*), but man, in that boundage of illusion, sharing the sentient life with the creation, goes on accumulating deeds, words, and commitments (*karma*), sunk in lust and desires and all forms of pettiness of spirit; that he is thus doomed to the eternal wheel of transmigration (*lun-huei*); that man, however, can liberate himself by escaping from the illusion and contamination by an intellectual or an intuitive effort; that he can let the mind-essence take command of the senses and the normal perceiving, discriminating mind; that this state of liberation from all finite, conditioned thought (whether of life and death or of other distinctions) is the indeterminate, unconditioned *Nirvana*; that equally the Wheel of the Law (*dharma*) turns eternally; and finally, that the path to deliverance lies in the three treasures, the Buddha, the Law, and the Church (*Sangha*). The whole theology is logical enough, which accounts for its intellectual and spiritual power to conquer the whole of the far Orient. (One may note here that the Buddhist transmigration of souls is different from the Chuangtsean "transformation of material things"—*wu-hua*. Chuangtse's concept seems more atomic; one part of a man may become upon his death "a rat's liver" or a cricket's leg or an inanimate object like a boy's sling.)

But the most distinctive notion is *karma*, which in Chinese is *nieh-chang*, or "the burden of sin." A simpler but less accurate translation would be simply "bondage." This bondage is something which drives us on in the multifarious businesses of life and of living, involving us deeper and deeper. *Nieh* is sin, and *chang* has the idea of an "obstacle" or a "screen" which prevents us from seeing the truth. Quite accurately,

Buddha could use the Biblical sentence: "Ye shall know the truth, and the truth shall make you free."

We can leave the Buddhist moral teachings alone; no religion in the world ever teaches deceit or stealing or adultery, dishonesty, hatred, or vengeance. One does not have to worry on that score. One need only point out that the result of the doctrine of transmigration is to teach kindness to all animals and forbid destruction of life, or eating slaughtered meat. The Chinese people never had a "zoo," although the imperial court had. The only thing was the "let-live pond" of fish in Buddhist temples. I always enjoyed looking at the fish in the famous let-live pond at Hangchow, where seventy or eighty big carp growing to two to three feet long in a pond supplied with a fresh mountain current had the chance to "live out the even tenor of their days," safe from human persecutions. In the eyes of a Buddhist, any one of those big carp might eventually be reincarnated as a human being and perhaps even become a Buddha.

As I said, the most distinctive concept in Buddhist teaching is *karma,* or sin. This sin, as a wit has said, is anything but original; it is common to all mankind. Buddha was deeply concerned with this universal bondage, this drive to follow the animal lusts and desires, which was Schopenhauer's "will to live" and "will to reproduce." Schopenhauer's will to live is of course Buddhism in European dress, and its famous pessimism is equally characteristic of the whole tenor of Buddhist pity. Buddha's commentary on human life could be summed up in five words: The pity of it all! And Schopenhauer came to the same solution for escape by asceticism and conquest of the ego sense—again, both Buddhist.

I think the Christian concept of original sin is too mystical. The sin of the first Adam is of course symbolic in meaning only; as we are born of this flesh, we are born with the same failings, same impulses, and destructive instincts which we inherit from our ancestors. It is original only in the sense that it is born, that no animal or human being is born without the instincts of hunger, sex, fear, hatred, and so on, which are necessary instincts for survival in the life of the jungle. But there is no need to make this "original sin" into a mystical entity, as if every baby were born a branded criminal and destined for Hell. Nor is it necessary to libel God, making Him punish a murderer for a hundred and perhaps a thousand generations in his children and grandchildren because of a single act. Even granted that criminal tendencies are "inherited," that is, "original," we do not punish a criminal for such tendencies until he has committed an act against the law. Very often Christians simply do not have the wit to understand this; they make original sin into a myth, wrapped up into a "package" of salvation for the buyer to take or leave. Men will be punished for the mere possession of *inherited tendencies*. That is why I have said, "I am so profoundly religious that the religions often make me furious." And nothing makes me more furious than the belief that a newborn babe with his big innocent round eyes is going to be sent to Hell by a Christian God which is all Love. It is against a mother's every instinct. It is against all human decency. And even God cannot violate the law of common human decency. God is not a sadist.

The fact of inherited sin, of inherited instincts useful for survival in the jungle, nevertheless remains. These instincts—criminal if you like—become sin only when they end in transgressions against the law and decency and public order. A dog can commit a nuisance in the streets of Manhattan because he is living in the Tao, unconsciously obeying natural instincts. A human child must be *taught* not to do so. And so with all the mortal sins. Sin is in every human heart, if you like, the desire to do certain things pleasurable on the instinctive level, but it is usually checked by either the social law without or the moral law within. Hence the world of suppressions, sublimations, dreams, and dream wish-fulfillments, and so on, opened up by Freud.

Freud, I believe, helps us to understand original sin better.

Now, in the world of thought, there are only four or five original minds. Excluding the scientists, these are Buddha, Kant,
Freud, Schopenhauer, and Spinoza. All the rest of us are
merely repeating what others have thought, though many have
made their own discoveries by some thinking of their own. By
"original minds" I mean the thinkers who broke unknown
grounds for human thought, whose thinking soared to heights
where others had not been before. Kant explored the limits of
the true nature of so-called human knowledge in exhaustive
German fashion. Buddha went further and explored and discovered an escape beyond all Kant's Pure Reason. Of course,
he saw an awe-inspiring beauty, the beauty of knowledge
which is as near God's own as possible. Schopenhauer discovered the basis of all animal and human life in the will to
live, to survive, to reproduce, arising actually more from a
collective racial instinct than from individual instinct—which
drive must in the last analysis account for the mysterious mi-
gration of birds, the return of the salmon to spawn, the growing of fangs and horns and fins and claws, and a thousand odd
biological facts. According to Schopenhauer, "A bull does not
gore because he has horns; he has horns because he means to
gore." Now this is what I call profound. Spinoza discovered,
like Chuangtse, the unity of all things and saw only the infinite substance (compare Tao) of which the finite existences
are only modes or limitations (compare Teh). But Spinoza's
"intellectual love of God" is only for the humanist, the intellectual. I daresay that if other religions were not at hand,
popular imagination would and could transform even this
"intellectual love" and invest it with saints and spirits to en-
liven the pantheistic universe and make it somewhat easier
to worship.

The point is, Buddha, Schopenhauer, and Freud, while
breaking new frontiers of thought concerning human life,
were all confronted with the fact of sin and desires. And all
three also discovered something in man to regulate sin and
desires, which implies that a struggle is going on all the time,

and that man need not lie prostrate before the tyrannical force of the instincts. Freud discovered, and in the oracular litany of psychoanalysis was forced to postulate, an "id"—the moral censorship of the superego. Buddha and Schopenhauer both advocated suppression of desires and asceticism, which I do not like because of the assumption that the desires are in themselves evil, which is clearly untrue and unconvincing to the modern man's consciousness. Spinoza discovered that man had, besides the basic instincts, also the noble instinct for good, to perfect himself. The others—Kant, Mencius, Wang Yang-ming—traced it to "conscience," as something as much God-given, that is, inherited and "original," as sin itself. Why does no theologian discover an "original conscience" and allow Calvin to run away with his "total depravity"? If they have failed to do so, it is not because Jesus did not say explicitly and bluntly, "The kingdom of God is within you." If the kingdom of God is within you, how can depravity be "total"? How difficult it is for this truth to penetrate theological minds! (I must say here that the Presbyterian Church is greater than Calvin. I believe in Jesus against Calvin.)

Freud, to my mind, is one of the most curious creatures. He had the instinct of a ground hog, whose first instinct is to head for dark, subterranean regions and ferret out the hiding places of things, throwing a lot of dirt above ground. For a thousand frauds there is only one Freud. These original minds are always interesting to read, because their thoughts are fresh and have not been handled and rehandled and mishandled until they begin to wilt and spoil. And Freud's discovery of man's inner self presents a picture not so different from Buddha's. What a nest of undesirable eggs within! All men are neurotic one way or another. The same is true of Schopenhauer's unknown, dark, primeval racial drives and racial urges. But at least we have learned from these moderns to understand sin a little better. We understand why Hebrew writers and others spoke of these forces as demons and personified them in Satan. Freud, too, speaks of the "tyrannical, autonomous" forces of the instincts beyond the rational mind's control. Speak of these instincts as demons if you like, but there is no need to hypnotize oneself with words.

And this is what I want to say about all religions and about Buddhism in particular. If religion means otherworldliness, I reject it. If religion means that we must run away from this present, sentient life and "escape" from it as fast as possible, like a rat abandoning a sinking ship, I am against it. One ought to, I think, with Chinese common sense, come to live with the world and make terms with it, bravely, in the sense of the acceptance of the grace of living as the Shan believers do. And I feel strongly that so long as religion, *any* religion, clings to an otherworldliness, this tendency to deny and escape from this sentient life which God has given us so abundantly, we will, by doing so, by just so much prevent religion, *any* religion, from being in touch with the modern man's consciousness. We shall be in a true sense ungrateful children of God, not even worthy cousins of the Shan believers.

If I had to make a choice between a run-away-from-the-world spiritualism, including mortification of the flesh, and a stark, heathen materialism, or if I had to make a choice between contemplating sin exclusively in some dark, cavernous corner of my soul, and eating bananas with a half-naked girl in Tahiti, entirely unconscious of sin, I would choose the latter. What I think and feel personally is unimportant, but if this is what many modern men feel, it is important for the religionists to think about. "The earth is bounteous and the fruit thereof," said St. Paul.

CHAPTER 6

Reason in Religion

I. Method in Religion

IN ANY discussion of religion, ancient or modern, Occidental or Oriental, a discourse in method is necessary. One does not open clams with a crowbar; nor, in the Biblical analogy, can one lead a camel through the Needle Gate. A wise surgeon does not cut a coronary artery with a pair of garden shears. It is just not done. Yet modern Westerners have always tried to reach God by Cartesian logic.

A *Discourse on Method* in religion at this point is essential. For much of the confusion with regard to religion in the modern mind is due to a fundamental error of method, and is even attributable to the dominance of the Cartesian method, to the overpowering emphasis placed on the primacy of cognitive reason, as such, and to an inadequate conception of the primacy of intuitive understanding. "I cannot forgive Descartes," says Pascal. Nor can I. For in the realm of material knowledge or of scientific knowledge of facts, the tools of reasoning by the categories of time, space, motion, and causation are supreme and unquestionable, whereas in the realm of significances and moral values—in religion and love and human relationships—this method is curiously unadapted to the purpose and in fact wholly irrelevant. The recognition of these two different realms of knowledge, the realm of facts and the realm of moral values, is fundamental. For religion, which is appreciation and wonderment and a fundamental attitude of reverence of the mind, is a gift of intuitive understanding by a man's whole consciousness, a total response to the universe by his moral nature, and this intuitive appreciation and understanding is a far subtler and higher gift and of a higher order of understanding than mathematical reasoning. The war of the scientific temper and the religious temper is due to this confusion of method, and to the subjugation of the realm of moral knowledge to the methods suitable to the exploration of the realm of nature.

Descartes made the first error in assuming that human existence had to go begging for proof of its reality through cognitive reasoning. His entire trust and dependence on cognitive reason, and the dominance of this method, which today is still the foundation of modern philosophy, have resulted in the horrible spectacle of modern philosophy degenerating almost into a branch of mathematics, entirely divorced from ethics and morals, and a little shy of God as something inscrutable, immeasurable, and outside its realm of competence. For in the realm of science, one must fight shy of all things that are not measurable, and God and Satan and good and evil are certainly not amenable to measurement by meters. There are minor errors and limitations in Descartes' method, for even in science a reasonable sizing up of the whole situation and of the "fitness of things" is part and parcel of the daily process of scientific thinking. What sight fails, vision must supply, or science can never make any progress at all. And Descartes made a second error in the entirely unwarranted separation of mind and matter, a thesis which is daily becoming more and more untenable in contemporary science.

The Chinese long ago, I believe by a sound instinct, repudiated entirely the role of logic in religion. The development of Zen Buddhism, as we have seen, is based on the distrust of logical analysis, and Westerners schooled in the Cartesian method of reasoning find Zen very difficult to understand. The most shocking thing about the Christian religion to an Oriental mind is the scholastic approach to religion which is part of almost all Christian theology. The error is almost unbelievable, but to a world dominated by the primacy of reason rather than by the primacy of feeling and man's total consciousness, the error is not even perceptible and is ignored. It is not that the scientific method is wrong, but that it is totally and wholly irrelevant in the sphere of religion. Always man wishes to define the Infinite in finite terms, and to speak of spiritual things as material things, being unaware of the nature of the subject he is dealing with.

I am always suspicious of people who lug in science to defend religion. Religionists like to get slips of evidence from natural science to bolster their ancient beliefs. This is a habit derived from the prestige of science, a prestige that is entirely deserved. But religionists, instead of standing on the primacy of man's whole consciousness, often like to filch scraps of natural science or confessions from natural scientists in the same way that sellers of patent medicines inevitably shout in a raucous voice, "Three out of four doctors recommend . . ." The public must be impressed, and so the sellers of patent medicines must cry their wares. No, Religion should not go down on its knees, begging for clinical proof from Science. It should have more dignity. The weapon of science is the microscope; the weapon of knowledge in religion is the still, small voice of the human heart and a warm, subtle awareness with an intuitive capacity to guess at truth. But what the modern man lacks is precisely that finesse and *Schicklichkeit*.

Hence the confusion of thinking about religion in the modern world. Hence the assumption that there is a war between science and religion, whereas this war exists only in the minds of people who are trained, consciously or unconsciously, in the

Cartesian, or, if you like, in the scholastic, method of reasoning.

On the whole, I must say that the most characteristic differences between Chinese and Occidental methods of thinking may be represented as follows:

	Chinese	Western
Science	Deficient	Reason and mathematics
Philosophy	Intuitive verdicts on ethics and principal concern with conduct	Growing invasion of mathematics, and divorce from ethics
Religion	Denial of logic and reliance on intuition	"War" between the mathematical mind and man's whole consciousness

Heinrich Heine gives an amusing picture of an argument about God and religion in his *Reisebilder:*

When the roast became too bad, we argued the existence of God. But the good Lord always had the majority. Only three of the dinner company were atheistically inclined; but even these could be swayed if we at least had good cheese for dessert. The most zealous deist was little Samson, and when he debated the existence of God with lanky Vanpitter, he sometimes became quite excited, and ran up and down the room, continually crying: "By God, that isn't right!" Lanky Vanpitter, a lean Frisian, whose soul was as calm as the waters in a Dutch canal, and whose words trailed as leisurely as a towbarge, drew his arguments from German philosophy, which he had studied assiduously at Leyden. He ridiculed the narrow-minded heads that attributed a personal existence to God. He even accused them of blasphemy because they endowed God with wisdom, justice, love and similar human attributes, not at all suitable to Him, since they were in a way only the obverse of human qualities, antitheses of human folly, injustice and hatred. But when Vanpitter developed his own pantheistic view, he was beset by a fat Fichtean, a certain Driksen of Utrecht, who stoutly confuted his vague conception of a God diffused throughout Nature, that is to say, existing in space . . . whereas in thinking of God, a man must abstract Him from all substance, and not think of Him as a form of extension, but as an order of events. God was no Being, but pure Act—the principle of a transcendental world-order.

At these words, little Samson was beside himself with rage. He ran up and down the room even more crazily, and cried more loudly, "God! Oh, God! By God, that isn't right! Oh, God!" I believe that in honor of God he would have drubbed the fat Fichtean, if his arms had not been so thin. As it was, he sometimes did attack him, and then the fat one took hold of little Samson's two little arms, held him quietly, and without taking his pipe from his lips, quietly expounded his system, now and then blowing his airy arguments along with his tobacco smoke into Samson's face, so that the little fellow was almost choked by fumes and fury, and wailed more and more pitifully: "Oh, God! Oh, God!"

But God never came to his aid, although he was defending His cause so valiantly.

This is an example of the futility of argument and disputation about the Divinity. What do all these bold sallies of the intellect amount to? To a thoroughgoing materialist, the spectacle of three students of religion arguing in a coffeehouse, three little human minds who were presumably descendants of the amoeba arguing about the nature and the character of God, must certainly be a very amusing and thought-provoking spectacle. The interesting point is, however, that God *never came to the rescue,* and anybody who has sense can see that these people will never get anywhere.

Essentially, however, the spectacle of the three students of religion has not changed from that of the fourth century in the Christian era during the debate on the Athanasian Creed. There was no tobacco smoke to be blown in another's face, but each was as desperately sure of himself as Vanpitter or Samson. What they were trying to do was to put the three members of the Trinity in a logical relationship, a very worthy subject for the bishops. The first point they agreed on was that the three members of God were three Persons but one "substance," a word which is somewhat ridiculous with regard to God but had, we must allow, a philosophical meaning. Even the word "Person" immediately involved definition in terms of human beings. The great debate was the difference between the three members of the Trinity. What an engaging topic! All three members were uncreate. However, the greatest difficulty was to define the logical relationship between two members of the Trinity and God the Father, and it was finally decided that God the Son was uncreate but "born" of the Father, whereas the Holy Ghost was uncreate, and not "born" but merely "proceedeth" from the Father, with the threat of perdition to all people who were wicked enough to disagree. When it was agreed that the Holy Ghost merely "proceedeth," the debate raged round the question whether it "proceedeth" directly from the Father or through the Son. On such scholastic pinpoints the Greek Orthodox Church separated from the Roman Catholic Church, and in the eleventh century the Pope and the Patriarch excommunicated each other for the glory of God. If this is not impiety, what is?

II. *Present Attitudes*

As a matter of fact, the confusion in thinking with regard to religion is not entirely due to the method made popular by Descartes, but was scholastic in origin. Only monks with plenty of time, security, and wine could produce such a brain child. Religion means many things to many men, and the present state of religious beliefs offers a wide variety of attitudes and opinions. William James, in his lectures *The Varieties of Religious Experience,* has given us a very varied picture of different kinds of religious practices and beliefs, including some which are absurd. In the luxuriant jungle of so-called religious beliefs and opinions, all the fallacies, the "Four Idols" of Francis Bacon, are present—all the prejudices and preconceived notions ("Idols of the Tribe") such as the idea that God must be a kind of human being, an anthropomorphic God; all the beliefs identified with personal or national prejudices ("Idols of the Cave") such as the current usage in which being "Christian" and being "white" have practically the same meaning; all the verbal fictions and confusions ("Idols of the Market Place"); and all the fantastic tenets based on philosophic systems created by man ("Idols of the Theater"), such as Calvin's doctrine of "total depravity."

The Bible itself furnishes us with some examples of the attitudes of the contemporaries of Jesus, still prevalent today. First there was the attitude of Salome, the daughter of Herod, who wanted St. John the Baptist's head. This is the attitude of contemporary Communism, the Salome attitude, the attitude in which one's sole desire is to see religion flayed and crushed. There was the attitude of Pontius Pilate, the attitude of neutralism which was made popular by Nehru, in any struggle between good and evil. Judged objectively and fairly, I do not think that Pontius Pilate's position was unusual or uncommon, and, according to his particular "Idol of the Cave," it was even justifiable. He had no reason to be mixed up with the quarrels among the Jews. He washed his hands of the matter, and he did say *"Ecce Homo,"* "Behold the Man," which was a sarcastic dig at Caiaphas, "Here, look at your criminal!" At least, Pontius Pilate's neutralism was a more real kind than that of Jawaharlal Nehru, who raised shrill cries against white imperialism during the Suez crisis, and was reluctant and perfunctory in the condemnation of Red imperialism during the Hungarian crisis. The attitude of King Agrippa and his wife, Beatrice, seems to be a slight improvement, when Agrippa says to St. Paul, "Almost thou persuadest me to be a Christian." He seemed to be more open-minded. The point is, he was carrying out his secular duties too, and he would have freed St. Paul; but the latter had chosen to appeal to Caesar, and Agrippa could do no more about it. I believe the attitude of King Agrippa is very much a contemporary one, an attitude of tolerant indifference. He was too "busy," and did not pursue the question further.

There is of course the Pharisaical attitude which Jesus repeatedly condemned, an attitude in which religion or Christianity is but a cloak of piety. Kaiser Wilhelm, in his first conversation as the Prince of Prussia with Bismarck, referred to a certain person he disliked as a Pietist. "What is a Pietist?" asked Bismarck. "A person who tries, under the guise of religion, to further his own selfish interests," replied the Prince. Heine, with his peculiar gift for satire, describes the Pietist in a verse:

> Ich kenne die Weise, ich kenne den Text,
> Ich kenne auch die Verfasser.
> Ich weiss, sie tranken heimlich Wein
> Und predigten öffentlich Wasser.

> I know the wise fellows, I know the text,
> I know also its author.
> I know they secretly drank wine
> And publicly preached water.

An extraordinary example of what passes for religion can be seen in George Fox. It is extreme, but I do not think that it is so uncommon among modern Christians. One day George Fox was going to Lichfield, and this is what he wrote in his Journal:

> Then was I commanded by the Lord to pull off my shoes. I stood still, for it was winter, but the word of the Lord was like a fire in me. So I put off my shoes and left them with the shepherds, and the poor shepherds trembled, and were astonished. Then I walked on about a mile, and as soon as I was got within the city, the word of the Lord came to me again, saying: Cry, "Wo to the bloody city of Lichfield!" So I went up and down the streets, crying with a loud voice, Wo to the bloody city of Lichfield! It being market day, I went into the marketplace, and to and fro in the several

parts of it, and made stands, crying as before, Wo to the bloody city of Lichfield! And no one laid hands on me. As I went thus crying through the streets, there seemed to me to be a channel of blood running down the streets, and the marketplace appeared like a pool of blood. When I had declared what was upon me, and felt myself clear, I went out of the town is peace; and returning to the shepherds gave them some money, and took my shoes of them again. But the fire of the Lord was so on my feet, and all over me, that I did not matter to put on my shoes, and was at a stand whether I should or no, till I felt freedom from the Lord so to do: then, after I had washed my feet, I put on my shoes again.

This is most curious indeed. It is true that there are more things which God can do than are dreamed of in man's religion, but it is equally true that much in religion is attributed to God that God never dreamed of doing. I do not mean to disparage the founder of the Society of Friends, for whom I have the greatest respect and admiration. But much religion of this type has brought upon it, and has deserved to bring upon it, the ridicule of the more rational-minded. We need not enumerate all the various experiences that pass for religion, from neurotic behavior, hallucinations, epileptic fits, rolling, and speaking of tongues, to all forms of religious revivalism.

Owing to this confusion of religious beliefs and the discrepancies of the churches, I once fought past the Scylla of damning hell-fire and the Charybdis of Pharisaism and called myself a pagan. I made my stand upon rationalism and humanism. Considering the epithets hurled by the different religions at one another, I believe that the word "pagan" avoids the opprobrium of many believers. For, curiously, the word "pagan" or "heathen" cannot be applied in English usage to the major religions of Christianity, Judaism, and Mohammedanism.

While the word "heathen" is usually a word of contempt, the word "pagan" has a fine ring of classical antiquity about it, for the whole brood of gods on Mount Olympus has at least the affectionate respect of modern Christians. Because of its association with the Renaissance and with eighteenth-century

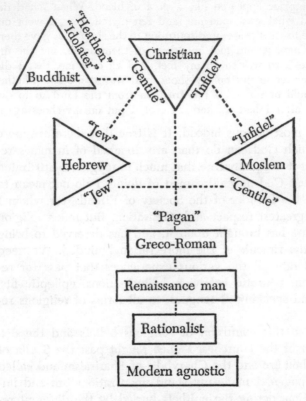

Epithets in quotations denote terms used by people in opposite triangles.

rationalism, as well as with classical antiquity, perhaps the stand I took suggests to many minds that of a rationalist, a stand rather envied by some as signifying the emancipation of the intellect and the coming of age of man's reason. A pagan always believes in God, but is afraid of saying so for fear of

being misunderstood. Indeed, there is much in the current
forms of religion which must forever make a more sober-
minded and educated modern man look askance at religious
exhibitionism, and there is just as much in humanism and
rationalism to command a modern man's respect. Certainly
modern man finds it easy to respect and admire the sober
humanism of Confucius, or the stoic meditations of Marcus
Aurelius, or even the poetic materialism of Lucretius. Certainly modern man finds nothing inherently objectionable in
the following meditation of Marcus Aurelius, even though he
called upon the name of Zeus instead of that of the Christian
God:

> Everything harmonizes with me, which is harmonious to thee,
> O Universe. Nothing for me is too early nor too late, which
> is in due time for thee. Everything is fruit to me which thy
> seasons bring, O Nature: from thee are all things, in thee
> are all things, to thee all things return. The poet says, Dear
> City of Cecrops; and will thou not say, Dear City of Zeus?

The above quotation shows how near to God the so-called
pagan always is, as I have shown with regard to the Chinese
humanists. "The fool has said, 'There is no God,'" says the
Bible. But there have been surprisingly few fools in the history of thought.

And this is what I mean. It is a highly uncomfortable,
and to me even an anomalous, situation, that the modern
educated man in Christendom should find it easier to sympa-
thize with a rationalist or humanist than with a religious follower. On the other hand, a self-declared pagan who publicly
returns to religion may be suspected of backing away from
full belief in the power of reason, and even of a weakening of
the intellect. For years I drifted, believing in God, but finding
it difficult to be attached to any church. I was never quite
satisfied with the situation, but in the confusion of religious
beliefs and creeds and dogmas it was difficult to give expression to one's belief in God.

III. *The Limit of the "Knowable"*

In any sane society, however, the religious man should be held in higher honor than a mere irreligious rationalist, or a man who merely attends to his secular duties and material comforts and is satisfied with them and is devoid of the higher spiritual yearnings, than a materialist who willingly and deliberately limits the field of human awareness and human insight and hugs a cozy chimney corner of human indifference.

We have seen where the confusion in method has led us to. Shall we say that a man who accepts God represents a higher and fuller and more mature intelligence than a mere rationalist? If so, why? Or shall we say that a man who is running toward God is necessarily running away from reason? What does one mean by reason? Is there a necessary antithesis between reason and religious perception? And if not, what is the relation between them? Which is a higher order of human intelligence, a mere rationalist mind or a mind which is capable of higher intuitive religious perceptions? What is reason and what is belief?

I believe that the best picture of man's reason and his ability to grasp the reality of the world around him is still that given by Plato. It is a picture of what the human mind can and cannot do with the world of phenomena. From Buddha and Plato to Berkeley and Kant and to the most modern natural scientists, the picture of human consciousness with regard to its ability to know truth behind the world of phenomena is essentially that of a man sitting with his back toward the entrance of a cave. Plato says in the *Republic:*

> And now, I said, let me show in a figure how far our nature is enlightened or unenlightened:—Behold! human beings living in an underground cave, which has a mouth open toward the light and reaching all along the cave; here they have been from their childhood, and have their legs and necks chained so that they cannot move, and can only see before them,

being prevented by the chains from turning round their heads. Above and behind them a fire is blazing at a distance, and between the fire and the prisoners there is a raised way; and you will see, if you look, a low wall built along the way, like the screen which marionette players have in front of them, over which they show the puppets.

I see.

And do you see, I said, men passing along the wall carrying all sorts of vessels, and statues and figures of animals made of wood and stone and various materials, which appear over the wall? . . .

You have shown me a strange image, and they are strange prisoners.

Like ourselves, I replied; and they see only their own shadows, or the other shadows which the fire throws on the opposite wall of the cave?

True, he said; how could they see anything but the shadows if they were never allowed to move their heads?

And of the objects which are being carried in like manner they would see only the shadows?

Yes, he said. . . .

To them, I said, the truth would be literally nothing but the shadows of the images.

Plato's analogy of the cave is much more appropriate and precise in the light of modern science than we might have supposed. Eddington says, "The frank realization that physical science is concerned with a world of shadows is one of the most significant of recent advances." And Jeans, pursuing the question of the quantum and wave length and ether, says, "The universe begins to look more like a great thought than like a great machine." The quantum became literally the quandary for physics. The quantum is where we first saw matter and energy cross the invisible frontier, to make us realize that the old concept of matter is no longer adequate. And as we pursued matter further, to the subatomic particles charged with a million volts, we simply lost it. That is the objective tendency of opinion today.

A world of shadows is all we can see and know, as Plato said so well. Our sensory perceptions give us a picture of the world of phenomena only: that is all that "reason" can tell us; behind the phenomena are the *noumena*, the *Ding-an-sich*, the thing-in-itself, the absolute truths of which we can never know by the reasoning faculties of our mind. What a pity! This is the sad announcement of the limits of human knowledge: that it is based on sensory perceptions, that *esse* of natural things is *percepi*, that what we regard as being is only perception and perhaps an illusion, and that, constituted as we are, we are doomed to see things, as it were, through a screen, but that we shall never see the face of absolute truth. Do what we will, something always remains behind: the *residue* of the knowable world. This is the insult to man's intelligence, the sad announcement of his mental predicament, against which man feels powerless to rebel. But Buddha preached it, Plato expounded it, and a host of philosophers, all of whom were engaged in a concentrated attack for three centuries on the mechanism and paraphernalia and laws of human knowledge, have sadly acknowledged it, and recent science confirms it. Let us therefore humbly accept it and know where we stand.

We sit, then, with our backs to the entrance of the cave, and all we can see is a procession of shadows, of men and animals and utensils and plants, projected on the screen of the cave wall. We might enlarge upon Plato's picture of slaves chained to sensory impressions, and, besides the light and shadows, add sounds and smells and the feelings of heat and cold. We might learn to associate the sound of braying with passing donkeys, of mooing with cows, and of barking noises with dogs as they run on the raised way; and we might say to ourselves that the animal with long ears makes a braying noise, the horned animal a mooing noise, and the small furry animal a barking noise. In the same way, we may smell a distinct smell when a camel or a horse is passing, and feel heat and cold in correlation to sun and shadow and passing rain. We might from experience learn to associate the images of moving flurries on the screen with snow and interpret broken vertical lines as rainfall. Though we might do all this, our knowledge of the real world outside would still be a world known to us entirely through sensory impressions received by a reasoning mind which makes the connections, the cognition, the knowing.

But over and above the shadows are curious changes of light and color between sunset and sundown, and we can even picture the sounds of holocausts of winds and storms and thunder. Now among the slaves so chained that their heads cannot turn round, there are some active minds more restless than the others, and these will be busily occupied with speculating on what the sounds of winds and snowstorms and the changes of temperature and light and the varying length of days and nights in the successive seasons mean. A mind like Newton's among the slaves so chained, with some knowledge of optics, will perhaps speculate on the existence of a source of light, the sun, and from the diffused light of the night deduce the existence of the moon and the stars. These, it must be noted, will be purely mental operations, apart from direct sensory impressions.

Now, what shall one call these creative guesses at truth? They are not part of our positive knowledge, for remember that in the Platonic analogy of the cave the world outside stands for the real substance, the absolute truths, the *noumena,* while the shadows on the cave wall stand for the world of sense perceptions, the *phenomena.* And these efforts of the more speculative minds to make creative guesses at the truth, these efforts to apprehend the ultimate cause and to comprehend the whole and establish a kind of unity, and not be satisfied with the procession of images—what shall one call these? They are speculative efforts; they are mental visions, not capable of direct proof, but perhaps belonging to a higher order of psychic faculties, a greater power of comprehension than the mere observance of the shadows and the sounds and smells and movements. What shall one call these beliefs? Are they unwarranted flights of the imagination or arrogant assumptions of the intellect, or are they manifestations of man's *higher reason?* Are they not perhaps the *total response of man's whole being* to the universe? Perhaps this situation may be likened to the relation of the human eye and the ultraviolet and infrared rays to which it is blind. Someone may be gifted with an extended vision of infrared and ultraviolet beyond the normal range, as some persons are color blind. Such a person will have psychic powers of vision, and he must seem crazy to us. Such a person must be killed. To Caiaphas, Jesus was clearly mad; He even forgave sins. That is why Jesus was crucified.

IV. *The Residual Area of Knowledge*

This is therefore what I call the *residual area of knowledge.* Something always remains behind and eludes our philosophical analysis. As soon as we enter the realm of ethic, we find that one can go thus far and no further. The realm of knowledge, the realm of moral values, can never be proved. We merely make creative guesses and have intimations. For this whole response of man's moral nature to the universe we have no appropriate intelligible name: some call it intuition, others call it faith.

Now, it is a tragedy that this residual area of knowledge is given the name of "faith" by scholastic minds. It is not amenable to the usual form of reasoning, but the word "faith" has come to have a certain accepted meaning. Because "reason" is Cartesian and mathematical, the residual area, being not amenable to such reasoning, is called faith, which excludes narrow, mathematical reasoning. At once an antithesis of reason and faith is set up. Once this antithesis of faith and reason is established, there is always the temptation to abuse it by mystifying it and putting more and more things difficult to believe in it, as an autonomous region of the unknowable, the wholly mysterious, the sacred and holy. Faith has come to mean almost the surrender of reason, if not contradiction to reason. Faith also means taking things on hearsay, something hardened and encased and inflexible, with the command to believe under the dire threat of eternal perdition. Faith smacks of coercion in belief, and at the time of the Inquisition it did mean coercion. From this rises the bad odor which has been associated with faith, and the Christian faith in particular. One can well understand the angry protest of Voltaire, "By what right could a being created free force another to think like himself?"

This is what sixteen hundred years of theology did to us under the influence of scholastic minds. We need only to remind ourselves of the Thirty Years' War and of the Massacre of St. Bartholomew and of the fact that Spinoza dared not publish his *Ethics* during his lifetime. It is axiomatic that as one becomes more and more theological, one becomes more and more bigoted also, and less and less pious. That is why Jesus said to the scribes and theologians of His day, "The publicans and harlots will enter the Kingdom of Heaven before you." No one can read the Gospels without seeing the violent hatred of Jesus for the priests and the professors of Mosaic law, which was revealed in frequent, periodic explosions.*

However, the secular philosophers did not call it "faith," but "intuition." The remarkable and fortunate fact is that Western man, after three hundred years of quixotic tilting at the windmill of knowledge, did allow some room for common sense in the residual area beyond reason, as soon as he entered the sphere of man's moral life and moral actions. The classical case is Kant's *Critique of Practical Reason,* and his famous "categorical imperative." (Contrary to Kant, I think it would

---

* I use the word "violent" advisedly here, and I believe most students of the Bible will agree. The invective includes not only "Woe unto you," "the blind leading the blind," "washing the outside of the cup," but also "whited sepulchres," "children of Hell," and calling them robbers of widows' fortunes.

be fairer to call these "categorical imperatives" unrelated to known sense perceptions "pure reason," and the operations relating to natural things "practical reason.") The extraordinary thing in Western philosophy is that since Descartes, himself a mathematician, set the fashion for a mechanical dissection of the mechanism of knowledge and an analysis of its contents, and after tomes had been written about the limits of the pure reason and positive knowledge, in which, among some theologians, God constantly threatened to become a mighty geometrician—after all this, the same speculative philosophers cavalierly dropped their analytical tools as soon as they entered the realm of moral knowledge and fell back on words like "intuition" and "categorical imperatives" (such as "do not lie" and "do not steal"), and on our innate intuitive sense, born of common sense, which we feel but cannot explain. Thus the late-comers Locke and Berkeley and Hume, after having followed the analysis of the world of phenomena 2,400 years after Buddha and agreed with him, and after the extreme flights into the rarefied atmosphere of metaphysics, fell to the ground clutching nothing more remarkable than two conclusions: (a) that "rational" beliefs are based on custom, observation, and expectations of experience (Hume—who is really better than Locke or Berkeley), and (b) that there is a "moral sense" or intuition, or unexplained and unexplainable command of conscience.

Nobody ever bothered to dissect this thing called intuition or moral sense. It is God-given; it is unconditioned; it is categorical; it is a command ("imperative"). At once, the speculative philosophers laid down their tools and accepted it as something very real and justifiable and without need and even without necessity of analytical proof. I do not disagree with this. Far from it. But had they been consistent, and accepted the role of common-sense intuition in the area of positive knowledge, such as the question whether you and I exist and eat and breathe together, they would have spared themselves the devastating chase of knowledge called epistemology.

Common sense wins. After all is said and done, Descartes practically said, "I am here and I am thinking, and therefore I know I must be real." And I know that you too are real, according to Berkeley, because you *speak to* me. And I know that God is real because God *speaks to* us through the vast creation. But if sense perceptions are illusions only, how do I really know that you *speak to* me? We do assume certain things, don't we? There is a kind of alternating, ruthless analysis on the one hand, and unwarrantable taking of things for granted on the other.

Chuangtse, the Taoist philosopher, and Hueitse, the sophist, once had an argument. They had strolled onto the bridge over the Hao, when Chuangtse observed, "See how the small fish are darting about! That is the happiness of the fish." "You are not a fish yourself," said Hueitse; "how can you know the happiness of the fish?" "And you not being I," retorted Chuangtse, "how can you know that I do not know?" "If I, not being you, cannot know what you know," urged Hueitse, "it follows that you, not being a fish, cannot know the happiness of the fish." "Let us go back to your original proposition," said Chuangtse. "You asked me how I knew the happiness of the fish. Your very question shows that you knew that I knew." The Western sophists, it seems to me, never took the last step of Hueitse. The dilemma was broken by Chuangtse falling back on actual experience.

I am glad, however, that the Western sophists, unlike the theologians, call this total response of man's moral being "intuition" and not "faith." Convenient, isn't it? More familiarly, we may simply call it conscience, the distinction between right and wrong. Schopenhauer's love of all men, compassion, is based on "intuition," an intuitive sense of the identity of all beings. Again, Kant calls it "intuition" and the "small voice of the heart within" and "categorical imperative," that is, a direct, unreasoned, and disinterested command. (In Kant's case, all forms of reason and of intuition are a priori.) Hume called it the "moral sense." Hume tried at first to show that this distinction of good and evil was an interested preference for what is good for ourselves, but gave up before the stupendous fact that man, that lowly speck of dust in the universe, does have a *disinterested* preference for what is morally good, without selfish interests and without expectation of gain. We are confronted here with a strange fact of the universe, the pure, blessed desire to do good, to love and to help others as a final fact without explanation. This is the wonder of the universe, that man strives toward the good, and feels compelled inwardly to perfect himself, almost as the salmon instinctively goes upstream to spawn. Can it also be that the will to believe, like Schopenhauer's will to live and will to reproduce, is one of the primordial urges of the race?

This is the stupendous fact about man and his spiritual development and his striving after God. It is not faith; it is not a contradiction of reason; it is merely a healthy instinct. It is the God-given moral sense. It is man's total response to the universe through his moral nature. It is not the antithesis of reason; it is the higher reason. It is *samadhi* of the Zen Buddhists, the flash of insight into the real thing-in-itself. And this residual area of knowledge happens to be the most significant area of human knowledge and of moral consciousness, in which God, the soul, and immortality and man's whole moral being are all involved.

CHAPTER 7

The Challenge of Materialism

IT WOULD BE beautiful to say, Render unto spirit the things that belong to the spirit, and render unto matter the things that belong to matter. Unfortunately, we cannot quite say that. When Jesus said, "Render unto Caesar the things that are Caesar's," implying a kingdom of Caesar and a kingdom of God, it was only to answer a question posed with malice. Jesus did not mean that the kingdom of Caesar and the kingdom of God were coextensive or even separate, or that they did not overlap. He meant that, as a Jew under a foreign conqueror, one should have a practical line of action. The problem of the Jewish fighters for independence lay in a separate political field which was far from Jesus' immediate concern with the kingdom of God.

I suspect that the general conflict of modern thought with religion stems from a materialistic interpretation of the universe, an interpretation that the entire universe can be explained mechanically by physico-chemical laws, without residue. That does not directly take God out of the universe, but it indirectly leads to such thinking.

The posing of the question is therefore all-important.

Whether we are for matter or for spirit, the dichotomy of
spirit and matter is wholly unsound. Defenders of the faith,
spiritual faith, are treading on unsafe ground when they build
their spiritual structure apart from matter. They are building
a house upon sand, and sooner or later, the tide of scientific
facts will wash it away. Human life and human consciousness
are a helter-skelter of material and spiritual facts, of biological
and psychological facts, mixed in an extremely curious and
extraordinarily complicated fashion—how extraordinary and
how complicated the biologists can best tell you. One day a
person may talk like a Brahmin with utter contempt for dress
and food and all things that belong to matter. The next day
he may read about tranquilizers or about insulin shock for
treatment of schizophrenia, proving that madness is chemical,
and the Brahmin will have nowhere to hide.

I think that all interpretations of the universe, with the
exception of the truly religious interpretation, can be classified
as follows:

1. Idolatry—too much God.
2. Humanism—a medium position.
3. Materialism—not enough God.

To the first class belongs animism. In the second, some room
is always provided for God in the universe and in human life;
a completely godless humanism is rare. The third category,
materialism, is either skeptical of God's existence (agnosti-
cism) or asserts outright that there is no God (atheism), which
is also comparatively rare in the history of thought. Confucius,
Socrates, and Voltaire all stood somewhat in the middle, dis-
believing in idols or popular gods, without denying God in a
higher conception, and quite willing sometimes to take part
in certain religious functions. Pure atheism, on the other hand,
is purely a synthetic product of a limited age, confined to a
limited fashion of thought. Contrary to common belief, materialism is seldom the standpoint of a thinker who pushes the
question of the universe to its logical conclusion, but rather

of one who stops near the borderline when things begin to appear strange and unfamiliar and confusing. For a hundred materialists who say, "I cannot know God," there is probably only one who says categorically, "There is no God," and he is a brave one.

Now, actually between the first and the third category, the idolater is, on the whole, nearer the truth than the materialist. The savage animist who believes that every tree is a spirit (that is, alive with feeling and power of its own) is closer to reality than the materialist who is concerned only with the accurate tabulating of the facts of observation and who does not ask for a final cause motivating the tree. For a crass materialist, the tree is merely a brown trunk with a thick bark, sending out its roots to the soil for food below and its branches to the sky for air. He makes himself into a clerk and a bookkeeper of the facts of the tree's growth, and tries to understand the physico-chemical processes involved in the growth and reproduction of trees in the flower-seed-tree cycle, or in the spring-summer-autumn-winter cycle. Now, a botanist who knows all the facts so far discovered and known about the tree is a good botanist; but if he is *satisfied* that he really knows the reason behind all these phenomena, he must be a shallow scientific clerk and bookkeeper, and not much good for anything else. You cannot help thinking that such a man is devoid of intellect. The majority of such botanists are of course not devoid of intellect; they have their private view of the First Cause, and many believe in God. When an international convention of botanists meets, its members meet only apparently as a great assembly of scientific clerks and bookkeepers, at home with many accurate data, and keeping strictly to the field of their competence. There is no special point or reason to advertising their ignorance of God, or their despair in trying to find out the *reason* for things.

When the intellectual disease of Europe began with Descartes' cutting up of the universe into two convenient separate compartments, mind and matter, it was not explicitly said that the deductive method was also to apply to the area of human life and human consciousness, as well as to the examination of the natural world. But the tendency was to do so. Insofar as the "spirit" of God or of man was amenable to this Cartesian method, it was a part of knowledge, and in the contrary case it was not. Inevitably, the material displaced the spiritual in man's attention; and the spiritual was increasingly associated with the supernatural and damned. This tendency then grew into nineteenth-century materialism as we know it. God and moral values steadily lost ground in that century. The full consequences were not yet apparent, for Victorian morality was still intact. Girls' names were still Faith and Patience. Lord Tennyson was still singing. The sweetness of the Blue Boy was not sneered at by artists. The pre-Raphaelites were "spiritual" in their outlook, and Ruskin was actually "preaching" goodness and truth and beauty. Carlyle was still thundering about the greatness of the human spirit. The House of Queen Victoria had not yet disintegrated, and man had not yet been left to choke on the bone of despair. It was Max Nordau who finally wrote a book about the coming despair and cynicism of the *fin de siècle*, around 1900.

With the advent of the twentieth century, the trend increasingly became one of moral cynicism. The sweetness and light of the human spirit were gone. Anyone who talks of sweetness and light now sounds woefully old-fashioned. Anybody can see the beauty of a woman's leg except an artist; anyone who does not admire the pregnant woman of Picasso with her big stomach and hulking legs is a hopeless anti-intellectual ignoramus. Then came the age of destruction. Picasso dissected the material world with as much pleasure as a naughty boy who takes a watch apart and spreads the wheels, pinions, coils, and springs before him, and calls it "inner vision." Stravinsky laughed at harmony, Gertrude Stein destroyed grammar, E. E. Cummings destroyed punctuation, Lenin destroyed democracy, Joyce destroyed idiom, and Dali destroyed sanity. Everyone was tearing up something, and by doing so received popular acclaim. It was the Brave New World with the emphasis on the word "brave." What was destroyed was unimportant; the important thing was the tearing up, for only by tearing up can mankind show "progress." These are our leaders, our intellectual elite, our *avant-garde* of the spirit. Artists and writers who mean to be progressive should think hard to see what next they can lay their hands on to destroy which somebody else has not already destroyed. I thought of inventing a new school of art by covering the canvas with amoeba-like splotches, but an American has already stolen the show, and made a great noise in Paris recently with a similar type of painting suggesting a world of molecules. Someday some poet will invent verse in which letters of the alphabet appear upside down, a form which Cummings has not, fortunately, yet thought of. And the camp followers will of course find no lack of words or formulas to suggest the spiritual meaning of the inverted alphabets. I can think of a name for this school—supersemanticism, meaning that the function of a word should be, not to convey sense, but supersense.

Freud played a curious role in the general destruction. He established his laboratory in the toilet and was able to analyze a number of things about man. Now any man who did so was bound to get very close to certain biological facts about man. Freud had something to say, and yet he had to create his own language. He found the word "soul" overused, and was extremely wise to use the word "psyche" instead. And then he went on to speak of the libido, the id, the ego, and the super-ego. The great word was of course the "unconscious." He opened up a new frontier of human knowledge. On the whole, the world of the unconscious was essentially the world of the primeval "instincts"; but by placing it against the conscious world and against the operation of conscious reason, he revealed new vistas which covered rationalization, defense mechanism, wish-fulfillment, inferiority complexes, and so on. Thus our knowledge of the mental processes, conscious and unconscious, was sharpened. Now, when a man discovers an entirely new world, the results are not simple. They cannot be. The immediate results are not pretty—any more than an anatomical operation is pretty. It stinks, and yet it fascinates. It is like assisting at a surgical operation and observing the bloody innards of man. It reveals man in the power of his instincts, lays open his self-deceptions, and shows him as a savage with a very imperfect mind. Man's behavior is anything but rational. If man is a thinking animal, his thinking is of a very low order. The report of the human soul by the Freudians, in fact, is just about on a par with a scullery maid's report of a duke's castle. I have written elsewhere:

No more privacy
Of mind and body; the students of mental history
Have stripped the fig leaves, dispelled all mystery,
Have sent the naked, shivering soul to the scullery,
And turned the toilet into a public gallery;
They've dulled the glamor of love, soured the wine of romance,
Plucked the feathers of pride, exposed to naked glance
The Inner Sanctum of sovereign mind, dethroned from its dais,
And crowned the rank-smelling Libido in its place.*

Yet, in the long run, the whole trend set by Freud's discoveries leads to a better and deeper understanding of man's "soul" (psyche), to a fuller understanding of sin, of the inner self and the office of the moral censor, and, through Jung, to a more "mystic" and less materialistic view of life, to a greater appreciation of the role of intuition and the collective unconscious—the racial desires and yearnings of man. In other words, any deepened understanding of the psychology of the individual is bound to apply to man's relations to his fellow men, and to lead to the deeper forces governing man's mind. The elevating of the importance of the unconscious automatically lessens the importance of reason in man's total response to the universe. It leads away from a materialistic, and, especially through Jung, toward a more spiritual and mystical view of life.

* *The Wisdom of India and China,* p. 575.

And the same development is true of the advance of physics, astronomy, biology, and chemistry. Materialism never dares go the whole way to pursue the subject to its "logical conclusion" for fear that matter might be spirited away. Now, as far as science is concerned, this attitude is correct and even admirable, that is, the attitude of not touching ground which one has no physical tools for knowing. The natural scientist is like an honest guide; he takes you to the frontier of the "knowable" right up to a closed door, and tells you frankly, "Beyond that door I do not know and cannot tell you."

If I were God (and therefore a master physicist and master chemist), I would be extremely interested in seeing how the chemists and physicists and astronomers and biologists on earth proceeded to unlock my secrets. I would of course remain silent and give no help, but I would be very interested in watching their scientific discoveries, giving them perhaps a century or two to pry open my secrets and think them over. Anything would do—an ant, a cricket, a spider, an eel, or a simple blade of grass. Take a spider, for instance. The problem of the Man-Scientist would be to exhaust the secrets of the spider by a physico-chemical explanation on a purely mechanical basis. I would tell Man that the spider is plainly mechanical, that is, that the spider is actuated by a physicochemical mechanism. Of course it is. First he would unravel the mechanisms of the mandibles, the digestive system, the defense system, and so on, which are comparatively simple, except for the venom of the black widow. How the black widow hits upon the chemical formula for its venom and produces it with such deadly simplicity may puzzle him; but I suppose he would not stop to think about it, so long as he was satisfied that he had got the chemical formula of the poison. Then there would be the problem of the viscous silk which does not dry up, for if it dried completely on exposure to air, it would not be of much good to the spider. A generation would pass, and Du Pont and Company would come up with an answer. Then there would be the problem of the anti-glue without which the spider's feet would be immobilized and the spider would not be able to move on its web. The problem is not new: the hydrochloric acid of the stomach digests meat but does not digest the wall of the stomach itself because the stomach provides its own antidote against the acid. Another generation would pass and the Sloan-Kettering Foundation in its research on cancer would accidentally discover the chemical formula for the anti-glue and would be able to make it synthetically. The professor of the Sloan Institute might even ask for permission to have an interview with God on the merit of this discovery, but he would perhaps be refused admittance.

I can picture what happened between God and the scientist. The scientist, still pursuing the mystery of the spider, would now face the really difficult problem. At this point the conversation between God and the scientist, if he were admitted, would be occupied with the problems of how the baby spider learns to make the web without the mother's instruction. The baby spider has to know, whether its mother stands by or not. They would then be lost in a discussion of instincts and genes and heredity, and the transmission or nontransmission of acquired characteristics. They would be lost in profound principles of biogenetics and biochemistry, and would be dealing with strictly chemical formulas. If acquired characteristics for adaptation to life were not transmitted, they would be of no use to the race of spiders; if they were transmitted, then there would have to be a "storage" of memory somewhere, to feed the information to the baby spider, telling him exactly what to do and when. Some scientist in Oslo or Berlin, say, seventy years later, would then unravel the chemical formula for this storage of racial memory, in the form of "tape information" concealed in the genes which contained code signals probably one-billionth of an inch in size that sent out instructions for certain enzymes to be formed to make possible certain chemical reactions, which will then withdraw and retire from the scene. On the basis of this discovery, the professor of Oslo or Berlin who had won the Nobel Prize in chemistry would be admitted to God's presence and would be given many compliments and encouraging words. The professor would come away from the conversation with God greatly impressed, having learned a few more complicated chemical equations which had only then been revealed to him —in any case much more complicated than the Ten Commandments which Jehovah had revealed to Moses. Just at parting, God might say to the professor:

"I have shown you the chemical formulas hidden in the genes."

"You have, God Almighty."

"And I have helped you to get a complete mechanical explanation of the spider's instincts and instinctive behavior."

"You have, Lord God, indeed."

"And you are satisfied?"

"I am. Don't You think I should be?"

"So you think you know now."

"I think I know. I always thought that if I could get hold of the chemical formulas for things, we human beings would be able to explain everything."

"Do you ever wonder?" asks God.

"Certainly I am impressed."

"That is not what I mean," says God. "I have given you these chemical formulas which show you merely *how* these things happen, but not *why* they happen. For the two questions *how* and *why* are different. I have let you know the *how*, but you still have not found out the *why*."

Tears fill the professor's eyes and he asks, "Oh, God, why? why? why?"

"That you will never find out by chemical formulas," says God. "But if you cannot find out the *why*, you still don't know the secrets of the spider."

"No, I don't."

I am not Chuangtse. But this is what Chuangtse might write in conclusion. "The professor woke up from his sleep with perspiration all over his body. His wife found him silent for seven days. On the seventh day, he began to eat, but never dared to go out into the garden again all his life. He had developed a spider phobia which the doctors pronounced incurable."

*

Especially in the last few decades, spirit and matter have moved closer, largely through the new vistas opened up by science. And, strangely enough, the rapprochement is due to matter yielding ground to spirit rather than spirit yielding ground to matter. Matter constantly threatens to evaporate; the old notions of ether and substance are no longer adequate. The stark, crude materialism of solid matter no longer seems tenable. And this time the spirit is no longer the "supernatural." The spirit has not become clearer, but matter has become perhaps more translucent. The trend of the last four or five centuries of thought seems to be in general as follows:

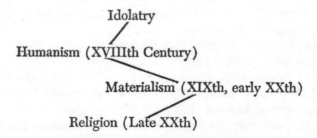

Idolatry

Humanism (XVIIIth Century)

Materialism (XIXth, early XXth)

Religion (Late XXth)

In support of the above diagram, I need quote only J. S. Haldane, the great British biologist. Writing in 1932 in his preface to *Materialism,* he says, concerning the argument of his book:

Although antiquated as a philosophical system, Materialism is still very much alive on the scientific and practical sides, and it is from these sides that I have approached the subject. Several well-known recent books have been concerned with the ultimate breakdown of traditional physical conceptions in connection with what we distinguish, however artificially, as the inorganic world. With this particular aspect of the breakdown the present book does not deal directly. What is dealt with is the impossibility of interpreting the phenomena of life and of conscious behavior in terms of physical conceptions, and the final necessity of a spiritual interpretation of our universe.

What a curious route to travel by way of materialism to God or to a spiritual interpretation of the universe! Such, nevertheless, seems to be the case. Of course, this is a simplified picture. A number of things happened between the Age of Enlightenment and the Age of Despair today.

Now when Voltaire, Diderot, and D'Alembert began the *Encyclopédie,* man's hopes were high. He was done with antiquated "supernatural" religion. He relied upon man's liberated reason. Man was looking toward a new era of reason, of rationalism and sanity, of true enlightenment—an era that would leave the Dark Ages behind.

And why not? Chinese humanism had continued for about two thousand years without anyone giving in to a materialist philosophy. There was only one Chinese atheist, Fan Shen, around A.D. 500. The Chinese remained philosophical idealists throughout, placing greater value on "virtue" than on material goods—at least in theory among the scholars—while the populace preferred idolatry and animism to a stark, godless materialism. This was principally because such atheism made less sense than a good healthy, luxuriant heathen animism. What changed the course of history of man's spirit in Europe was the materialistic outlook provided by the natural sciences, which because of their steady and glorious advance gradually invaded the humanistic sciences and the view of human life in general. As a consequence, the proper development of humanism was truncated by the advance of materialism in the following century, the nineteenth.

One of the strangest flowers of the invading materialism

was of course Karl Marx. But one should not forget Karl Marx's and Friedrich Engels' intellectual backgrounds in the middle of the nineteenth century. Everybody was still hopeful. The materialistic and naturalistic viewpoint was steadily gaining ground. Aping the natural scientists, the humanistic students also tried to introduce the naturalistic and materialistic outlook into the humanities, such as the economic interpretation of history as a consequence of a biped moving inevitably in the direction of potato supplies; or that the Roman Empire fell not because of decay of the moral fiber of man, but because of mice; Napoleon was not defeated by the courage and strategy of Wellington at Waterloo, but by the lack of sugarbeet supply in France, and so on. It came down straight to Parrington, who, however, had the virtue of writing well.

Let us remember that, toward 1850, the prestige of the materialistic method was mounting every day as an academic fashion, and invading the moral sciences and the humanistic studies. The scholars all wanted to find the "fundamental laws" of the "growth" of "organisms" in man's affairs. Auguste Comte, the positivist, intended to build humanism into a religion of humanity by repudiating metaphysics and revealed religion. Comte spoke of society as an "organism." Mommsen was writing his *History of Rome* in the 1850's. Taine wrote in 1856 in his preface to the *History of English Literature* that "vice and virtue are products just as vitriol and sugar are." How charming! So morals becomes physics, and human society or the soul of human individuals grows, gets sick, and decays exactly like a plant. Taine not only had a literary gift; he had the generous vision of building an intellectual structure of *race, milieu, moment,* and *faculté maîtresse.* Every literary personality could be explained by this material formula of race, environment, moment, and individual talent. Taine gives the clearest expression of the open desire to copy the method of the natural scientists. Taine says: "The natural scientists have observed that . . . In the same way, the his-

torians can establish . . . The natural sicentists show that
. . . By a like method, historians can show that . . ."

The year 1859, when Darwin's *On the Origin of Species*
appeared, is of crucial importance. When Karl Marx wrote
Das Kapital, the first volume of which was published in 1867,
the materialistic trend of thinking, of explaining everything
by mechanical scientific laws, was at its zenith. Both Taine
and Renan, gifted artists of letters, conceived of themselves as
scientists; as Darwin wrote the *Origin of Species* and as
Taine wrote the *Origines* of contemporary France, dissecting
it "like a doctor," so Renan wrote the *Histoire des Origines du
Christianisme*, beginning with *The Life of Jesus* in 1863.
Renan was not a theologian, a spinner of theological cobwebs;
he was an Orientalist and archaeologist, and his life of Jesus
embodied research carried out in Phoenicia and Jerusalem on
the spot. Epoch-making discoveries were being made in the
1860's. Pasteur, Virchow, and Bunsen were opening new frontiers in light spectrums and the world of bacteria. The year
in which Marx published his first volume of *Das Kapital*, 1867,
was also the year in which Zola inaugurated the autopsy
school of naturalistic fiction. Marx wrote as the natural child
of the bitch-goddess of his age. That was why he claimed to
have found for the first time a "scientific Utopia" in which
Cartesian-Hegelian logic combined with a naturalistic façade
of science to produce "inevitable" materialistic laws of human
development. The phrase "materialistic dialectic" was a large
mouthful. But Marx intended it to be a large mouthful of
quasi-scientific social science. Thus arose the "infallibility" of
this child of a narrow sectarian school, without the humility
and caution of Darwin or the artistic gift and comprehension
of Taine or Renan. Marxist materialism was as infallible as the
fashions of Empress Eugénie at the time. It would have been
of course impossible to suggest that Empress Eugénie's high
waistline was not the eternal and infallible guide to feminine
beauty. In the same way, Marx became "infallible." Whereas

Darwin's caution has saved him from many contradictions of fact, Marx's lack of caution (that is, his pseudoscientific pose) has left him open to contradiction by a thousand facts on every one of his tenets. The reason is that Charles Darwin stayed strictly in his field of natural science, but Marx claimed that the rigorous economic laws of development possessed the "inevitability" and "objectivity" of natural science while dealing in the area of human activities and "social science." Stalin himself is probably the best rebuke to Marx for his assertion that in history environment is everything and man, nothing. At least, Taine had the large perspicacity of the French spirit, and allowed room for the individual, as well as for the *milieu*. The fanatic theoretician of Cologne did not. He was led to this pretense by the fashion of the age. Class war had to be inevitable, or it would have lost its scientific, that is, mechanistic, character.

I. *The Impasse*

Modern discoveries about the atom and subatomic particles cannot but change a man's religion or view of life, whatever it may be. It is altogether too upsetting. When I say, as I have said above, that spirit and matter are moving closer together as a result of recent discoveries, and that this moving closer together is being done by "matter yielding ground to spirit, and not spirit yielding ground to matter," this seems to be a case for religion. Yet it is not altogether that. We have unconsciously equated spirit with energy; when we see matter disappearing into energy, superficially we think it is a case for the spirit. Yet really we have only changed our conception of matter; the inexplicable force of millions of volts of energy driving some infinitesimal subatomic particles, appearing and disappearing as "matter," changes our idea of matter, but a universe consisting entirely of energy would still be strictly a mechanical, that is, material universe. Therefore I say that spirit has not become clearer; matter has merely become less opaque, that is, less solid. Such a revelation of matter does not necessarily destroy "materialism."

Yet in a larger sense, matter and spirit have moved closer together. We have found nothing new about spirit, but the conventional view of matter is no longer tenable. It is not solid; it is in fact empty, and is not always visible. Matter has changed its hue and complexion. And what happens to spirit? Spirit has become less "supernatural," but enters into the fabric of matter itself; or at least we can say the seen and the unseen threaten to merge into one. In this sense, at least, it is now easier to have a more educated view of the world and human life and what it is all about. What has become "supernatural" is not spirit, but rather matter itself. If a glass of water contains enough nuclear energy to run a train from New York to Washington, then the natural becomes the miraculous, and the miraculous, the natural. We are prepared for anything now. There is a new sense of wonderment. I tried to express this thought in the following verse, on reading an article by Stephen Leacock in the *Atlantic Monthly* about the atom, a few years before Hiroshima:

> The fairy tales of science can now be told,
> Surpassing the brave dreams of manhood's youth,
> When faith was a creative guess at truth,
> Investing Nature with elves and sprites of old;
> Or our own childhood fancies, free and bold,
> When kinship love made all the universe move,
> When twinkling starlets whispered from above,
> And the beetle's back was prettier than gold;
> Till adolescence shed a cold, gray tinge,
> And bat-eyed reason paled the magic lure,
> And all is matter dead, exact and sure,
> All mysteries gone, and nothing wondrous strange.
> But the earth is alive! Once more we can
> Recapture the joy and wonder of ancient man.
>
> Ah, eerie is Nature, magic in the flesh!

The atom is a prison of fairy ions—
The insubstantial fabric which our science
Is weaving into a cosmic, ethereal mesh;
While she forges the cipher key to crash
The phantom fortress by a million volts
And pry loose the infinitesimal bolts,
So freeing ions to serve mankind afresh.
This was the vision which the sages saw
That matter wore a spiritual hue.
And somewhat chastened now, we stand anew
Before a speck of dust, staggered with awe.
Such the new faith: the stars of heaven pour
A golden liquid same as a blade of straw.

I like it; I am all for an improved, better, clearer, sharper, perhaps more real view of the universe. I will not deny matter, and if matter becomes force or energy, I am going to like force and energy, too. In short, I like to comprehend the universe we are living in. I like even an adequate mechanical explanation of the universe, if such is possible. The expanded view of the universe deepens the mystery. Darwinism only deepens the mystery of creation. A mechanical explanation of the universe, starting with cosmic rays shooting off in all directions and developing finally into human consciousness, also deepens the mystery.

There is, however, a dilemma for "materialism" which is very stubborn and which threatens to remain. If any scientist can help to solve this dilemma in my lifetime, I shall be very grateful. I like something which makes sense. I am not a scientist, but, like any educated modern man, I am anxious to know, to find something satisfactory, and not be led up to a "closed door." I want to understand the universe, and how it operates, and how life comes into being.

I suspect that the "materialist's" dilemma is of the obdurate, insoluble kind. In the conversation with God pictured above, I pointed out that all physico-chemical explanations show only the *how*, but not the *why*. All science will show the *how*, but not the *why*. For instance, we already know, concerning the mystery of a blade of grass, that it has the chemical property of utilizing sunlight to synthesize food by means of chlorophyll. Perhaps we do not know yet the chemical reaction in precise detail, but we know that it happens. It helps our knowledge of the life of plants. As to *why* the blade of grass should have that "supernatural" power to perform that chemical reaction, we know nothing, and shall never be able to find out. In effect, then, we have discovered the chlorophyll, but we know no more than the African savage who already knows that a plant needs sunlight for growth. And that dilemma will always continue to bother us.

Darwinism throws this dilemma into a clear light. I am all for Darwin and Darwinism, as any average modern man is. The Pope, I think, believes in evolution too. The process of continuous creation is more inspiring than the creation of the world, figuratively speaking, of course, in seven days. On the whole, the concept of survival of the fittest cannot be denied, but the origin of "species" (constant forms) is rather a matter of faith, an intuitive guess, open to question, and may or may not be right. I do not know. No scientist knows for certain. There are quite a few conceptual difficulties in such "faith." No doubt, in the hands of Haeckel, the faith became a beautiful, almost poetic structure—the *Lebenswunder*. Still, as a theory, evolution, as the mere work of blind chance given limitless time for the wheel of fortune to hit the right number, is simply full of holes. I like to see a theory make sense. I have been informed by one qualified person, no less than someone long connected with the Sporting Club of Monte Carlo, that in his lifetime the number zero once came out five times in succession. I have seen zero come out in succession three times myself. In roulette no one has yet seen an unbroken series of 1, 2, 3, 4, 5, 6, 7, 8, 9 appearing in orderly succession. Conceivably, in a million years that too will happen. To build a scientific theory of life based on such blind chance, however, sounds shaky to me. Blind chance means "luck," and a universe of a myriad forms built by luck sounds more like credulity than like objective science. If the numbers 1, 2, 3, 4, 5, 6, 7, 8, 9 do appear in that order, the layman's healthy reaction is to suspect a croupier, that is, a conscious design.

The basic conception of evolution holds, but the explanation of the processes and how they happened seems very faulty. It supposes and presupposes too many things. The succession of 1 to 9 is fairly simple; it *can* happen by chance. The evolution of the giraffe's neck involves processes far more complex. What happens is that every attempt to explain Nature's transformations involves metaphysics, that is to say, short of blind chance, as soon as we ask the question *why* evolution took place, it transcends the sphere of strict "physics." The moment we ask why, we are forced to assume many things. There are indeed many contradictions in the theory of "blind chance." First, it supposes that an organism survives when it is "fittest" for a certain purpose and that it came to be fit for that purpose but without purpose. The existence or nonexistence of purpose is pure metaphysics. And evolution, so stated, becomes a purposeless change for a purpose, which makes even less sense. Second, the origin of constant forms ("species") has not been supported by connecting forms in between, not even in fossils covering millions of years; in theory I like the daring supposition that they have so evolved; only, the proof is wanting. One is forced to talk of a "descent" on a staircase without rungs, or rather a staircase of rungs without the connecting support. Third, Schopenhauer supposes in *The Will in Nature* that the evolution of forms useful for survival and adapted to conditions of living presupposes the *will to adapt.* I agree with this. In other words (and this too is metaphysical), adaptability presupposes the will to adapt; otherwise, adaptability would be merely the act of shuffling a tray of five hundred pieces of a jigsaw puzzle an infinite number of times, say ten thousand times, in the hope that the pieces will finally fall into place. Now that would be a miracle, and science does not like miracles. I can well believe, in theory, two pieces which fit in first would show "adaptability"; on the supposition that two such pieces are firmly held together, it is possible to believe that, like Karl Marx's theory of disappearing capitalists, the small pieces would become fewer but bigger pieces, and eventually the few big pieces too would "adapt" themselves. A beautiful theory that may convince myself, but not others. Fourth, the infinite variations are damnably teleological. Voltaire spoofed "teleology" by saying that the nose is made by God for wearing spectacles and the legs for wearing stockings, seeing how perfectly fitted they are for each other. But one cannot deny after all a certain convenience, if not exactly "survival" value, in the fact that the human nose points downward. The orthodox view would be that infinite chances caused noses to be born in all directions, turning upward, to the right and to the left as well as to the ground, and that the last one finally "survived" because it was more "adapted" to conditions of living. Clearly, an upward-turning nose would be highly inconvenient during a rainfall. Variations seem, as I say, cursedly teleological. And such an adaptation as a downward-pointing nose is only a minor fact among ten thousand other physicochemical facts happening inside a human body, even before the body can function properly.

Perhaps I can sum it up by stating the enormous difficulties of the *arrival of the fittest,* and the enormous difficulties of inheritance of a characteristic of the fittest after it survives. I do not know the chemical composition of the venom of the rattlesnake. I take a chance by saying that a chemist would call the synthetic reproduction of that venom a highly complicated process. It is the venom which helps the snake to survive, although I wish he didn't have to be that nasty. On the theory of blind-chance variations, that venom could be formed by the snake without thought and by blind chance one in 10,000,000 chances. The purely fortuitous *arrival* of the darting tongue and the poison sac for the necessary and effective injection of that poison would be again one chance in

10,000,000. But the inheritance of that capacity to form exactly that chemical compound in the second generation by a
sheer fluke of accident would be perhaps one chance in
1,000,000,000. Such a simple thing, with all the saints and
angels in heaven helping, would stand the chance of happening in one chance to one followed by 23 zeros, or:
$$\frac{1}{100,000,000,000,000,000,000,000}.$$ The mathematical odds are
rather steep. And yet that chance had to happen before we
could have a poisonous rattlesnake. The survival is easy, the
arrival enormously difficult. And this is true of any vital natural characteristic, such as the skunk's emission or the cuttle-
fish's black ink. Therefore Schopenhauer must be right: "The
bull does not gore because he has horns, but has horns because he means to gore." Science indeed! It is all metaphysics. Evolution is good sense, and it may even be obvious,
but it is not as simple as one supposes. Many have been forced
to postulate some form of "vitalism" to account for the arrival
of the fittest, like the *"force supermécanique"* of the chemist
Dumas (teacher of Pasteur, who said to the latter when he
wanted to find out about the origin of life, "I would not advise
anyone to spend too much time on that subject"), the "life-
force" of many (Bernard Shaw included), the "soul" in Haeckel's crystals, and so on.

"Vitalism" does not answer my question. We oversimplify
things, invent a word for an answer, but do not test it on every
occasion to make sure that it proves satisfactory. There is a
bird, the warbler, which is called in Chinese "painted eyebrow." This bird, as in the North American variety of black-
and-white creeper, has a white streak above its eyes, from
which it derives its Chinese name. That painted eyebrow
should make any philosopher stop to think. For what is involved in the evolving of this eyebrow is something *extremely
difficult to explain mechanically as well as chemically.* The
beauty of flowers can be explained by symmetry, but not this.
The white streak seems like a painted line, but is actually

formed by a number of separate feathers individually colored at a certain point for a certain length, so that when they come together they form a straight white line. Any of the separate feathers or down, taken apart, would show a black line, interrupted by a section of white of a given length, situated at a different point so that as the bird's feather grows, it is black, then turns white in the middle, and turns black again after crossing that imaginary frontier, including all the barbs and barbules in its path. A number of such feathers would be seen as in the following schematic diagram:

It is not a chemical problem; it is a matter of turning black and white and black again while the feather is nourished by the same element. The determination of the exact point for turning white in any single feather is very difficult to explain by mechanical or any other means. The presence of enzymes, even if they exist, only begs the question. And this is a fairly common phenomenon in all birds and fish and animals that have streaks or circles or graphic designs (such as the striped bass, the peacock's golden rings, and so on).

This is my impasse. I do not know the answer. I merely point out the dilemma. I stop thinking. I am not prepared to go into a fit of mysticism over it. I simply say that the processes involved in the law of evolution, observed by a serious student and not superficially accepted, lead to and always end in metaphysics, that is, in assumptions beyond the law of physics.

II. *The Void*

It were well to let humanism develop without the specter
of materialistic philosophy following in its wake. It were also
well, on the contrary, that we had been able to arrive immediately at an adequate mechanical explanation of all nature's
phenomena without residue and that we knew where we
stood. But we are held in suspense and in ignorance. The
common man's view is that we know much about the physical
universe; the scientist's opinion is that we know less than one-
tenth of what we ought to know and one-hundredth of what
remains to be known.

I do not think that the disappearance of moral convictions
today is due to the progress of natural science, but rather to
the tendency of the social sciences to ape the natural sciences
in their methods, and above all in their outlook. Any scientist
can tell you that science is concerned with true and false, not
with good or bad, or right or wrong. The scientific method
must be an *amoral* method, rising above good and evil, and
concerned only with facts and not with values, commercial or
moral. A scientist is not concerned with a diamond's commercial value, but only with its weight, its degree of hardness,
and its absorption or deflection of light. Now when Comte
announced that he was going to found sociological ethics, he
did not mean to start the fashion for destroying values—rather,
the opposite was the case. But he already talked of society as
an "organism," presumably like a plant or animal. Once that
stand was taken, the tendency of the humanistic studies—history, sociology, psychology, and so forth—to become "objective" and "amoral" was inevitable. In the long run, such a
tendency must end in the disappearance of convictions, moral
or religious. There is no morality in the study of rocks, but
there is, and should be, morality in the study of man. A scientist can hide behind his fortress of objectivity and do the
world no harm while he is studying rocks. But when a student

of human society and human psychology hides behind such a fortress of objectivity, regarding praise or condemnation as being of no concern of his, he inevitably leads the way to a void of values, whether he wants to or not. And when such a mode of thinking becomes general or even fashionable, society must increasingly tend to lose all convictions.

Now all the academic jargon of the psychologists and sociologists reveals a desire to appear scientific, and a desire to understand, but not to evaluate moral significances. I may be old-fashioned, but I think it will be a long time before you will hear an educational psychologist dare to say that a child's behavior is "right" or "wrong," "selfish" or "unselfish." To say that a certain type of behavior is right or wrong would be to imply lack of objectivity, a tendency to condemn or praise, which is none of science's business. The phrase "a selfish person" implies condemnation, but the phrase "a maladjusted individual" does not. Therefore when a person is selfish, he is merely maladjusted. And so we go on to "patterns of behavior," "Oedipus complex," "emotional instability," "childhood inhibitions," "atavism," straight down to "amnesia," "split personality," and "temporary insanity," the last of which can and does excuse murder. The emphasis is always toward placing the blame either on heredity or on environment, never on the will and the responsibility of the individual. If the newspapers would agree to stop using the phrase "juvenile delinquency" and start using "young lawbreaker" or "young criminal" instead, we could probably cut youthful crime by 50 per cent. Obviously, no teen-age boy minds being called a juvenile delinquent, which is of Latin origin and charmingly colorless and remote, but every one of them—I have seen such "juveniles" standing six foot tall on the pavements of Manhattan—hates to be branded a "young criminal." The psychologist means to say that he is an unfortunate victim of circumstances and is juvenile and temporarily delinquent, and does not know right from wrong. I think that these six-foot fellows know very well what is right and what is wrong, and know exactly what they are doing when they murder or rob. Any Asiatic boy of twelve knows what is right and what is wrong, and to say that an American boy of sixteen or seventeen still does not know right from wrong (and therefore has no moral responsibility for his actions) is an obvious travesty of the American people, and implies immaturity on the part of the adolescent "social scientists." A socially maladjusted individual is not just a socially maladjusted individual; he is, in plain English, just an ill-bred brat. Now the human constitution is such that if you call a brat a brat, the brat disappears; but if you call an ill-bred shuffling sneak or shirker of duties just an emotionally unbalanced personality, he rather likes it and is proud of it and wears his hair and his dress in a manner to advertise it.

I am old-fashioned, and I do not feel the esthetic charm of artistic despair or of moral cynicism. I even like a little spanking in schools, which does no bodily harm but which most emphatically registers a sense of wrong and shame in a child's mind. In all fairness, I think of England as a society where invisible standards still prevail, where something is regarded as wrong because it is "just not done," because it is "not cricket." I think that in English society certain ideals and values still exist, not on paper, but in the actual conduct of men. Now, no human society is perfect, but isn't it in England that the word "gentleman" not only exists on paper but also embodies a real, a living ideal? What more does one expect of men? Isn't there somewhere in this world—perhaps in England—a place where human culture has reached the stage of true civilization, of having a definite ideal, and where that ideal is still coherent and visible, where the young growing up have a visible ideal to aspire to? And isn't that the essence of true culture? Isn't the essence of culture to see beauty in good form? And where that ideal does not exist, is it not society as a whole which suffers?

The gradual disappearance of moral enthusiasm, beginning as a sophisticated fear of sweetness and light, may or may not

be due to the two world wars. They probably helped. Hence
the post-Versailles fashion for despair, and the post-Potsdam
"beat" generation. The beat generation, by calling themselves
"beat," merely point up the fact that they have found a moral
void, the absence of something convincing and good and fresh
to live for and fight for. The tragedy of liberalism in America
is that it has nothing to fight for today, which was not true of
liberalism thirty or forty years ago. Liberalism is a child, and
must have something to play with to keep it out of mischief.
Having nothing to fight for and finding time heavy on its
hands, liberalism, even church liberalism, is fighting for sympathy with, allowance for, and recognition of a foreign police
state and foreign tyranny which is Red China. Where are the
moral values? A good Christian thinks nothing of condemning
ten million free men to totalitarian slavery. No moral principles
seem to be involved, or if they were, they are unaware of it,
having been taught to think "objectively." But why wonder?
Moral principles disappeared when we were fighting the Second World War. No leader tried to make us think that we
were fighting a war to make the world safe for democracy;
we were fighting strictly for savage survival, for unconditional
surrender, and not for self-determination as a principle. The
haziness of moral principles in World War II, as compared
with World War I, in the official pronouncements of its leaders, is in itself an index of increasing moral cynicism.

Now, I think moral chaos is against man's instinct. I think
men like to have a cogent ideal of life. A society with a clear
ideal is an easier society to live in than one without it. It
breeds fewer neurasthenics, fewer frustrations, and fewer
mental breakdowns. I believe that the instinct to worship
something is in every man, and that no society exists, not even
atheistic society, which does not worship something. The
Soviet experiment in a godless society, the only large-scale
experiment of this type, has not been a happy one. The ubiq-
uitous portraits of Soviet leaders in Moscow or Peking declare the necessity of worship of some god or other even in a

"godless" society. The only difference is that new gods, new dogmas, new heresies, and new litanies have replaced the old ones. Judging by the number of portraits and idols being carried about during the parades, the compulsory salutes to and te deums sung in praise of these new gods, and the abrogation of the right of the individual to think for himself, I think the Communist countries are the most abjectly idolatrous in the modern world, in the true sense of the word. It is unfortunate that the god they happened to worship for thirty years turned out after his death, according to Khrushchev, to be a murderer and a master of frame-ups, a gangster whom 200,000,000 persons worshiped for thirty years without being able to find out the truth about him. But let us call it an accident of history. Even so, the theism of an atheistic society must go on forever, the infallible lord of this religion being Karl Marx, its prophet of revelation, Lenin. If this revealed religion is not held up strictly and worshiped as sacred, the whole atheistic church must crumble to pieces.

This is the void we have arrived at. Modern liberalism seems to be attracted toward that void. Liberalism is uncomfortable with itself. And nature, we know, abhors vacuums, which are the most dangerous things in the world. Isn't there light somewhere in this terrifying darkness to save humanity? Confucius says, "A man who does not say to himself, 'What to do? What to do?'—indeed, I do not know what to do with such a person."

CHAPTER 8

The Majesty of Light

"BLOW OUT the candles! The sun is up!" said a great recluse philosopher when Emperor Yao mounted the throne. Such is the natural imagery when mankind sees an incomparable light. The world of Jesus is the world of sunlight by comparison with that of all the sages and philosophers and the schoolmen of any country. Like the Jungfrau which stands above the glaciers in the world of snow and seems to touch heaven itself, Jesus' teachings have that immediacy and clarity and simplicity which puts to shame all other efforts of men's minds to know God or to inquire after God.

Whence came this dazzling light of Jesus, which put Him in a special category by Himself among all teachers of men? Whence came the "prepossessing" power of Jesus, as Emerson called it?

Quite apart from the content of Jesus' teachings, I think the light and the power (dazzling light always has power) of Jesus came from the manner and the voice of His teaching and from His personal example. Jesus spoke as no teacher of men ever spoke. Jesus never expounded His faith, never reasoned it out. He spoke with the simplicity and certainty of

223

clear knowledge. At most He said, "How is it that ye do not understand?" He taught without hypothesis and without argument. With the utmost naturalness and gentility, He said, "He that hath seen me hath seen the Father." With perfect simplicity, He said, "These things I command you, that ye love one another." "He that hath my commandments and keepeth them, he it is that loveth me: and he that loveth me shall be loved of my Father, and I will love him, and will manifest myself to him." That is altogether a new voice in history, a voice never heard before. "Little children, yet a little while I am with you. Ye shall seek me; and as I said unto the Jews, whither I go, ye cannot come; so I say unto you. A new commandment I give unto you, that ye love one another; as I have loved you, that ye also love one another." It is the very same voice which later said, "Father, forgive them for they know not what they do." Such simple words have power, as do the following: "Peace I leave with you, my peace I give unto you: not as the world giveth, give I unto you. Let not your heart be troubled, neither let it be afraid." There is a note of authentic nobility about it, as in: "Come unto me, all ye that labour and are heavy laden, and I will give you rest." That is the gentle voice of Jesus, and at the same time the compelling voice, a commanding voice that has haunted the understanding of men for the last two thousand years.

I do not think there is anything in the contention that St. John may have put these sentiments in his own words. Assuredly, these words written by the author of the Gospel of St. John were not a verbatim report. But they were words as St. John heard them, or as he remembered them years afterward. Nor, for that matter, are the Socratic Dialogues the exact words of Socrates. I have always thought of the *Phaedo* by Plato and the Chapters XIII to XVII of the Gospel of St. John as being among the most moving bits of writing concerning two great thinkers' discourse as they approached death; but, although St. John was not a writer like Plato, these four or five Chapters of St. John are incomparably the most moving

thing in literature. They are different from the *Phaedo* for the
simple reason that they contain such superior beauty, the
beauty of a voice that the world has not heard repeated since
Jesus' death. Granted that St. John, let us say, knew about the
Greek *Logos* philosophy when he wrote this. Such a passage
as "I am the Way, the Truth and the Life" may be Greek
philosophy. (It is not in Matthew's Gospel when Matthew
speaks about the same message.) But there are surprising
touches in John's Gospel; for instance, when Jesus begins to
wash the feet of his disciples, or when there is a sudden turn
in the language, and Jesus calls his disciples "friends": "Ye
are my friends, if ye do whatsoever I command you. Henceforth I call you not servants; for the servant knoweth not what
his lord doeth; but I have called you friends." These are not
sayings that John could have invented. There is an authentic
quality about his Gospel even as there is an authentic quality
in certain novels.

Thus it is that the world of Jesus contains both that power,
and something else—the absolute clarity of light, without the
self-limitation of Confucius, the intellectual analysis of Buddha, or the mysticism of Chuangtse. Where others reasoned,
Jesus taught, and where others taught, Jesus commanded. He
spoke out of the fullness of the knowledge and love of God.
Jesus communicated the feeling of the immediate knowledge
and love of God, and further, immediately and without quali-
fication, equated that love of God with obeying His commandment, which is to love one another. If all great truths are
simple, we stand here in the presence of a simple truth which
contains the germ of the principle for all human development,
and is sufficient.

His teaching was of a different order from that of previous
philosophers. No more the positivism and common sense of
Confucius, no more his staid occupation with human relations only, or his counsel of gradual self-cultivation; nor the
phantasmagoria of a world of eternal transformations of Taoism, of Being returning to Not-Being; nor the mighty intellec-

tualism of Buddha and his heroic effort at conquest of the perceiving mind, with the hope of escaping into the infinite and the unconditioned. All these have been worthy flights of the human mind into the upper sphere of divine truth, worthy attempts to explain the nature of life and death. Confucianism is eminently practical, nonabstract, easy to follow and to understand, but it balks at any close scrutiny of the true nature of life and the universe. It teaches honor and a sense of responsibility and a continuous aiming at our human best. Taoism and Buddhism, on the other hand, teach freedom of the spirit as the ultimate goal. Of the two, the Buddhist method, apart from Chan, is intellectual rather than mystic. Indeed, the Taoism of Chuangtse contributes most directly to the emancipation of the spirit; it has a largeness of comprehension rare in lesser philosophers of reason. The Chuangtsean standpoint was, like that of Pascal, really religious, as we have seen. Laotse at times rose to immense heights in his belief in the power of love and humility, and in his contempt of all human measures, like government, punishment, and war, for giving peace to man. Laotse and Jesus are brothers in spirit. Jesus said, "I am meek and lowly," and Laotse said, "Hold on to meekness and the lowly position." Both established the kingdom of the poor in spirit, a phrase which enraged Nietzsche, but Jesus exemplified it by washing the feet of his disciples, a thing which Laotse conceivably might have done, but there is no record of his doing so.

We live in a world without belief, a world of moral cynicism, of collapse of valid human ideals. And all of us are paying for that collapse of human ideals. Insofar as our usually accepted ideas for the betterment of this world relate to a "higher standard of living," and insofar as modern thinkers propose to tackle the ills of society by economic measures, on the whole it is true to say that we are living in a "materialistic" age. Now, of course, the Western world also believes in two spiritual values, democracy and freedom, but places limitations on both of them. The general assumption is that

the white man wants freedom but the yellow man wants
rice, which simply shows that the white man does not understand freedom as an instinct inherent in all men, and
not a special Anglo-Saxon spiritual yearning. Modern pun-
dits assert again and again that the men of Asia care first
of all for rice, that they do not know what freedom means
nor do they care for it, and that while tyranny is hateful
to the white man the yellow man can tolerate it. This simply proves how materialistic and how generally superficial
these Western observers are and how mistaken they can be in
their conception of the mind of Asia. At this level, the West's
thinking is more materialistic than that of Confucius, for the
latter said that a nation could go without an army, if necessary; that it could even go without food, but that no nation
could exist without faith.

This materialism will not do. We know of nothing that will
change it except for the basic doctrines of Jesus. All social-
istic reforms, inside or outside Soviet Russia, tend only to
strengthen the materialistic, the economic approach, and, as
Chuangtse would say, "only bring us into greater confusion."
Confucius said, "Of all means for the regeneration of mankind, those made with noise and show are the least important." Confucius, in his own way, as I have tried to show,
believed with Jesus in the silent revolution, the revolution in
the man from within. Albert Schweitzer, that great Christian,
in his oration at Frankfurt in 1932, on the hundredth anni-
versary of Goethe's death, said:

> In a thousand different ways mankind has been persuaded
> to give up its natural relations with reality, and to seek its
> welfare in the magic formulas of some kind of *economic and
> social witchcraft* [italics mine] by which the possibility of
> freeing itself from economic and social misery is only still
> further removed!
>
> And the tragic meaning of these magic formulas, to what-
> ever kind of economic and social witchcraft they may belong,
> is always just this, that the individual must give up his own

material and spiritual personality and must live only as one of the spiritually restless and materialistic multitude which claims control over him.

Renan, another great student of Jesus, said:

> All the social revolutions of humanity will be grafted on this phrase [the "kingdom of God"]. But, tainted by a coarse materialism, and aspiring to the impossible, that is to say, *to found universal happiness upon political and economical measures* [italics mine], the "socialist" attempts of our time will remain unfruitful until they take as their rule the true spirit of Jesus, I mean absolute idealism—the principle that, in order to possess the world, we must renounce it.

Depth is what we need, and depth is what we do not have.

Insofar as the West believes in freedom and democracy, it directly follows the core of Jesus' teachings, although it appears that the West does not completely believe. If the "freedom" of Alaska is threatened, the United States will fight for it, but if the freedom of the Hungarians or the Chinese or the Russians is at stake, we do not believe in it deeply enough to care. Freedom therefore has not yet a universal character; it is not, in the present decade at least, a passionate faith. The root of such a universal religion of freedom and of democracy is in the words of Jesus, which will one day yet make themselves felt. How this is related, I shall make clear.

Christianity stands for the common man. We are acquainted with the power of Christianity in the past history of the Western world. But even more important, that power is here today, ready to bring about the silent revolution and make for mankind's progress, a vital force always. Peculiarly, Jesus' teachings are such that they cannot be affected by any changes in fashions of thought or in economic or physical concepts. Jesus has no dogmas, no creeds, no rites, and no rituals. Jesus taught a principle, or rather two principles in one: that the kingdom of God is within you, and, almost in the same breath, that the meek and the humble shall inherit the earth. The first

teaches the inner freedom of man's spirit; the second, the
worthiness of the "least of these my brethren." In other words,
the humblest man is free in spirit, and the humblest man shall
win. These are the spiritual principles behind all freedom and
all democracy.

The materialist believes the opposite. He believes that all
will be well if the humblest man is given rice. The true materialist would vote for more equitable distribution of wealth
against more individual freedom if he had to make that choice.
Somehow man will be happy if he has rice.

I believe that anyone studying the teachings of Jesus, even
as a human teacher only, could not but be struck by this
anomaly, that Jesus taught as no man ever did. Even taking
Renan, who is a fair test of objectivity, we see that Jesus' life
and teachings *compelled* this French scholar to say, "Jesus remains an inexhaustible principle of moral regeneration for humanity." He summed up the life of Jesus at the end of his book
in what really amounts to an apostrophe to Jesus, even though
he denied the strict divinity of Christ:

> This sublime person, who each day still presides over the
> destiny of the world, we may call divine, not in the sense
> that Jesus has absorbed all the divine, or has been adequate
> to it (to employ an expression of the schoolmen), but in the
> sense that Jesus is the one who has caused his fellow-men *to
> make the greatest step toward the divine* [italics mine]. Man-
> kind in its totality offers an assemblage of low beings, self-
> ish, and superior to the animal only in that its selfishness
> is more reflective. From the midst of this uniform mediocrity,
> there are pillars that rise toward the sky, and bear witness to
> a nobler destiny. Jesus is the highest of these pillars which
> show to man whence he comes, and whither he ought to tend.
> In him was condensed all that is good and elevated in our
> nature. . . .
>
> As to us, eternal children, powerless as we are, we who
> labor without reaping, and who will never see the fruit of
> that which we have sown, let us bow before these demi-gods.

They were able to do that which we cannot do: to create, to affirm, to act. Will great originality be born again, or will the world content itself henceforth by following the ways opened by the bold creators of the ancient ages? We know not. But whatever may be the unexpected phenomena of the future, Jesus will not be surpassed. His worship will constantly renew its youth, the tale of his life will cause ceaseless tears, his sufferings will soften the best hearts; all the ages will proclaim that, among the sons of men, there is none born who is greater than Jesus.

Thus Renan wrote about the death of Jesus:

> Rest now in thy glory, noble initiator. Thy work is completed; thy divinity is established. Fear no more to see the edifice of thy efforts crumble through a flaw. Henceforth, beyond the reach of frailty, thou shalt be present, from the height of thy divine peace, in the infinite consequences of thy acts. At the price of a few hours of suffering, which have not even touched thy great soul, thou hast purchased the most complete immortality. For thousands of years the world will extoll thee. Banner of our contradictions, thou wilt be the sign around which will be fought the fiercest battles. A thousand times more living, a thousand times more loved since thy death than during the days of thy pilgrimage here below, thou wilt become to such a degree the corner-stone of humanity, that to tear thy name from this world would be to shake it to its foundations.

Who but a Frenchman with the delicacy and depth of the French could express it so well and so eloquently?

Theology, of whatever kind, always detracts from the power and simplicity of Jesus' teachings. Surely, the Apostles' Creed requires many questions and answers. There is nothing to catechize in Jesus' own words, nothing which the average man cannot understand for himself. There are in Jesus' words no mysterious definitions, no dangerous deductions, no self-deluding dialectic, no "Five Points." To dissect them is to kill them; to improve upon them is to spoil them. If the theologians

knew what they were doing! For no theologian, however great
he is, has the mind of Jesus. As soon as he enters into a discussion, the tone, the voice, changes. We must ever talk of the
things of the spirit as if they were material things: we cannot
help ourselves.

Many of us who had to "learn Shakespeare" in school acquired such a permanent distaste for Shakespeare that we
never wanted to touch his work again for the rest of our lives.
Then, one day, John Gielgud or Laurence Olivier came along,
and did not "teach" Shakespeare but merely pronounced
Shakepeare's own words, and the scales fell from our eyes.
We refused to believe that *that* was Shakespeare. Why, Shakespeare is beautiful! Why did we never learn to appreciate it
in school? I have been kept away from Jesus' teachings just as
a permanent dread of Shakespeare is bred in schoolboys. It
has seemed to me that Christ's teachings enclosed in theological dogmas are like a portrait by Rembrandt enclosed in
a five-and-ten-cent frame. The five-and-ten-cent frame detracts
from and obstructs the virtue of the Rembrandt. I have said
that there is nothing in Jesus' words which an unlearned man
cannot understand for himself. If some things are slightly unclear, nothing serious is; if the King James version is obscure
at times, it is a part of the light and shadow of the portrait.
Shall we retouch it? I like it as it is.

I am not talking about the doctrinal differences of the different Christian churches, but rather about the *futility* of discussion of doctrinal differences at all. Such discussions are all
too familiar and shopworn, but above all they are futile. To
enter into such a discussion is to drag oneself down to the
scholastic level and offend the truth. What I am saying is that
what prevents men from knowing Jesus is exactly these doc-
trinaire busybodies, that their confusion of creeds and dogmas kept me away from Christianity for thirty years, and that
their five-and-ten-cent theology prevented me from seeing
Jesus. I am not alone in this. It is the reason why J. S. Haldane, who argues most effectively for the recognition of the

spirit of Christ and of God in human affairs, finds it impossible to join any church. "As you probably know," he said at a
luncheon talk at St. Martin's Church, Trafalgar Square, in
May, 1932, "I am a member of no church, because there is so
much that I cannot accept in the theology associated with
existing Churches" (*Materialism*, page 220). And Albert
Schweitzer is fully aware of this, too. Schweitzer wrote in the
Christian Century, on November 21 and 28, 1934:

> I am going to discuss religion in the spiritual life and civili-
> zation of our time. The first question to be faced, therefore,
> is: Is religion a force in the spiritual life of our age? I answer
> in your name, and mine, "No!". . . . There is (however) a
> longing for religion among many who no longer belong to
> the churches.

Now I may be permitted to make some personal observa-
tions. In actual fact, Christianity in China never made converts
by doctrines, but it did make converts whenever a Chinese
came into personal contact with a Christian personality who
followed the Christian teachings; namely, those few words
"Love ye one another." At the time when I was moving away
from Christianity at Tsinghua, an orthodox Confucianist, a
classmate of mine, was being converted to Christianity. How?
Not by catechism. I knew Meng as anyone knows his classmate. He was excellent in Chinese, and he came from an old
Confucian family near Soochow and was dubbed "descendant
of Mencius" because of his surname Meng. He had come to
St. John's for English. But his background was diametrically
opposite to mine. At Tsinghua we were both teachers of English and shared the same house, each occupying one room, my
room door opening opposite his. I was in Western dress but
he never was. I used to admire him sitting erect in his hard
chair all day, which was a part of his severe Confucian training. The thoroughgoing severity of a Chinese family upbringing had been bred into him, and he was brilliant and of a
high integrity of character, respected by everyone. While at

St. John's, we had both laughed at Sherwood Eddy's revivalist tactics. One of his tricks was suddenly to pull a Chinese flag (then of five colors) out of his coat pocket and declare that he loved China. Such melodramatics didn't go with us, for Meng was an intellectual, although a number of students went up after the speech and "signed up for Jesus." Why, then, did Meng become a Christian? I know the psychological background only too well. An American lady on the teaching staff converted him—a saintly character who, in her tone and her words, showed Christian kindness. "Love" is a debased word; there was nothing remotely romantic here. The lady was, I believe, about fifty. She was just a good Christian lady, and she cared for the Tsinghua students deeply. Her care, her regard for the individual was a remarkable thing. This American lady had the Christian virtue of love. She taught Meng the Bible, and it won him over. It was an altogether different world from the world he had known. Meng's own Confucian family life was as austere as anything I know. It was a world of duties and obligations and moral discipline. He could not help feeling the warmth of the new world opening up before him in which Christian law superseded the rigorous Confucian way of life. He felt, I believe, as the first Christians felt about a new law superseding the laws of Moses.

This is true of my own case. The sight of a Christian who actually practices Christian kindness and concern for individuals always tended to bring me closer to the Christian Church. This formula works as no doctrine works. The exceptions also prove the rule. There were missionaries in my boyhood days who cared nothing about the Chinese converts and who did not love them as individuals, as Jesus undoubtedly would, or as missionaries should. Now the Chinese are an intensely practical people. We size up missionaries and judge them, not by what they preach but by what they are, and classify them simply as "good men" or "bad men." You cannot get away from these final simplicities. There were in my boyhood days two missionary sisters who never loved the Chinese

boys and girls but who worked for them, I imagine, as a form
of self-mortification for God. They made a bad impression on
us, and we boys christened them with unmentionable nick-
names. They lived in a high mansion overlooking the sea and
a beautiful landscape, and were served by Chinese sedan-
chair coolies, cooks, and amahs. The combination of Christian
evangelism and "white prestige" was bizarre. Now, where
there is love for fellow men or interest in others, one senses it
immediately; what we boys sensed in that house was a continual annoyance with the Chinese people. And the sisters
fully deserved the names we called them. On the other hand,
in my period of paganism it was my confrontation by a Christian lady which reminded me of another world. I remember
once, while crossing the Atlantic, meeting a foreign lady who
wanted to reconvert me to Christianity, and almost did so by
her humility and gentleness. I daresay that if the voyage had
been longer by ten days, I would have turned back to Christianity then and there. In this connection I must mention an
adorable lady, now ninety-four years old, living in New Jersey.
She knew me as a boy at the beginning of this century when
she was a missionary in Amoy. Now, this lady shines with the
Christian spirit of regard and care for others. It is remarkable,
but after half a century of absence she called me by my first
boyhood name. That she should have remembered at all! I am
sure the two sisters so wrapped up in their own communion
with God could not remember my name if they were living
now. It is just that: If ye remember my Commandment, ye
will love one another. Every time I came near this grand old
lady, I stood in the presence of the true spirit of Christianity.
It always worked as a reminder of a lost world. In other words,
Christians breed Christians, but Christian theology does not.

I cannot overemphasize the necessity of keeping to the core
of Jesus' teachings. I am quite sure that it is this spirit which
is behind Schweitzer's compulsion to work in an African jungle. Let us respect what Schweitzer says, because his words
are highly important and pregnant with meaning:

We wander in darkness now, but one with another we all have the conviction that we are advancing to the light; that again a time will come when religion and ethical thinking will unite. This we believe, and hope and work for, maintaining the belief that if we make ethical ideals active in our lives, then the time will come when peoples will do the same. Let us look out toward the light and comfort ourselves in reflecting on what thinking is preparing for us.

In his extremely important Epilogue to *Out of My Life and Thought*, which should be read by every thinking man, Schweitzer makes the point about the "thinking" referred to above, and shows the necessity of a "new rationalism" which does not renounce thinking but which will one day refocus man's thinking on the primary problems of man's relations to life, to God, and the universe. He shows why modern man has lost the capacity for this type of thinking and why by the study of speculative philosophy, psychology, sociology, and the natural sciences he has come to look at the problems of human life "as if he were not a being who is in the world and lives his life in it, but one who is stationed near it, and *contemplates it from the outside*" (italics mine). But the other point he makes in the above quote about the union of "religion and ethical thinking" is equally important and in fact shows the way to do it. It seems to me that Christian theology is largely responsible for shifting the emphasis of Christ on "bearing fruit" and doing his commandments to some easy-to-take, near-magical formula for salvation which does not require moral effort on the part of the individual and is therefore more palatable. It is true that the Christian Churches also teach repentance and a rebirth, but on the whole the emphasis has been the other way round—that, since Someone has already died for you, the salvation is yours anyway if you merely "believe" or call upon His name, "Lord, Lord." The working of the Doctrine of Atonement appears to be automatic and foolproof; that is what the priests have wanted their congregations to believe. Jesus taught otherwise. In a dozen parables about the vine, the seed, the fig tree, the talents, and so on, He makes salvation or forgiveness conditional upon "bearing fruit" and doing His commandments. Forgiveness is by no means automatic or unequivocal. Worship is less important than service: "Leave there thy gift before the altar . . . first be reconciled to thy brother"; "But if ye forgive not men their trespasses, neither will your Father forgive your trespasses"; "Condemn not and ye shall not be condemned: forgive and ye shall be forgiven." This was the emphasis Jesus laid on ethical living and individual effort. Not all the blood of the Lamb can wash away one's sins if one does not do His commandments and love and forgive but only "repents" and "believes." Salvation is neither automatic nor assured. Once this original emphasis is restored and Christians "bear fruit" in their lives, nothing can withstand the power of Christianity.

*

Since this book is about my personal journey from paganism back to Christianity, I believe a word more must be said about this change. The reader may have felt that I never stopped believing in God and that my quest for a satisfactory form of worship never ceased. But I was deterred by the theology of the churches. I was repelled by things that are coldly intellectual, haughtily deductive, and even uncharitable toward God. My position was that of many modern men who are born Christians but who, for various reasons, feel there is something in churches that instinctively keeps them away. In all honesty, I believe there are millions like me. I was kept away from paying attention to the Rembrandt by the horrible thing called its frame. There was, in fact, no cataclysmic "conversion," no mystic vision, no feeling of someone heaping red coals upon my head. The return to the church of my father was merely finding a church which was adequate for me and did not repel me by dogmatism. It was a natural thing when it happened.

I must say that, during the period of my paganism, my

casual attempts to attend church services had always resulted in discouragement. It is sad, but sweet reasonableness is so often wanting in Christ's churches. My wife always read the Bible in bed and attended church services wherever she could. I admired and secretly envied the true spirit of piety in her, the essence of which I believe is humility. Once in a while, I would accompany her, but usually returned discouraged. With the best will in the world, I could not bear a second-rate sermon. Seeing me squirm in my seat, she thought it just as well for her to go alone. Once in a while, by chance I would tune in on a radio program, only to hear a voice shouting and ranting about sin and eternal damnation, urging us to come to God in the typical voice of a crier at a village fair. I do not think that this is an unfair picture. I think a great deal of religion in America today is still motivated by fear of eternal damnation. Many Americans accept that, but many Americans cannot. It is most unfortunate that the true fellowship of Christ and the love of God which, in the world of Jesus, falls like the gentle dew from heaven, is so rare, and that the divine nature in all men is so rarely mentioned and damnation so often insisted upon. But this seems to be the case. Church worship still very largely consists in an angry minister preaching damnation in angry words about an angry God. Sin is almost as essential to ministers as disease and death are to doctors. Jesus Himself never mentioned sin but to forgive it. I don't seem to remember that He ever damned even Judas Iscariot. Judas was actually and literally forgiven from the Cross.

Now I have found a church where I do not squirm in my seat, but listen in rapt attention from beginning to end. After having heard the first sermon by Dr. David Read, I went Sunday after Sunday, because I was richly rewarded every time. What a feeling of relief to be allowed to come near to God and worship as I always wanted to worship! It happened naturally, so that when the matter of joining the church officially was brought up, there was not even a family discussion about it. We had been going to the Madison Avenue Presbyterian Church Sunday after Sunday for half a year before we joined, and joined gladly. I want only to add that Dr. Read always kept to the problems of the Christian life in his sermons; he did not do as the minister at the Memorial Church at Harvard did when I was there years ago, sometimes take George Eliot for the subject of his sermon. There *are* so many problems of the Christian life to talk about without having to go off on a tangent. It therefore became a pleasure to go to church because to be in church was to be near the true spirit of Jesus Christ. I believe there are churches in New York and elsewhere where it is still possible for a modern, educated man to go and worship and come out renewed because of the fresh contact, feeling a better man for it, instead of more like a doomed sinner escaping damnation by Someone else's effort. To deny this possibility is to deny the richness of the Christian life and of the world of Christ. Isn't the peculiarity of Christ that He made one feel a better and worthier person instead of a sinner in His presence?

As for the doctrinal differences, I am willing to take Christ and leave all the sinners to Calvin. I know that there has been such a steady weakening of the intellectual framework of Calvinism that the modern Presbyterian Church no longer insists on the belief in "total depravity" and denial of "free will" invented by that haughty man who burned Servetus at the stake. To defend Calvinism by saying that determinism and free will can co-exist is just quibbling. I have an instinctive distrust of any man who insists on a "total" this, an "unconditional" that, and an "irresistible" something else—all by means of a pre-Marxist materialistic dialectic. The gall of that predeterministic emetic! The denial of the kingdom of heaven within you and me! Buddha assured his disciples: "No teaching which is unkind can be the true teaching of Buddha." Calvinism has been terribly unkind to God and man. With permission from Calvin, his God would like to burn a few more honest, stubborn men like Servetus at a bigger and better stake!

Meanwhile, a cogent ideal of life is there in the incomparable teachings of Christ, the highest that man has been privileged to hear. We tend constantly to think of Jesus' revelation of God as an act belonging to the past. But anyone who reads the Gospels today cannot help feeling that sense of present revelation of God as love, clear and unmistakable and convincing, and that His whole life is itself a "revelation," that is, the spirit of God made visible and concrete for us to see. When Jesus taught, "Inasmuch as ye have done it to the least of these my brethren, ye have done it unto me," I knew and felt that He was indeed the Master and understood why He was not only respected, but adored by all wherever His word was heard. That light of God's truth was a light of dazzling purity of spirit, without compare in the teachings of men. And when He went further and taught forgiveness and exemplified it in His own life, I accepted Him as truly Lord and Saviour of us all. Only Jesus, and no one else, could bring us to that direct knowledge of God. Morally and ethically, it is a world of incomparable beauty. And here, if the world still wants an ideal, is a perfect ideal for human guidance.

That teaching is enough. It is adequate. Therein lies the majesty of light. But it is also greater than the world of men can digest or realize or put into practice. The goal has been set high enough to become a lodestar for future human spirits to follow, always. The light which dazzled St. Paul on the road to Damascus will continue to shine through the ages, unobscured and unobscurable. So at last the spirit of man has been uplifted to join the spirit of God through Christ. The essential worth of man is justified. For that reason, mankind will always adore Him. And that simple doctrine of the essential worth of man, however humble he may be, will yet prove to be the greatest liberating force of history.

One more word and I shall have done. There are form and

content in any religion, and religion always expresses itself through form. In the case of Christianity, the content was given by Jesus in all its plenitude, but the form was added by man. Jesus founded His church without dogmas, solely upon the basis of the majestic force of love He created in His disciples. That force of compelling love of the disciples for the Master was the beginning of the Christian Church. As for form, according to Jesus, man was free to worship in spirit and in truth, "neither at this mountain, nor at Jerusalem." Now form is conditioned, based on tradition and historical development. There has been much bigotry in this matter, the division between the Catholic Church and the Protestant, and among the Protestant sects. No intelligent Methodist of to-day, I believe, thinks evil of a Presbyterian or of an Episcopalian or of a Catholic. Is it possible that form is so important? Is it not true that one must worship God in spirit and in truth, and that the form is as inconsequential as the language one chooses to worship God in, whether it be French, German, English, or Latin? Each man must find the form which suits him best, and by that I mean the form which least interferes with his habits of worship and habits of belief. Even when outward compliance is given, every man believes in God in his own way, with relative points of emphasis conditioned by his past experience. It must be so. And as long as man worships God in spirit and in truth, the forms are only means, different for different individuals, to reach the same end. The forms are valuable or valueless only as they lead us to that goal which is the fellowship of Christ.

Index

Index

243

ABOUT THE AUTHOR

LIN YUTANG's family name is Lin. Nevertheless when people call him "Mr. Yutang," he rather likes it because it is so Chinese. In a nation of ten million Changs and ten million Wangs, naturally such a custom developed. But "Mr. Lin" would also be correct. Born of a Presbyterian minister in 1895 in an inland village on the southeast coast of Fukien, he considers his upbringing in a village in deep mountains had a permanent influence on his character.

He took his degrees from St. John's (Shanghai), Harvard, and Leipzig. He considers he got all his English before coming to Harvard. In the Widener Library he first found himself, first came alive; never saw a Harvard-Yale football match. He was a teacher at Tsinghua University, Peking, in 1916-19; married and went abroad with his wife to study, 1919; studied in the School of Comparative Literature under Bliss Perry and Irving Babbitt at Harvard in 1919-1920; worked with the Y.M.C.A. for Chinese laborers at Le Creusot, France, to support himself, 1920-1921; studied at Jena and Leipzig, 1921-23; was professor of English at Peking National University, 1923-26; and Dean of Women's Normal College, 1926; was chased out of Peking by the Dog-Meat General in 1926, blacklisted among the radical professors; became Dean of Arts in Amoy University, 1926; joined the Wuhan Nationalist Government as a secretary to the Foreign Ministry at Hankow in first half of 1927; "liked the Revolution but got tired of the revolutionists." Since the summer of 1927, he has devoted his time entirely to authorship. He was editor of the literary fortnightlies, *Lunyu, Jenchienshih,* and *Yuchoufeng,* 1929-35 in Shanghai. Now the only important things to him are his books and his family, including two grandchildren, Niuniu and Didi.

This book was set in

Weiss and Caledonia types,

printed, and bound by

The Haddon Craftsmen.

Typography and design are by Larry Kamp.